No US citizen has ever been killed or injured, no facility, large or small, in that vast and rich territory has suffered the slightest material damage as a consequence of any action originated from Cuba.

CUBA,
The Untold Story

Editorial Capitán San Luis
Havana, Cuba, 2014

Design:
Francisco Masvidal
(National Award for Design, 2002)

Design (section on dengue and Elián):
Roberto Chávez Miranda

Selection, organization of texts and editing:
Juan Carlos Rodríguez Cruz

Style:
Asunción Rodda Romero

Researchers:
Juan Carlos Rodríguez Cruz
José Sáliva
Pedro Echeverri
Secundino Palenque
Marilyn Rodríguez

Production:
Francisco Masvidal
Eduardo A. González Hernández
Yariva Rivero Marchena
Norma Ramírez Vega
Julio Cubría Vichot

Translation:
Karen McCartney

All rights reserved
First edition, 2005
© Juan Carlos Rodríguez Cruz, 2014
© On the current edition
Editorial Capitán San Luis, 2014

ISBN: 959-211-255-X

Editorial Capitán San Luis, Calle 38 no. 4717,
entre 40 y 47, Playa, Havana, Cuba
Email: direccion@ecsanluis.cu
www.capitansanluis.cu

TERRORISM:

An account of violent attacks carried out to spread terror.

La Coubre

March 4, 1960

At 3:15 on the afternoon of March 4th, 1960, the steamship La Coubre, with a cargo of Belgian-made grenades for FAL rifles, blew up on the dockside in Havana. The explosion caused 101 deaths, over 200 injuries and an indeterminate number of disappearances.

The U.S. government had put the Belgian authorities under pressure not to send the arms shipment to the island, and from January of that same year the CIA had unleashed an underground war against the Cuban Revolution.

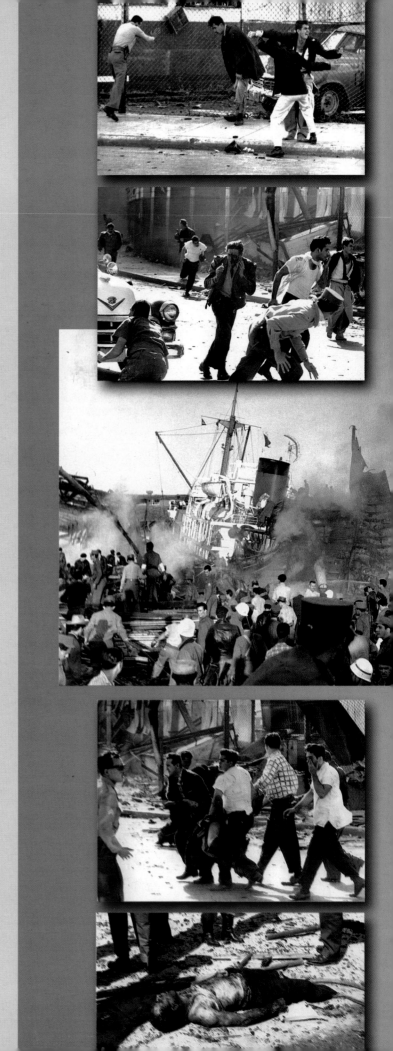

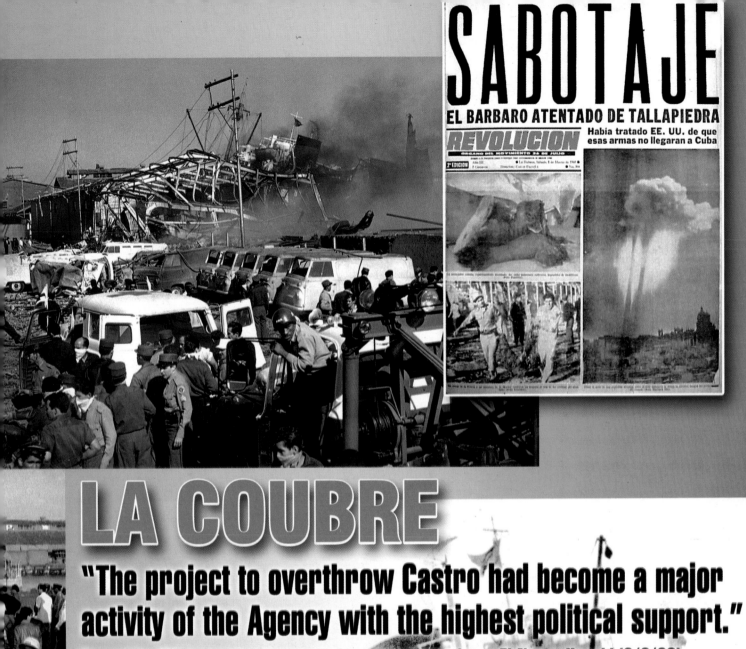

LA COUBRE

"The project to overthrow Castro had become a major activity of the Agency with the highest political support."

Report by CIA inspector, Lyman Kirkpatrick, Taken from *El Nuevo Herald* (2/3/98)

The factory from which these weapons had originated in Belgium had been under US pressure not to sell arms to Cuba. The U.S. consul in Belgium and a military attaché at the embassy had personally put the factory and the Belgian Foreign Ministry under pressure not to sell the weapons.

The Cuban authorities had received a substantial amount of confidential information regarding both official and unofficial pressure applied by the United States to prevent the sale of weaponry to the Ministry of the Revolutionary Armed Forces.

This act of sabotage deprived Cuba of 44 tons of grenades and 31 tons of munitions.

In the case of previous shipments, the entire cargo had been loaded via barges in the Bay of Amberes. Nevertheless, on this occasion the munitions and the general cargo had been stowed directly at the docks.

"As I said to President Castro, I understand the suspicions that have arisen. **We had begun to carry out some sabotage** at that time, but this was not amongst them, as far as I know..."

Robert Reynolds, head of the CIA station in Miami from September 1960 to October 1961. Academic Conference "Bay of Pigs, 40 years later", held in Havana in March of 2001. (Editor's Note.)

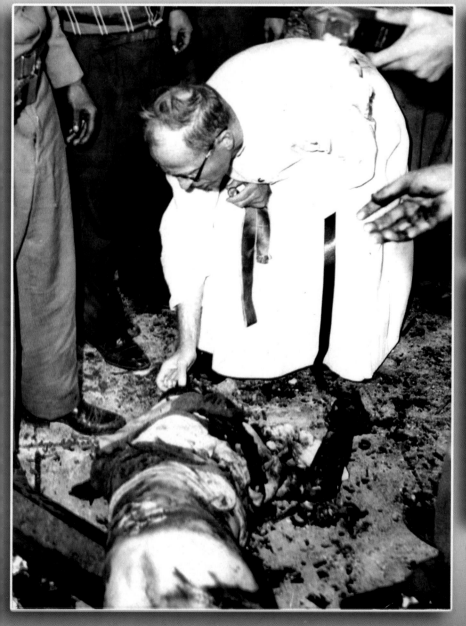

Six French sailors lost their lives.

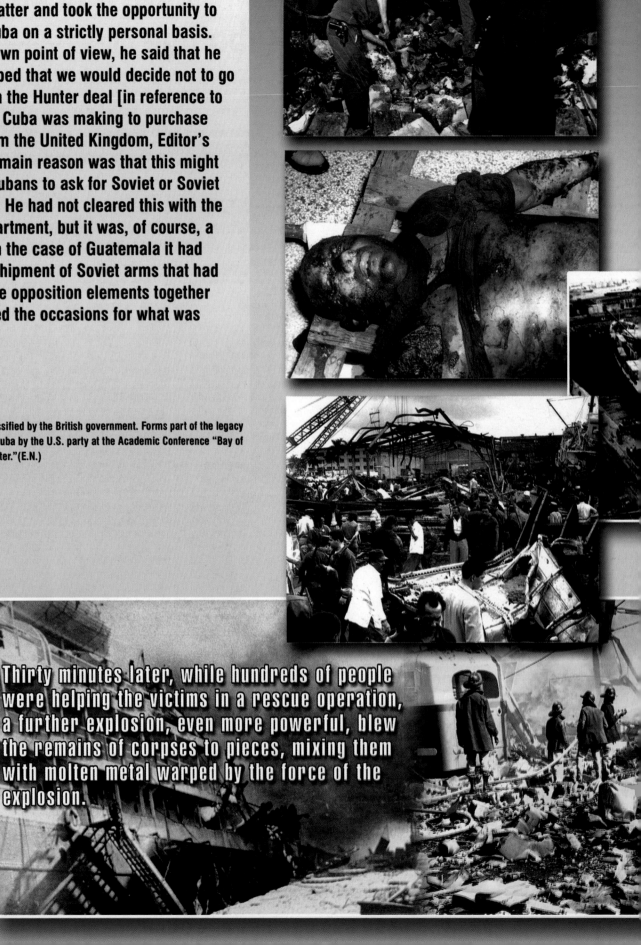

Coded. Top Secret. November 24, 1959. From Washington to British Secret Service. "I had to see Allen Dulles this morning on another matter and took the opportunity to discuss Cuba on a strictly personal basis. From his own point of view, he said that he greatly hoped that we would decide not to go ahead with the Hunter deal [in reference to the moves Cuba was making to purchase planes from the United Kingdom, Editor's note]. His main reason was that this might lead the Cubans to ask for Soviet or Soviet bloc arms. He had not cleared this with the State Department, but it was, of course, a fact that in the case of Guatemala it had been the shipment of Soviet arms that had brought the opposition elements together and created the occasions for what was done."

Document declassified by the British government. Forms part of the legacy handed over to Cuba by the U.S. party at the Academic Conference "Bay of Pigs, 40 years later."(E.N.)

Thirty minutes later, while hundreds of people were helping the victims in a rescue operation, a further explosion, even more powerful, blew the remains of corpses to pieces, mixing them with molten metal warped by the force of the explosion.

"There was no doubt that the ship had been sabotaged, that it was not an accident caused when transporting a case of anti-tank grenades amongst the cargo. . .

"Quite simply, there was a general belief that this had been an act of sabotage, carried out by the CIA."

Fidel Castro Ruz.
Academic Conference "Bay of Pigs, 40 years later."
Held in Havana, March 2001. (E.N.)

"Once the first explosion had taken place, I came out and the shock wave carried me out onto the street, Calvet was scorched. . . .There were few people with the first one, in the second workers from all parts of the docks had come running, as well as local people, firefighters, people came and started to help. There was no way of controlling them, the helpers, all anxious to cooperate, took the full impact, and that was the reason why there was death on such a massive scale at that time."

Alfredo Vidal Carrero

"There is one case in particular out of the many comrades who died that I can never forget. I have never spoken about it before, but I will now. . . . I gathered up the remains, I remember the eyes, which left an impression on me, as if they were alive, and I covered them with a dressing. Later on a child approached me asking about his father who had disappeared. I looked at him and knew immediately who he was looking for. 'Those are my father's eyes,' he said by way of confirmation.

He was a young man who was not even fifteen years old. I asked him not to tell the rest of his family about what he had seen and I prepared a coffin full of wood to approximate the weight of a corpse and that was where I put the eyes, and that was what the family mourned for later."

Nurse Gloria Azoy

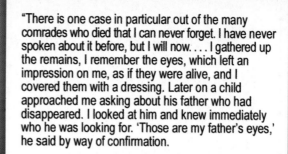

"We belonged to the War Material unit of the G4 Logistics Section.

"Once the ship had docked, the time available to put an explosive charge in the hold, in the cases, was not enough to place the charge firstly, because we had to get into the hold, and secondly, because a large number of cases had to be lifted within the hold in order to place the two charges inside it. Practically speaking, this was not possible and, in addition, more than one person would have been required to take part in the activity, which we believed to be impossible on account of the security measures taken. Experts put the charges in place in the cargo hold in Europe. There is no doubt about that.

"As we have already mentioned, we had handled large quantities of munitions before. Besides, those grenades had a detonator, two types of safety devices, one for transportation purposes and another, which was secured during the voyage. Huge mechanical efforts would have been required to detonate one of these grenades. Also, given the way in which they had been packaged, in a wooden crate, in a zinc container and inside a cardboard case, a fall or something similar could not have been accidental. Following the La Coubre explosion, an order was given at the highest levels to throw these types of crates from a plane at high altitude and they did not explode. In other words, there is no possibility whatsoever of an accident during the process of unloading the ship's cargo."

Estanislao Figueroa del Pozo

"My mother asked when the explosion occurred, 'What's happened at the docks?' And she added, 'My son is dead.' We had three brothers working at the docks; we didn't know where they were. The others appeared, and the only one missing was Guillermo. At the time of the second explosion the police wouldn't let me through. If they had, then I too would have died. We went to the hospital, by the bay. Only half of our next-door neighbor was found. The eight brothers who remained alive searched for him. What the imperialists have done to our people, to this island that has sacrificed so much, is unmentionable. Four orphans were left crying inconsolably for their father.

"We didn't find anything, in the bay or anywhere. For those four children who were orphaned, justice also has to be done."

Testimony by Zenaida Capetillo,
sister of one of the victims of the French ship
La Coubre.

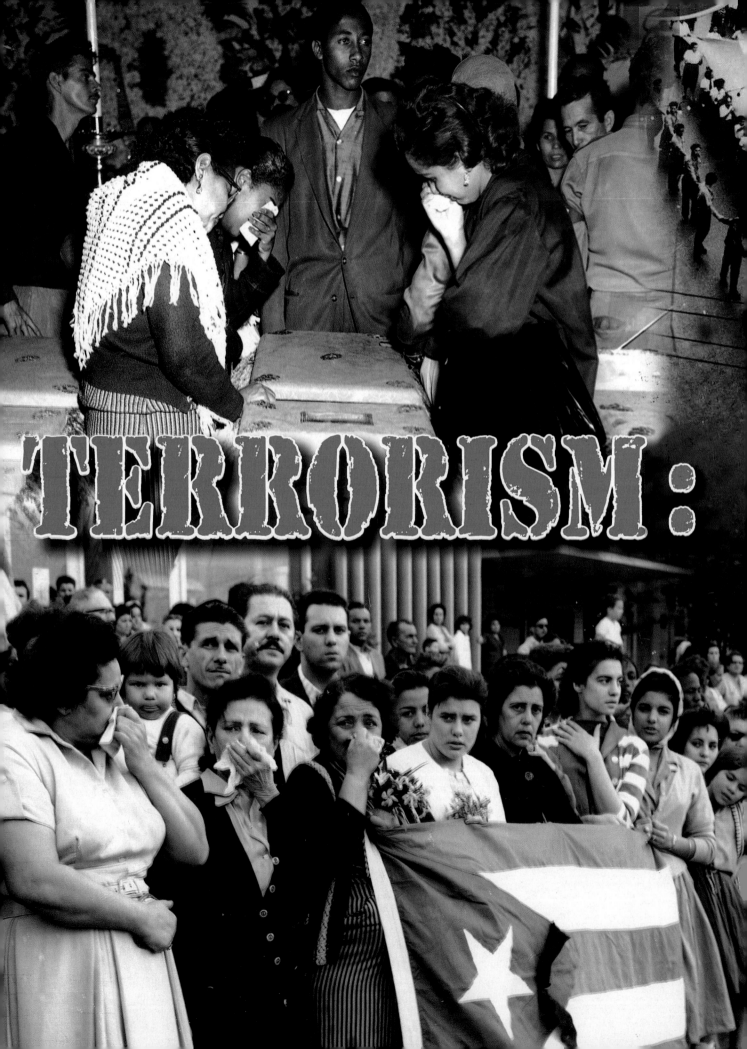

TERRORISM:

An account of violent attacks carried out to spread terror

"Freedom means even more now. Freedom means country and our choice now will be

Homeland or Death!"

Fidel Castro, March 5, 1960

It was evident that terrorism had killed, but it had not terrorized the Cuban people.

A country with a population twenty-five times smaller, and so much smaller in terms of surface area, than the United States has seen the blood of its citizens flow due to terrorist acts, organized and carried out from U.S. territory, on a larger scale than all the U.S. deaths during the Vietnam war.

"We had begun to carry ou

NOBEL
ACADEMY

some acts of sabotage..."

Robert Reynolds, head of the CIA station in Miami,
(Sept. 1960 to Oct. 1961).
Academic Conference "Bay of Pigs, 40 years later."
Havana, March 2001. Memoirs.

EL ENCANTO

TEN CENT

W WOOLWORT CO

LA NUEVA

CESAR de la CANDELA
ABRIMOS
FED. DEL COMERCIO

F W WOOLWORT CO

RABIOSA POR SUS DERROTAS APELA
AL SABOTAJE LA CONTRARREVOLUCION

NOTICIAS DE
HOY
UN DIARIO AL SERVICIO DEL PUEBLO

Airada condena femenina
al vil bombardeo yanqui

CINE CANDIDO
CINE RIESGO

orticóse

CRIMINAL A
DEL RIO: L

También 14 adu
recibieron ho

Lanzaron materias inflamables en
en la tanda infantil. Investigacion
los autores del salvaje hecho. In

PINAR DEL RIO,
mayo 26. (Raúl Luis,
por teléfono). — Un
nuevo y bárbaro aten

tado que ha lleva
hasta indignación
do al pueblo, pi
se llevó a cabo

REVOL
ORGANO DEL MOV

2ª EDICION
10 Centavos

Perú viv

Se llama Rigob

Vestíbulo del Teatro "Riesgo". Por estas puertas estrechas, acosados por
el humo y las llamas, fueron evacuados los niños.

Homenaje a héroes de Girón

ENTADO EN PINAR
IONADOS 26 NIÑOS

26 DE JULIO

...iro Madera: siete años;
...te quemado. ¿Besa usted
...da noche, mister Ken-
nedy?

...ernández. Cubano y niño: dos motivos suficientes
...ra que lo rociaran de fósforo vivo.

Frente al Hospital Civil
asistidas las víctimas,
reunirse una ciudadanía
e indignada.

20 CARTRIDGES
5.56 MM
BALL M193

20 CARTRIDGES
5.56 MM
BALL

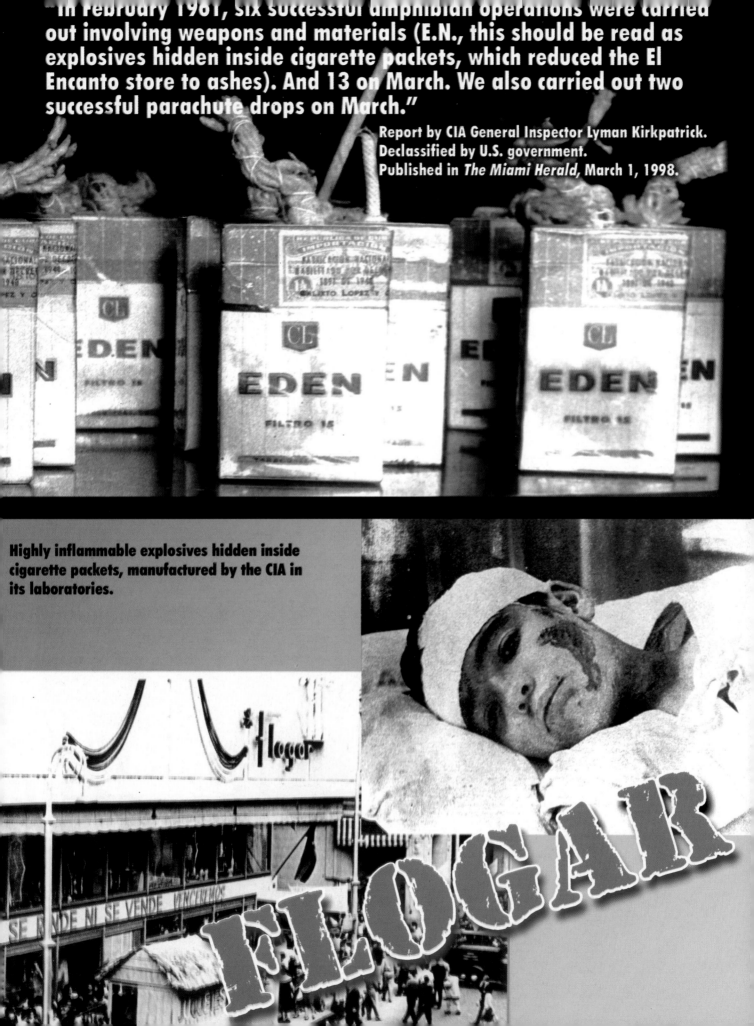

"In February 1961, six successful amphibian operations were carried out involving weapons and materials (E.N., this should be read as explosives hidden inside cigarette packets, which reduced the El Encanto store to ashes). And 13 on March. We also carried out two successful parachute drops on March."

Report by CIA General Inspector Lyman Kirkpatrick.
Declassified by U.S. government.
Published in *The Miami Herald,* March 1, 1998.

Highly inflammable explosives hidden inside cigarette packets, manufactured by the CIA in its laboratories.

FLOGAR

GIRON (BAY OF PIGS)
APRIL 17, 1961

Arthur Schlesinger, Jr., Assistant to President Kennedy, author of biographies on John and Robert Kennedy, Pulitzer prize-winner, who did not show very much enthusiasm for the plans to invade Cuba, would say years later, "Historically we have assumed a double role in Latin America. Sometimes we are the good neighbor, some times we are the bully of the hemisphere. Therefore, Latin Americans feel a mixture of hate and love for the United States. They react warmly to Dr. Jekyll and fear and detest Mr. Hyde. We would feel the same way if we were Latin Americans. Dr. Jekyll promotes the long-term interests of the United States. Mr. Hyde leaves bitter feelings behind him wherever he goes. The Bay of Pigs was the work of Mr. Hyde…"

L DAMAGE

"When they left Caletón they were going to take the Jagüey Grande road, at Playa Larga and Jagüey Grande junction, that's where they appeared and machine-gunned the open truck. They could see it was loaded with civilians, children, women and an elderly person. Nora, my daughter, was in the middle, and Dulce María was there too, as well as María Ortiz, their great aunt, was also there. The mercenaries appeared and machine-gunned the truck and my daughter Dulce María was killed instantly; she was only fourteen years old. María Ortiz, who was accompanying her sister to help out, was also killed. Ramón Mel, Amparo's husband, died too. There was also Cira María García, who was injured, and I don't know what happened after that, but in the end she died. That was my daughter, this was her aunt. This is the memory that I have of my family, which was destroyed by the U.S. government. Forgive me, but it is unbearable, and they have paid nothing to compensate for the suffering they have inflicted on the Cuban people. Because there are so many mothers and fathers, families that are suffering because of what happened."

Hirtolidia Angulo Cabrera,
mother of the girl seen in the photo.

COLLATERA

"Then we saw the other plane, which was flying very low, almost touching the road, and my father said to my mother, 'Bang hard against the cabin to make the driver stop.' Then he pushed my brother and shouted, 'Get down, that plane is going to land on the road.' I was sitting on a wooden box full of cans of condensed milk and was holding my six-month-old nephew at the time. Then the plane opened fire. My mother fell down, wounded in the stomach and arm. My grandmother was hit by a bullet in the spine and was left an invalid. My sister was hit in the leg and arm. I got down and my mother opened her eyes. I asked her if she had been hit. She raised her arm and wanted to touch me but she was too weak. Then my father got me off the truck. I said, 'If my mother isn't taken off then I'm not going, she's alive.' My father had covered her with a sheet and the wound in her abdomen couldn't be seen. That's why I thought she was alive. Then a breeze lifted the sheet and I saw the injury. Everything had come out. I saw my mother's insides."

Nemesia Rodríguez Montalvo

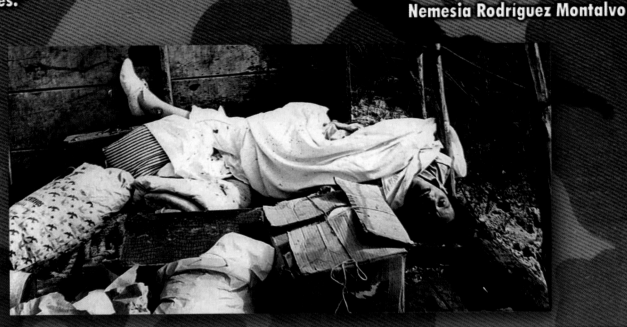

L DAMAGE

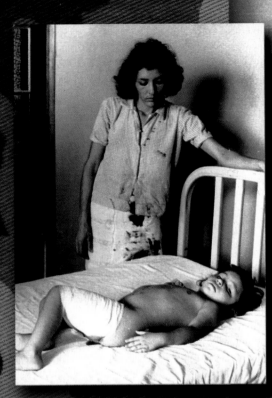

LIQUIDADA LA INVASION
Aplastante derrota del enemigo

REVOLUCION
ORGANO DEL MOVIMIENTO 26 DE JULIO

2ª EDICION   Año IV • La Habana, Jueves, 20 de Abril de 1961   No. 139
5 Centavos • Director: CARLOS FRANQUI

OCUPAN TANQUES PESADOS
YANQUIS SHERMAN Y ARMAS

HEROICA CONDUCTA DEL EJERCITO REBELDE Y LAS MILICIAS REVOLUCIONARIAS
TOMADA POR ASALTO PLAYA GIRON, ULTIMO REDUCTO DE LOS ENEMIGOS

PRESENTO ROA PRUEBAS DE
LA INTERVENCION YANQUI

On January 5, 1961, the volunteer teacher Conrado Benítez and peasant Heliodoro Rodríguez were tortured and murdered in the ESCAMBRAY mountains by a group of counterrevolutionaries. Conrado was 18 years old and he was a high school student when he volunteered to be teacher and headed off for the mountains.

"It was as if there had been a party in the camp that night. We were all shouting at him at the same time in the corral, we threw stones at him, we spat, swore and Osvaldo even said to Conrado Benítez 'If you join us we'll spare your life.' He replied that he was, above all, a revolutionary. You know, to tell that right in Osvaldo's face. . . .I repeat, it was as if we were having a party. First they got hold of Conrado Benítez, who had to practically run with the rope around his neck in order not to be dragged, while all those present beat him with sticks and cut him with knives."

"When he was under the tree chosen for the execution, the rope was thrown over a branch and the literacy teacher looked around him as if he were asking himself whether we were people or animals. The body was lowered and raised a few times, as if he were a puppet, until he was dead, then we left him hanging there. Even though he was clearly dead, Osvaldo ordered him to be stabbed and beaten."

Testimony by former counterrevolutionary Mirio Pérez Venegas.

The initial phase of paramilitary operations comprised the development, support and orientation of dissident groups in three areas of Cuba: Pinar del Río, the ESCAMBRAY and Sierra Maestra mountain chains. These groups were to be organized on the basis of guerrilla action against the regime.

Report by CIA General Inspector, Lyman Kirkpatrick.
Document declassified by the U.S. government.
Published in *The Miami Herald* on March 1, 1998.

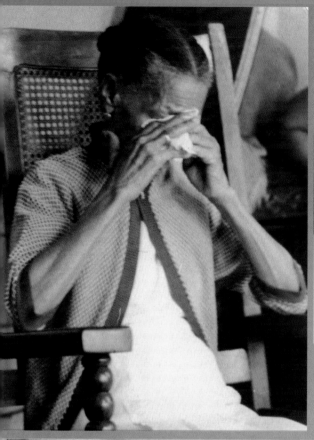

"As a father I used to ask myself why they perpetrated this criminal savagery against a young student who had not harmed anyone, and who only wanted to teach his fellow human beings?

Diego Benítez López, father
of the murdered teacher.

The reaction of Cuban young people to the barbaric act was to join on a massive scale the literacy brigades, named after the murdered teacher. A total of 105,664 students, with an average age of between 12 and 18, left for the mountains to teach reading and writing.

LITERACY CAMPAIGN

¡VENCEREMOS!

FABETICEMOS

The price the enemies of the Revolution

LITERACY CAMPAIGN

"When we reached the tree, I looked at Manuel: his black hair had fallen somewhat over his forehead, his lips were blackened, his tongue was violet colored with clotted blood around the edges. I noticed that his eyes were not bulging out of their sockets, as is almost always the case with those who have been hanged; that convinced me that they had hanged him up like that, dead. He also had a deep welt on the neck, and the laryngeal cartilage was fractured, which was detected by forensic examination.

"His genital organs were examined and contusions were observed, a sign that they had been subjected to pressure and abuse. There were fourteen stab wounds of varying degrees of depth.

"Beside him was Pedro Lantigua: with dark hair, somewhat reddish in color, his face covered with marks, he was entirely rigid, visible indication that he had fought against his murderers and signs that he had been dragged by a large number of men, been beaten, and a ecchymotic welt on the neck."

Rubén Dario Zayas Montalván, examining magistrate.

made them pay for such noble work.

LITERACY CAMPAIGN

"Operation will be planned and executed in support of guerrilla bands which exist or may emerge in the hills of Cuba utilizing both air and maritime operations for the delivery of arms and supplies and for the infiltration and exfiltration of personnel."

U.S. Foreign Relations 1961-1963, Cuba 1961-1962, Volume 10, Department of State, Washington, U.S. government, 1997.

"Manuel was like a brother to us, we led a normal life with him, we swam together in the river, rode the horses and harvested coffee. He was a nice guy, and when the counterrevolutionaries arrived he was teaching my brother Pedro."

Jacinto Lantigua de la Viña, son of the murdered peasant Pedro Lantigua Ortega.

"I have suffered the greatest possible pain that a mother can endure; in the ESCAMBRAY region they murdered my son, Manuel Ascunce Domenech, on November 26, 1961. . . .One of those gangs murdered my son, cruelly, they were merciless with his young body, he was only sixteen years old. And even though we regard human life as priceless, Yankee imperialism is unforgivable and I believe that they should pay for the damage they have done and the hurt they continue to cause us.

Testimony by Evelia Domenech, mother of Manuel Ascunce.

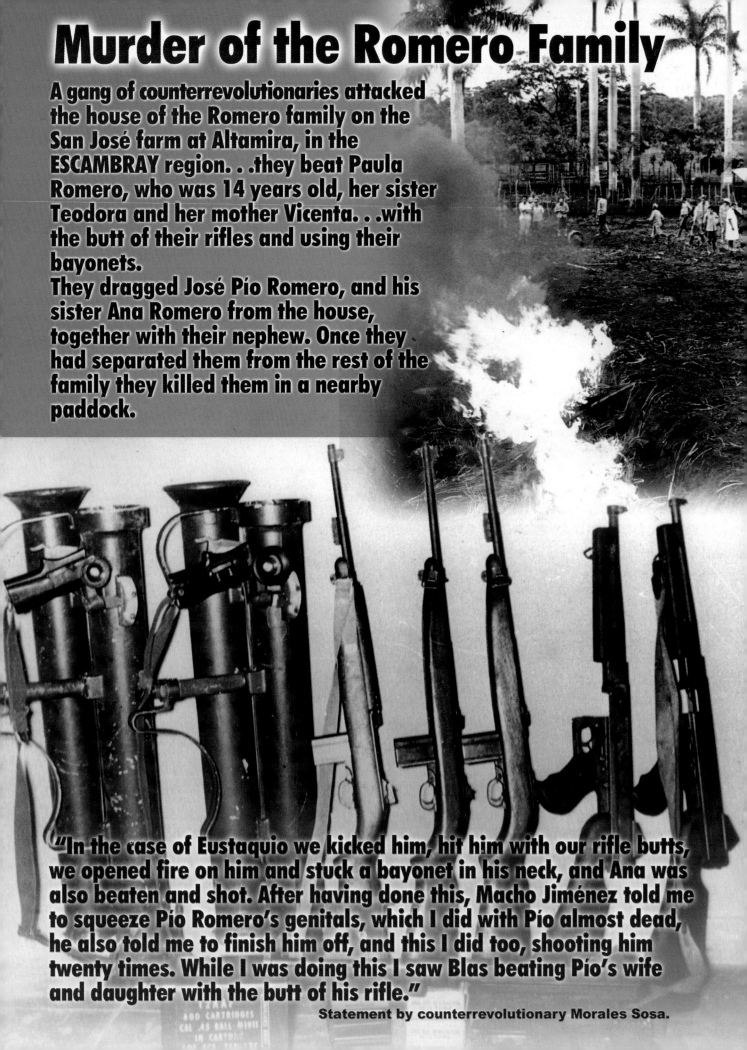

Murder of the Romero Family

A gang of counterrevolutionaries attacked the house of the Romero family on the San José farm at Altamira, in the ESCAMBRAY region. . .they beat Paula Romero, who was 14 years old, her sister Teodora and her mother Vicenta. . .with the butt of their rifles and using their bayonets.

They dragged José Pío Romero, and his sister Ana Romero from the house, together with their nephew. Once they had separated them from the rest of the family they killed them in a nearby paddock.

"In the case of Eustaquio we kicked him, hit him with our rifle butts, we opened fire on him and stuck a bayonet in his neck, and Ana was also beaten and shot. After having done this, Macho Jiménez told me to squeeze Pío Romero's genitals, which I did with Pío almost dead, he also told me to finish him off, and this I did too, shooting him twenty times. While I was doing this I saw Blas beating Pío's wife and daughter with the butt of his rifle."

Statement by counterrevolutionary Morales Sosa.

"They came out beating the family, until they reached the edge of the farmyard and then they opened fire. While my family was on the ground, they split open my cousin's forehead with gunfire, ripped off my aunt's breast and bayoneted my father in the neck."

Testimony by José Pío Romero, Bartolo Rafael Romero's son.

RECORD OF CONSTITUTION AND INQUIRY

On the San José de Altamira farm. . .on July 3, 1962, Rubén Darío Zayas Montalbán, the municipal judge, assisted by the expert military doctor from the ESCAMBRAY mountain division, arrived on the scene in order to carry out the procedures for an inquiry and the recovery of three corpses lying in the farm's paddock and put the following on record:

First: That the body of a person of white origin, who appears to be around twenty four years old, and who is known as Eustaquio Polo Romero, shows clear signs of being lifeless. He was found lying on the ground, face upwards, in a pool of blood. Having carried out an external examination, there were signs of bullet wounds caused by a heavy caliber weapon in the frontal parietal region, with the ensuing destruction of the brain, of the base of the nose, and the destruction of. . . .and other such injurie. . . .

Second: . . .Named Pío Romero y Rojas. . .who has numerous injuries to the face, cranium, arms, neck, testicles, caused by a heavy blunt instrument. . .wounds caused by a highly powerful heavy caliber firearm in the right cervical region with the total rupture of the jugular, and other such injuries. . . .

Third: The body of a woman aged around fifty. . .Ana Romero. . .wounds throughout the regions of the face and cranium apparently caused by a blunt instrument, in addition to massive hemorrhaging from the mouth. Injury, after injury, after injury. . . .

The Bolondrón Children

"Just a short time before the children had been revising their school lessons. I was worried because the dogs kept barking; I was even afraid to look out of the door. At around 9:30 p.m., I managed to settle them down for the night. Fermín had to rest because he had been working hard helping his father cut cane. . . .I remember because Fermín said to me, 'Mamá, I have worked out all the problems they set me at school. . . . Next year I am going to military school because I am old enough now.'

"At around eleven o'clock at night I heard a group approaching calling out to us, 'Comrades, comrades, get up. We are lost and can hardly see a thing.' A voice shouted. . .but I kept quiet to see whether they would leave, but they remained where they were and shouted out again,

'Could it be that you are traitors or are you afraid?' I couldn't keep quiet any longer and told them to look at the door of the house if they wanted to know whether or not we were trators. . .that's where the Cuban flag was hanging. Then they asked me to let the child take them to a nearby farm.

"I got up to open the door, Felicia had also woken, Gregorio was already in the living room. I open the door a little to see the face of the person who was talking. I asked him, 'Do you want to come in and sit down?' Then the nightmare started; it all happened at once. Gregorio realized that they had come to kill us and ran out of the house to look for a shotgun he had hanging on the wall. At that point, another voice coming from behind the door asked him, 'What are you waiting for? Shoot, corporal.'

"The man lifted his weapon and fired. Felicia, who was walking into the room, doubled over and fell onto a chair. In the window of the room where the children were sleeping, another burst of gunfire could be heard. They ran off into the darkness and were gone; I don't want to recall what I saw when I went into the room. My little son, Fermín, was there covered in blood; he had been dressing when was killed. Yolanda and Josefita were in bed; they woke up with bullet wounds in their little bodies. . .they didn't complain. I remember that in my despair I began to scream."

Nicolasa Díaz, mother of the murdered children.

Eduardo Ferrer, former CIA pilot, claims in his book "Operation Puma, the air battle of the Bay of Pigs," that between the months of September 1960 and March 1961, 68 air missions of weapons and explosives were supplied to insurgent groups over the Cuban mountains.

Operation Puma, Miami Dade Community College.
First edition in English (4-17-82).

REVOLUCION SEGUNDA EDICION

por el frío en toda Europa

POR QUE SE debe cortar a ros de tierra la caña

Cobarde y miserable acción

ASESINAN LOS GUSANOS EN BOLONDRON A UNA NIÑA DE 11 AÑOS Y UN NIÑO DE 13

ZONA REBELDE

la "Alianza" yanqui: an de explotación

Asaltaron por la noche una indefensa casa

HIRIERON TAMBIEN A LA MADRE Y A OTRAS DOS MENORES

ASESINOS ¿POR QUE, C

"What didn't we do to get rid of Castro?" mention is made of the different "pretexts" taken from a memorandum written by the President of the Council of Chiefs of Staff of the U.S. Armed Forces, April 11, 1962, sent to Secretary of Defense Robert McNamara.

Simulate an attack on the Guantánamo naval base using Cubans (Cubans resident in the United States, E.N.). They would be disguised as attacking forces launching mortars, destroying aircraft, facilities, before being captured. (Using this pretext the United States would launch a direct counterattack. E.N.)

Blow up a ship without crew close to a major Cuban city. The United States would simulate a rescue operation of non-existent crew, the list of victims would appear in the U.S. press with the resulting wave of national indignation.

Sink a boat loaded with Cubans heading for Florida.

Introduce weapons into a Caribbean country and send planes disguised as Cuban MIGs giving the appearance of a subversive act backed by Castro.

Blow up a U.S. plane without crew or passengers, with a false list of passengers. Cubans would be blamed for bringing the aircraft down.

US News & World Report journal,
October 8, 1998

Remember the Maine

Following the defeat of Brigade 2506 on the sands of Girón beach (Bay of Pigs), the United States government gave the go ahead for Operation Mongoose.

The largest CIA base was created within the context of this plan. This base continued to function on U.S. territory itself, even after Operation Mongoose had come to an end.

According to declassified U.S. documents, and other sources, some 600 officials of the Company operated out of the JM-Wave base, for whom between 3,000 and 4,000 agents of Cuban origin worked.

They controlled several hundred counter-Revolutionary organizations that operated as a screen in the permanent and incessant aggression against Cuba.

A complex infrastructure was set up in the city of Miami to operationally back up and supply actions against Cuba.

Training camps were set up in the keys and in the swampy areas of the Everglades for commando groups responsible for carrying out special operations

The camps were provided with planes for air attacks against economic and social targets, as well as naval bases. Resources included the mother ship, motorboats and speedboats that were heavily armed to attack merchant vessels of countries trading with Cuba, fishing boats, ports and coastal villages, and could also be used to get agents in and out Cuba, as well as weapons and explosives.

Agents of Cuban origin were directly responsible for these actions aimed at causing suffering and death to hundreds of Cuban families.

Following the deactivation of JM-Wave, and the support of U.S. authorities these Cuban terrorists based in Florida continued on with their activities.

N4365P

TERROR

TERRORISM

RRORISM

ISM:

AN ACCOUNT OF VIOLENT ATTACKS
CARRIED OUT TO SPREAD TERROR

AIR TERRORISM

The destruction of sugar mills and the devastation of the sugar cane crop via the use of incendiary devices was not only directed at Cuba's main industry, but also aimed at spreading fear among the peasant population who lost their homes and their lives.

17/01/1965: A bomb was dropped 13 km from the Niágara Sugar Mill, Consolación del Norte, in the Pinar del Río province, by a plane originating from the United States. It landed on the farmyard of the peasant Domingo Baños, and by some miracle it did not explode. Had it done so, the entire family would have perished.

On January 17, 1965, Orlando Bosch was given the responsibility of dropping napalm and live phosphorous bombs on the Niágara Sugar Mill, in the Pinar del Rio province. In a statement to the Miami press he declared, "IF WE HAD MORE RESOURCES, CUBA WOULD BURN FROM ONE END TO THE OTHER."

Three bombs were dropped from a plane originating from the United States, one of which damaged the roof of the Tarafa port, in the proximity of the thermoelectric plant of Nuevitas, in Camagüey; the other two did not explode.

Three bombs were dropped from a "pirate" plane on the "Cepero Bonilla" plant (formerly known as Cubanitro) and the "Frank País" fertilizer factory, in the western area of Matanzas bay, destroying a thousand cement fiber blocks and raw materials.

An aircraft originating from the United States entered Cuban air space on September 5, 1963, over the province of Las Villas. One of the bombs, which it dropped, exploded in the house of a teacher, Fabric Aguilar Noriega, killing him and injuring four of his children.

"I was in the living room, putting Alfonsito to sleep, the only one who was unharmed; after the crash I looked out of the room and saw my husband blown to pieces and the children hurt in the midst of wreckage. Because of that cowardly attack my young children never got to know their father, and they were almost killed. They injured 3 year old Sofia, 2 year old Abraham and 5 year old Francisco."

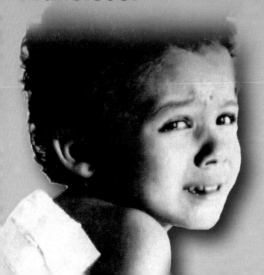

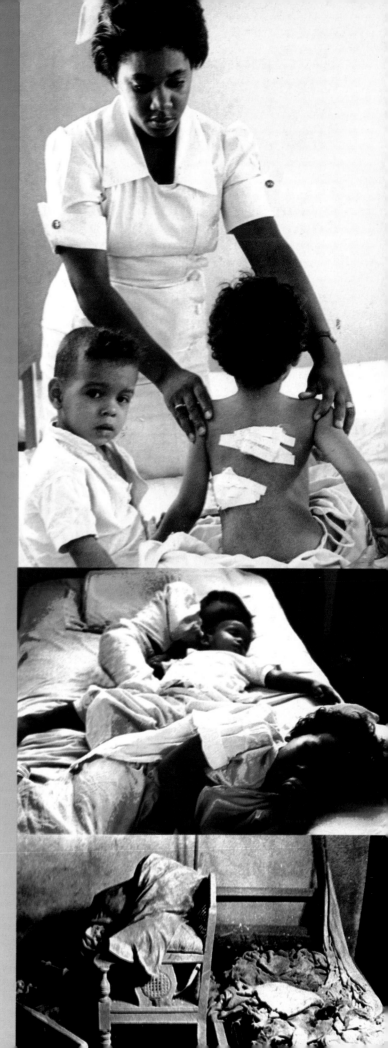

Bill Johnson, a former CIA pilot, according to the Miami press, declared that he together with Orlando Bosch had taken part in missions, under contract, in air incursions, against Cuban sugar mills.

"As a Rebel Army combatant, Cabrera was posted at that time in the region of the Punta Alegre sugar mill (today known as Máximo Gómez) in the province of Ciego de Avila; it was the first to be bombed following the success of the Cuban Revolution.

"There were no deaths because the first device exploded against a rail at the highest point of the mill and the shrapnes did not hit the people who were working below on the lathes, but it did, however, hit the metal structures about eighty times. The other device landed, without exploding, at the feet of a worker who was on duty nearby.

"Cabrera Estupiñán recalls, how, without any experience as a sapper, in order to avoid the death of innocent people, that he carried this last bomb on his right shoulder for a distance of around 500 meters to the garrison. There he discovered, when deactivating it, that it was filled with munitions and some 12 pounds of explosives."

On April 13, 1961, four peasants were burned to death: Eduardo Harga (53 years old), José María Soa (62 years old), Rogelio Pena Simón (33 years old) and Santiago González Linares (43 years old) while they were trying to put out a fire. The fire was caused by a napalm bomb dropped by a small plane, from the United States, on sugar cane plantations at the Venezuela Sugar Mill, in Ciego de Avila.

Fire! The cry for help was heard all around and everybody, some on foot and others on horseback, rushed to the scene.

The flames were huge. Smoke was everywhere. The sound of machetes, of bunches of sugar cane tops and branches of brushwood seemed like some terrible symphony of the deaf. The four peasants opened up a breach in the sugar cane plantation in the attempt to stop the fire from spreading.

Within a few minutes they were lost in the fire. They were not aware that the fire had surrounded them and, when they tried to turn back, it was too late. They were dead on arrival at the hospital.

Several sugar cane plantations were set on fire by planes, from the United States, which dropped the inflammable material "live phosphorus" on the Río de Palma region, Martí, in Matanzas.

They were bombed by a "pirate" plane that dropped the inflammable substance napalm on the sugar cane area of Ziskay, burning 100,000 kilos of cane for the "Boris Luis Santa Coloma" and "Rubén Martínez Villena" sugar mills.

During the night, two 50-pound bombs were dropped on the grounds of the Cunagua (Bolivia) sugar mill in the municipality of the same name, in Ciego de Avila, by a "pirate" plane, endangering the lives of local people who were asleep in their homes.

A "pirate" plane that had departed from the United States bombed the oil reserves at the port of Casilda in Sancti Spíritus. One of the rockets launched hit and set fire to one of the 24 train wagons which were on the railway line, while another destroyed a house.

REVOLUCION

La Habana, Sábado 2 de Abril de 1960

Quema 300mil arrobas en Matanzas

The Jaronú (Brasil) sugar mill in the municipality of Esmeralda, Camagüey, was bombed by a plane coming from the United States. Five 50-pound bombs were dropped, which exploded in the surrounding areas of the mill.

A second attack was carried out on the Jaronú (Brasil) sugar mill in the municipality of Esmeralda, Camagüey, by a plane originating from the United States, which dropped five 50-pound bombs that exploded in the area surrounding the Brasil sugar mill. One of the bombs destroyed several nearby rooms, without loss of human life.

Three bombs were dropped on the Reforma ("Marcelo Salado") sugar mill in Caibarién, Las Villas province, by a Cessna 205 plane belonging to the American Aviation Corporation, in Miami, registration number N 8365-Z, coming from the United States.

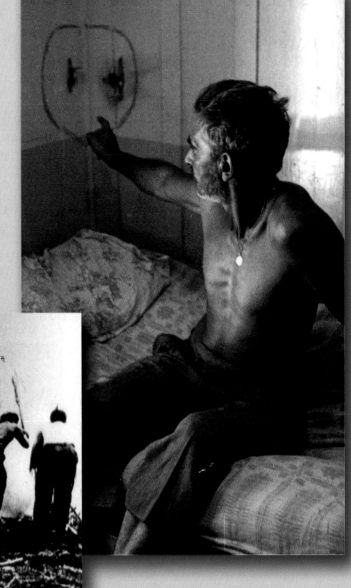

On June 11, 1965, *The Miami News* published an article on terrorist activities over a three-year period, carried out from the United States, under the direction of Orlando Bosch Ávila and the organization known as MIRR. The writer stated that Bosch and five of his men had been detained by authorities in Zellwood, Orlando, Tampa, when they attempted to export "without a license" eighteen aircraft bombs.

"Export" refers to transporting the bombs out of the United States in planes to be dropped on Cuba (E.N.)

¡SENSACIONAL! ¡EXCLUSIVO!

ESTOS SON LOS AVIONES QUE BOMBARDEAN A CUBA

Un Reportaje de
RENE HERNANDEZ

1.- Actuan impunemente en la Florida los criminales de guerra.

2.- Transportan armas y pertrechas en pleno día.

3.- Cobraron 3 mil dolares por el ataque a Cojímar y Regla. Mil por incendiar cañaverales.

"IF WE HAD MORE RESOURCES, CUBA WOULD BURN FROM ONE END TO THE OTHER."

Orlando Bosch, January 17, 1965, in a statement to the Miami press.

The Cuban vessel "San Pascual" and the British boat "New Lane," which were loaded with sugar, were machine-gunned by a "pirate" ship armed with artillery off Cayo Francés, in Sancti Spíritus. The Cuban ship was hit eighteen times, while the British one was hit thirteen times. On September 18, "Alpha 66," the U.S. based terrorist organization, assumed responsibility for the attack. Antonio Cuesta Valle, Antonio Quesada, Ángel Pouxes, and other terrorists took part in the attack.

63/03/17
The Soviet cargo ship "L`Gov" was hit by gunfire, while anchored in the port of Isabela de Sagua, in Las Villas province. The chimney and one of the ship's ventilators were damaged by the "pirate" boat.

TERRORISM AGAINST

MERCHANT SHIPS

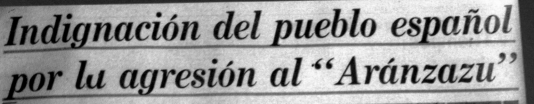

Indignación del pueblo español por lu agresión al "Aránzazu"

REMOLCADO A ORIENTE Y AUN ARDE

Hipócrita r...
de Rusk de l...
culpabilida...

● El criterio del go...
que Estados Unidos...
"por todo lo que ocurr...
donde fue atacado el "...
zazu", no fue compartid...
tario de Estado, Dean...
le urgente entrevista r...
entre el funcionario n...
el embajador de Espa...
Merry del Val, Dura...

Declaraciones de FIDEL

ESTADOS UNIDOS
TIENE DERECHO
INVADIR A CUBA

El ataque al barco "Sierra Aránzazu" fue
acto de revancha contra el gobierno espa...
por su comercio con nuestro país

Por LUIS BAEZ

El ataque al "Sierra Aranzazu"

RESPONSABLE DE ESE BARBARO HECHO EL GOBIERNO DE EE. UU.

Denuncia MINFAR el cobarde crimen pirata

ESPANA TAMBIEN ACUSA

Murieron el capitán y dos miembros de la tripulación

● El Ministerio de
las Fuerzas Armadas
Revolucionarias d l a
a conocer un impor-
tante comunicado so-
bre la bárbara y cri-
minal agresión per-
petrada por mercena-
rios cubanos al se...

REVOLUCION

Represalias del ...bierno uruguayo ...ntra periódicos

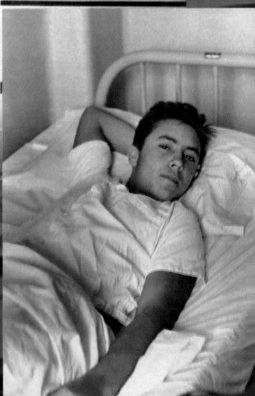

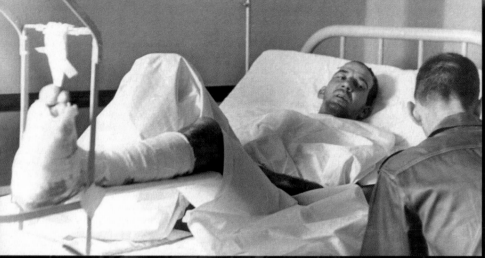

64/09/12
The Spanish ship "Sierra de Aranzazu" was attacked by "pirate" boats while transporting cargo to Cuba, cargo that included toys for Cuban children. The attack took place 75 miles to the north of Maisí in Guantánamo province.

Captain Pedro Ibargurengonitía lost his life in the attack and several crew members were injured.

63/03/26
The Soviet ship "Bakú," loaded with Cuban sugar, was attacked by a "pirate" vessel in the port of Caibarién, in the province of Las Villas. The ship was hit numerous times by shells fired from a 20-mm cannon and 30-and 50-caliber machine guns. The explosion of a magnetic mine blew open a four-meter long and half-meter wide crack.

For the attack on the "Bakú": the terrorists prepared an explosive charge inside an empty oil drum, to which they fixed a magnet. The improvised mine was attached by hand to the side of the ship, pressing it into position. At the same time, other terrorists opened fire on the deck of the Soviet ship to prevent the sailors from firing at them.

TODO MATANZAS SE MOVILIZA PARA EL SABADO 30

DOS MILLONES
de arrobas de caña
cortadas por el E.R.
(Vea Columna SIETE)

REVOLUCION SEGUNDA EDICION

1ro. DE ABRIL
fiesta socialista
por la emulación
(Vea Columna SEIS)

La Habana, Jueves 28 de Marzo de 1963

ACUSA FIDEL A E. U. POR ATAQUE PIRATA A OTRO BARCO DE URSS

Cuba se verá precisada a adquirir
bombarderos de largo alcance y los
equipos navales necesarios para la
escolta y repeler a los agresores

Inician Congreso de
Solidaridad con Cuba

Piden a Goulart de
garantías para
esta reunión

Trasmitirán a
todo el país
el discurso de
Fidel Castro

Atacó una lancha pirata
un mercante de la U.R.S.S.

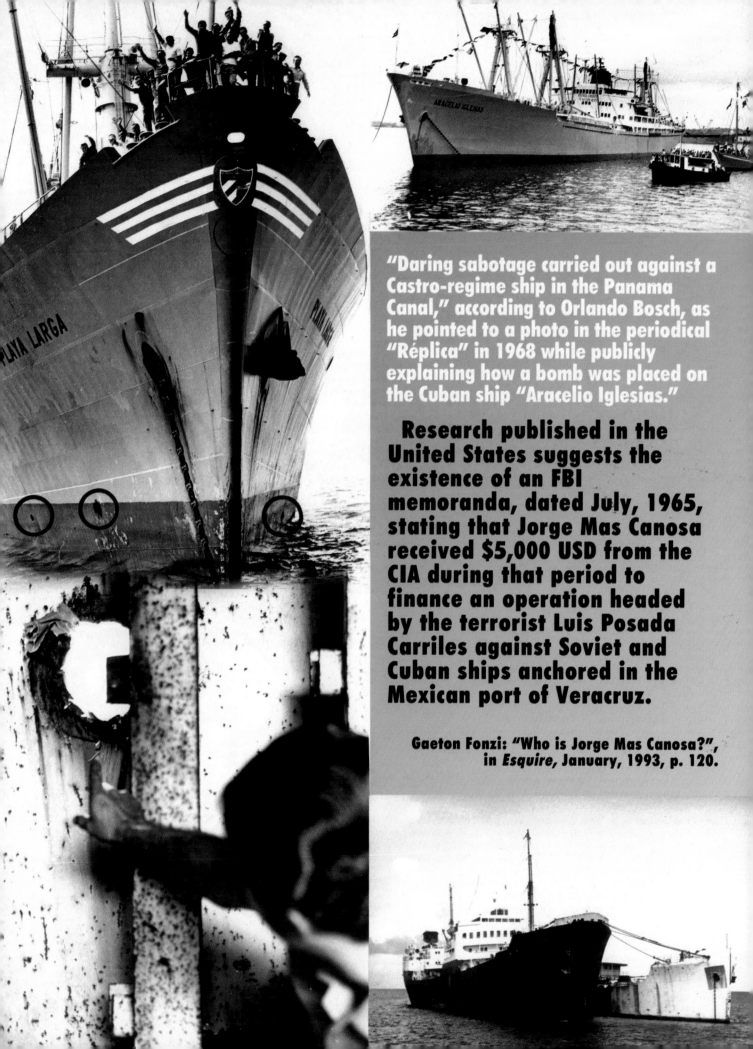

"Daring sabotage carried out against a Castro-regime ship in the Panama Canal," according to Orlando Bosch, as he pointed to a photo in the periodical "Réplica" in 1968 while publicly explaining how a bomb was placed on the Cuban ship "Aracelio Iglesias."

Research published in the United States suggests the existence of an FBI memoranda, dated July, 1965, stating that Jorge Mas Canosa received $5,000 USD from the CIA during that period to finance an operation headed by the terrorist Luis Posada Carriles against Soviet and Cuban ships anchored in the Mexican port of Veracruz.

Gaeton Fonzi: "Who is Jorge Mas Canosa?", in *Esquire*, January, 1993, p. 120.

The British ship "Lancaster Prince" was the target of a terrorist attack, and the Canadian textile company Morton Textile Co., based in Montreal, suffered serious damage to its merchandise in Cuba when incendiary devices, hidden amongst several packages, exploded and caused a fire on arrival at Nuevitas port, in Camagüey, in the Cuban cargo ship "Río Damují."

70/05/10
The fishing vessels "Plataforma I and IV", from Caibarién, were attacked in open sea, and their crew of eleven fishermen were kidnapped.

"I just don't understand it. I'm very upset. It is completely underhanded what they have done to Orosmán and the others. They are only fishermen."

Aida Morales, wife of the kidnapped fisherman Orosmán del Río.

"If they were handed over to me I would tear them apart. Sons of a bitch!"

Blanca Vasallo, Aida Morales' mother.

"No one was able to understand why ordinary workers were taken, kidnapped and mistreated. It is against all the rules and yet they went ahead and did it. It was happening and it was happening to us.

"When they were parallel with the ships they began to circle them while their crew displayed all kinds of weapons. They ordered one of the boats to be lowered from 'Plataforma 1,' and everyone to get on, and board 'Plataforma 4.'

"Then another of them climbed aboard with a pack of dynamite and a long fuse. There were about ten red cartridges, taped together.

"When 'Plataforma 4' was about a mile away an explosion was heard from 'Plataforma 1.' Around four in the afternoon we arrived at a key.

"They said they were from Alpha 66. Once on land, packs of dynamite were passed from the boats that were for the ship. They wanted to blow it up and sink it quickly. So they exploded the charges."

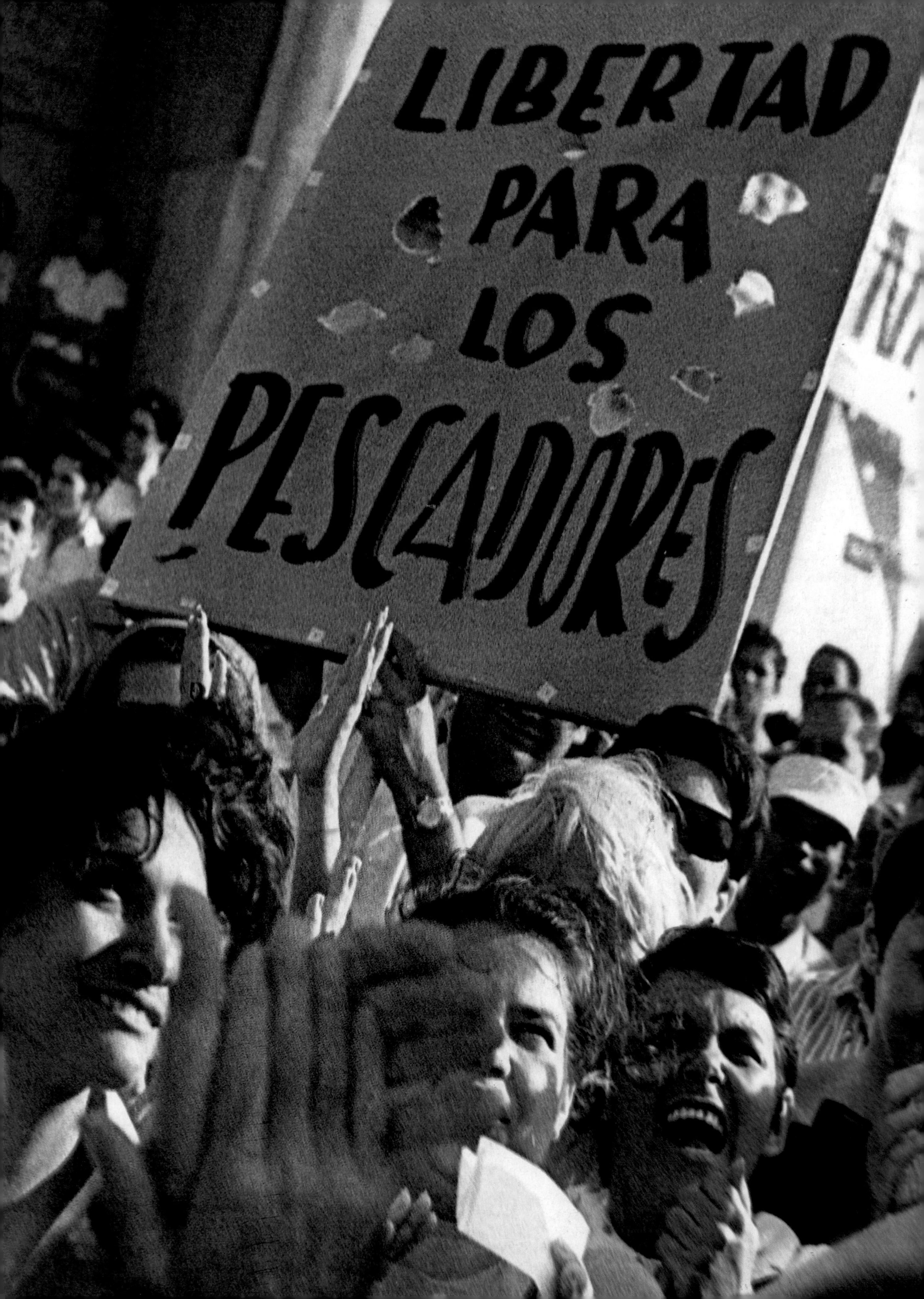
LIBERTAD PARA LOS PESCADORES

"It was really sad. Another ship could have replaced it but it wouldn't have been the same. Those who work at sea know that ships for us are like family, like a strong and kind father who has to be looked after. And what really hurt was that it was destroyed for no good reason, there was no logic to it, no decency and no respect. The night was a long one because of mosquitoes, gnats and then the cold, which we hadn't expected. Three days and nights were spent there, until there was no food and water. Finally, on the morning of the fourth day, the boat that had left first, appeared. Nazario Sargen was on board.

"Several days were spent like this. Then a plane appeared. It circled three times and then made a parachute drop of concentrated food comprised of bars of chocolate and tablets. It also included a message: 'Don't move. You have been rescued. International Red Cross.'

LOS HIJOS DEL PUEBLO NO SE CAMBIAN POR GUSANOS

Gramma

EDICION UNICA

ORGANO OFICIAL DEL COMITE CENTRAL
DEL PARTIDO COMUNISTA DE CUBA

¡VICTORIA!

CONFIRMADA LA NOTICIA

ABANDONAN LOS
MERCENARIOS DE LA CIA
A LOS PESCADORES EN LAS

200,000 PERSONAS DESFILARON FRENTE A LA GUARIDA YANQUI

Más de doscientas mil personas participaron ayer domingo en la ininterrumpida manifestación
contra el secuestro de nuestros 11 pescadores por una banda mercenaria al servicio del gobierno
de su justa indignación frente a la guarida yanqui

CDR

"They traveled to Nassau because the plane could not land at Andros. Afterwards we took the Cubana flight, changed into clean clothes, met with Fidel and attended a huge public rally in Havana.

"There was massive uproar in the port when people found out what had happened. People ran from house to house and everyone poured out into the street shouting with joy. Those who suffered most, as is always the case, were the families, the mothers, the women and the younger children. Orosmán's little daughter, who was only five years old, told me that her heart ached because she had cried so much."

Text comprised of statements made by family members of abducted and murdered fishermen.

On April 6, 1976, a "pirate" boat attacked two Cuban fishing vessels, sinking them; one of the crew was murdered and three others were injured. The attack took place around eight o'clock in the evening, when the "Ferro 123 and "Ferro 119" ships were between Anguila and Key Sal. Heavy caliber machine guns and other automatic weapons opened fire on them.

The crew of "Ferro 123" were abandoned in the middle of the channel at the mercy of strong winds and heavy currents. Two days later they managed to reach Key Anguila, where they were rescued by "Ferro 24" and taken to the base in Matanzas. Pérez Tápanes, Duquesne and Díaz Pérez, who died a few days later, were injured. The boat responsible for the attack immediately turned on "Ferro 119" and killed one of its crew members, 28-year old Bienvenido Mauriz Díaz. The owner of this boat, the crew, and the corpse of Mauriz Díaz were rescued by a Norwegian merchant ship and taken to Miami, where they demanded that the authorities return them immediately to Cuba.

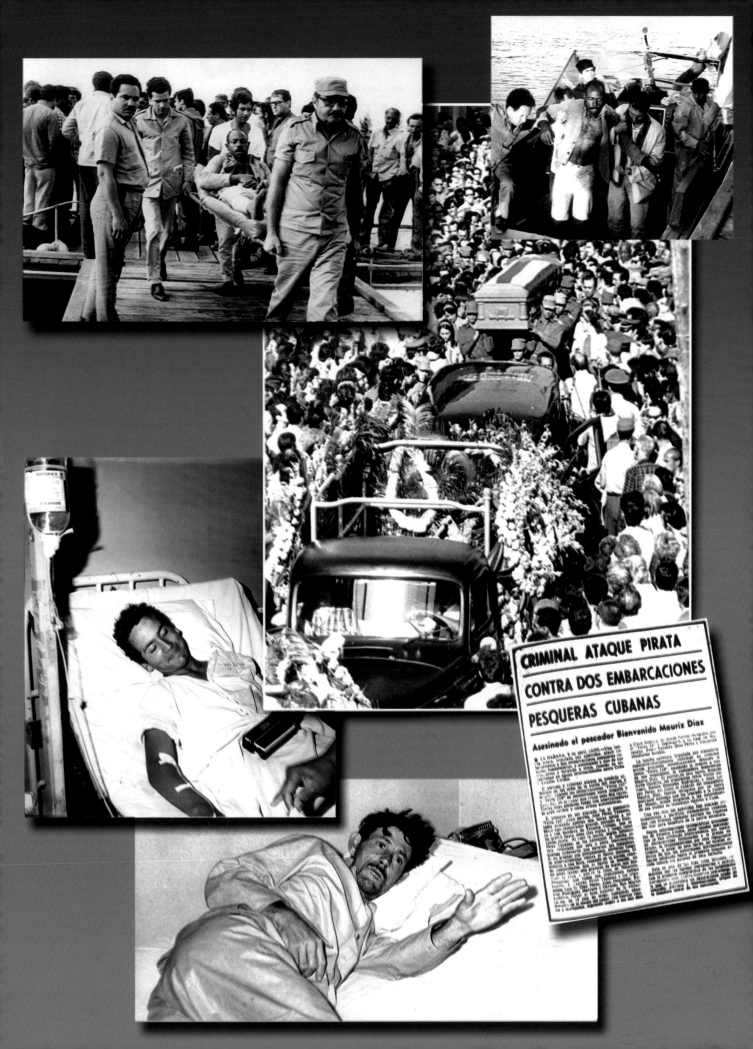

CRIMINAL ATAQUE PIRATA
CONTRA DOS EMBARCACIONES
PESQUERAS CUBANAS

Asesinado el pescador Bienvenido Mauriz Díaz

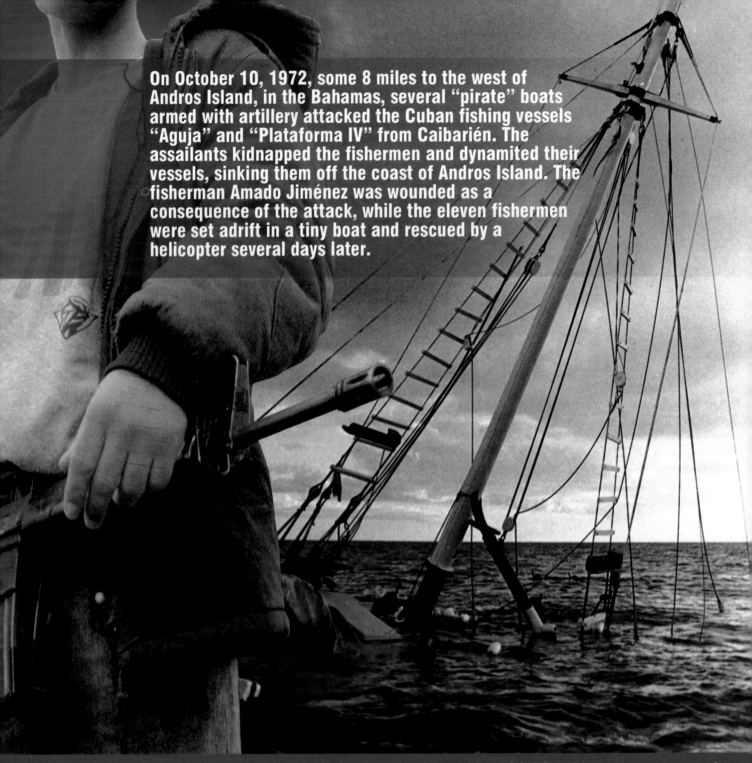

On October 10, 1972, some 8 miles to the west of Andros Island, in the Bahamas, several "pirate" boats armed with artillery attacked the Cuban fishing vessels "Aguja" and "Plataforma IV" from Caibarién. The assailants kidnapped the fishermen and dynamited their vessels, sinking them off the coast of Andros Island. The fisherman Amado Jiménez was wounded as a consequence of the attack, while the eleven fishermen were set adrift in a tiny boat and rescued by a helicopter several days later.

"They went to sleep around ten o'clock in the evening and at 11.30, when everyone was in a deep sleep, two boats approached in silence and they boarded "Plataforma IV." The crew awoke to the sound of Amado's shouts, crying out that he had been wounded. They had stabbed him three times in the throat, it was a massive wound, and he had to swallow huge amounts of blood in order to breathe. We couldn't work out why they had cut Amado's throat, they had nothing to gain from it; they caught him sleeping. That's when they covered his mouth and cut his throat, just for the sake of it, to slit him open, to see the blood of a human being spilled out.

"They arrived in two boats, one was large, another was an 18-foot inflatable rubber dingy; both were equipped with artillery. They dynamited the "Aguja" and set fire to her. It is always the same: to sabotage the boats, to destroy the fleet, to obstruct fishing, to frighten people. Then there is Amado, a living and perpetual reminder of what took place with a scar that runs across the whole of his neck."

Pilar Rodríguez Guevara,
mother of four kidnapped fishermen.

On October 4, 1973, the same year in which Cuba and the United States signed the bilateral accord known as the Memorandum of Agreement on the Hijacking of Aircraft and Seagoing Vessels and other Crimes, the Cuban fishermen of the "Cayo Largo 17" and "Cayo Largo 34" vessels, which were fishing in international waters, close to the Bahamas, were attacked by armed "pirate" boats, belonging to the Miami-based terrorist organization National Front for the Liberation of Cuba (FNLC, Spanish abbreviation).

As a consequence of the machine-gunning of the defenseless fishing boat, a fisherman, Roberto Torna Mirabal, died due to bullet wounds. The rest of the crew had to be rescued while they drifted at sea in rubber dinghies, without food or water.

"On the night of the fifth, it was announced that a ship had rescued the crew, which had disappeared, and that Roberto was among them. All the news became public at the same time. I said to myself, the one that has disappeared is Roberto and I am sure he is dead, because he always said that he couldn't put up with any of those people.

"Afterwards, the whole story was told. The "pirate" boat closed in on them and opened fire. Uberman ran to the bow where the radio was in order to warn the people back at the base, and Robert followed him. In a question of seconds there was a hail of bullets and that's when Roberto was hit; they say that when he fell to the deck he was already dead. They were in uniform, had their faces covered and wore Alpha 66 armbands.

"No one ever confirmed that he was dead. He was always classified as missing, and I waited without saying a word to anyone for him to walk in through the door, and twenty years went by that way. We will never know the truth about what happened. And the problem is that we cannot accept a death of a loved one until we see and touch the body.

"My daughter was 19 years old and was eight months pregnant at the time. The baby would have been his first grandson; she had to spend the final month of her pregnancy in hospital. Her blood pressure went up and the birth was premature. The baby was born with problems. He has asthma, kidney and psychological problems.

"I was about to lose my entire family, to be left alone in life. I had lost Roberto, my daughter was seriously ill and my grandchild was in intensive care.
I can hardly bear to think about what happened and in my despair I used to ask myself, 'Why me? My God, why me?' I am still waiting to see what might happen. Officially he has been pronounced as dead, and I am still hopeful; perhaps it is just me being stupid, but I can't accept it.

"I have old-age complaints, but nothing serious, and I love life and want to live it to the full, but what I have never managed to cope with, and will never be able to cope with, is the anxiety I feel when my grandson goes fishing; I cannot rest until I see him reach shore with the tide. Because my grandson is a fisherman. What else can he do?"

Testimony of Maria, widow of the murdered fisherman
Roberto Torna Mirabal.

TERRORISM AT SEA

Cobarde agresión a dos embarcaciones pesqueras cubanas

SAPARECIDOS SUS TRECE TRIPULANTES

NA DE LAS EMBARCACIONES FUE HALLADA SEMIHUNDIDA Y ARDIENDO, Y LA OTRA AL GARETE, EN LAS BAR...

QUEMADOS Y HUNDIDOS DOS BARCOS PESQUEROS CUBANOS

LA ACCION SE REALIZO AL SUR DE LA ISLA ANDROS. SE IGNORA LA SUERTE DE SUS TRIPULANTES

62/10/13
The fishermen Filiberto Suárez Lima and Miguel Cao Medina were seriously injured after their vessel was sunk during a terrorist machine gun attack, carried out with 30-caliber weapons from a "pirate" gray PT boat close to Key Blanco, 23 km off Cárdenas, in the province of Matanzas. The fishermen were kidnapped and taken to Miami in the United States. They were returned to Cuba 30 days later.

63/02/13
The fishermen Armando and Ramón López Ruiz were injured during an attack on two fishing Sigma vessels ("Sigma 15" and "Sigma 2"), belonging to the cooperative in Cárdenas, in the province of Matanzas. The attack was perpetrated by a boat, armed with artillery that had come from the United States, in the proximity of Key Roque, in Cárdenas. The attackers seized both vessels and took them to Key Elbow, in the Bahamas, and the injured crew members were left to fend for themselves.

On January 28, 1973, a Cuban fishing vessel was attacked in the Bahamas. The Cuban fisherman Ibrahim Ruiz was injured and his boat was seriously damaged. A Miami-based terrorist commando group claimed responsibility for the attack.

los familiares de los pescadores cubanos

"CUANDO VIMOS AL "AGUJA" QUEMADO Y SEMIHUNDIDO, DIJIMOS: ESTO ES OTRA AGRESION"

Expresa Alberto Perdomo, patrón del cayo largo "Plataforma 13", quien encontró al pesquero "Aguja" sumergido a pocas millas de la isla Andros.

CAIBARIEN — Alberto Perdomo Córdova, 54 años, 4 hijos, una vida consagrada al trabajo en el mar, fundador de la cooperativa "Capitán Miguel A. Rojas", patrón del cayo largo "Plataforma 13", fue el hombre que encontró sumergido a unas pocas millas de la isla Andros perteneciente al archipiélago de Nassau, al pesquero "Aguja", sin tripulantes y ardiendo por la banda de barlovento.

De izquierda a derecha (al centro) está Adelaida Córdova, esposa de Amado Jiménez (herido).

"No me he sentido sola un momento Todos han venido a alentarme"

"We decided to turn back after we were certain that no one remained on board the 'Aguja.' At that point we heard weak groaning and I said to my comrades, 'That is one of Jiménez's dogs.' And the truth is that there they were, in the prow of the dynamited boat, almost dead from hunger and cold, two small dogs that we rescued and brought to land."

Alberto Perdomo Cordova, owner of the "Cayo Largo" and "Plataforma 13."

Every time a terrorist attack is perpetrated against Cuban fishing vessels, a fleet takes to sea.

Attack on Boca de Samá

October 12, 1971

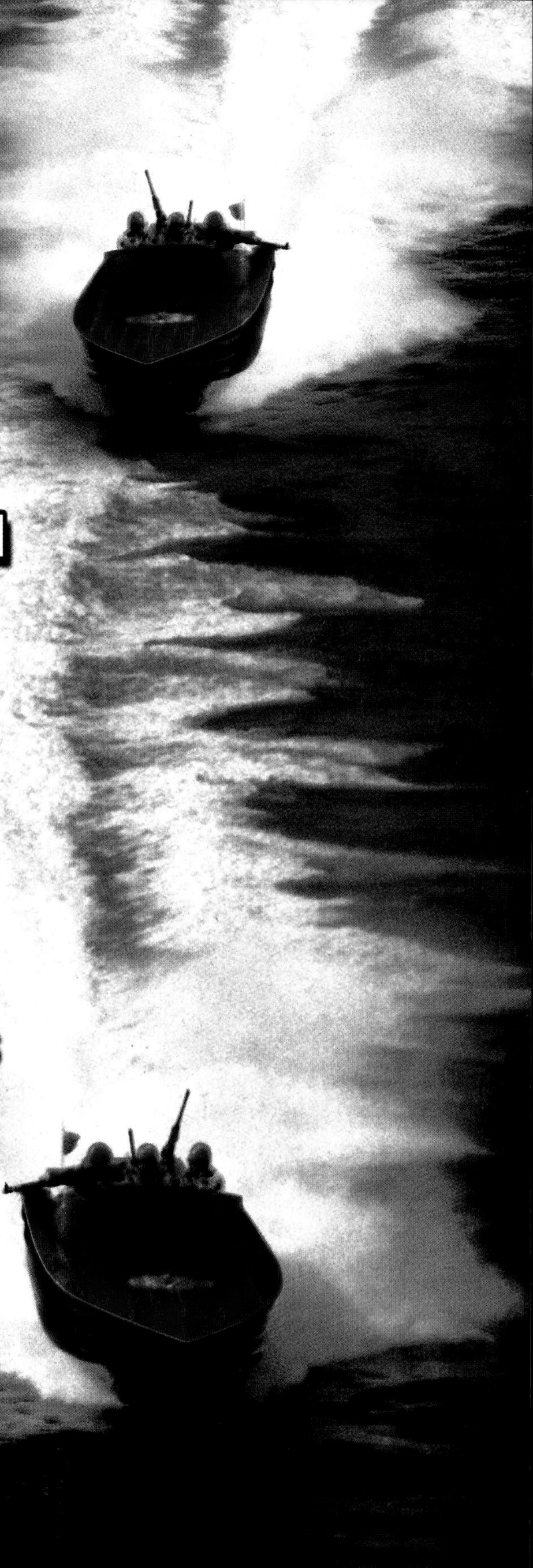

During an attack perpetrated by a group of terrorists who manned the two "pirate" boats coming from Florida against the village of Boca de Samá, in Banes, in the east of Cuba, Lidio Rivaflecha Galano and Ramón Arturo Siam Portelles were killed and the sisters Nancy and Angela Pavón Pavón, 15 and 13 years old, respectively, were injured. The former lost a foot. Also wounded were Carlos Escalante Gómez and Jesús Igarza Osorio.

EFEC...DO UN COMBATIVO ACTO DE MASAS
EN BOCA DE SAMA, EN REPUDIO A LA AGRESION
MERCENARIA PERPETRADA A ESE CASERIO

● HABLO ARMANDO HART, MIEMBRO DEL BURO POLITICO
● EL SEPELIO DE LOS CAIDOS

● Armando Hart Dávalos, miembro del Buró Político de nuestro Partido, habló en el ac... masivo de condenación a la... | memente respondieron al artero ataque. / Armando Hart describió al ... de Boca de Sama... | y puso como ejemplo a Cuba y a Viet Nam. / Refiriéndose nuevamente ... | nunció las palabra... dida...

"...My husband was killed in the cowardly attack against Boca de Samá, in Holguín; he was called Lidio Rivaflecha Galano....That was terrible, and I thought I was dying because of the suffering I had to endure. But I found the energy to bring up four children who never saw their father again. I did it alone, with the help of the government, but it was hard going. At that time my youngest daughter was two, and she loved her father; she waited for him every day to come back. She was the one who suffered most because she had learning difficulties during the early years of school. After that she overcame it."

Juana Vargas González

"...I lost my son Ramón Siam Portelles. No amount of money can pay for the life of a child; my son was only 24 years old and he had a six-month-old daughter who he was never able to give his love to...."

Josefa Caridad Portelles Tamayo

"We saw the leaflets, which they had distributed throughout the town, signed by Alpha 66, and a flag that they had attempted to hoist, but couldn't. They had been to three homes and taken some of the local people prisoner. They tried to convince them to take them to the border control post, with the aim of attacking it and killing the chief and his staff. In spite of threats the neighbors refused."

Carlos Andrés Escalante Gómez

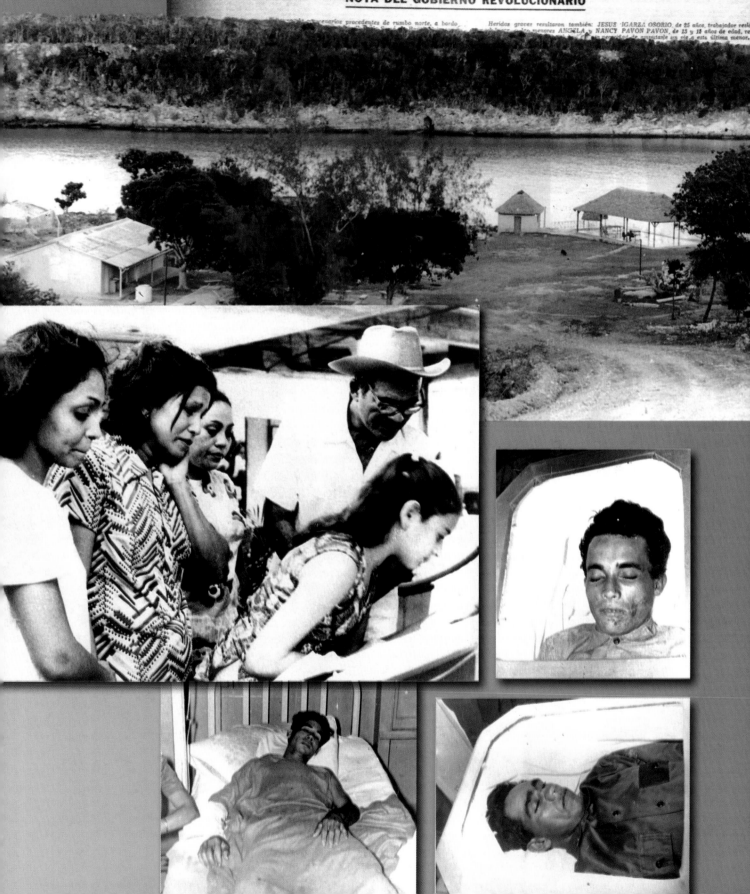

Gramma

ÓRGANO OFICIAL DEL COMITE CENTRAL
DEL PARTIDO COMUNISTA DE CUBA

LA HABANA, JUEVES 14 DE OCTUBRE DE 1971 / AÑO DE LA PRODUCTIVIDAD / Año 7 / No. 246 / Precio: 5 Ctvs. / CIERRE: 4:00 ...

EDICION

Ataque pirata al caserío de Boca de Samá, al norte de Banes, Oriente
Dos muertos y cuatro heridos por la criminal acción

NOTA DEL GOBIERNO REVOLUCIONARIO

"That night I was sleeping when I heard gunfire. My mother began to cry because there were small children around. A 50-caliber bullet hit her and I was hit in both feet; one of them was cut to pieces, as if I had been attacked with a machete. My father said, 'Let's see if we can get out of here with the children, otherwise they are going to bleed to death.' We had to leave the house in the midst of the shooting. My father tried to make it back into the house to get sheets to stop the flow of blood, and just as he was arriving they fired a cannon and the house shook. They operated on me and amputated my right foot. I spent nineteen months in hospital. It will soon be 28 years since that day and the prosthesis has begun to give way inside, and that upsets me. When I was fifteen years old my dream, when comedies were performed in school, was to be able to wear high heels one day. I was never able to because of those pigs that destroyed my life. I have never been happy because of my foot. . . ."

Nancy Pavón Pavón

After carrying out an attack on the island the Alpha 66 terrorists return to Miami, where they live.

Photo released by Alpha 66 to the Miami press.

HEADING NORTH...

" . . . They destroyed my youth. I have never been happy because of my foot."

Andrés Nazario Sargen
PRIVATE ADDRESS
2443 NW 29th St., Miami, Fl. 33142
ALPHA-66
1714 W Flager St., Miami, Fl. 33135

"From the time of the first commando attack in 1961 the war was galvanized. . . .Our whole purpose is to destroy everything we can inside Cuba."

Andrés Nazario Sargen

The U.S. government will defend the law with regard to all those who attempt to violate it. U.S. legislation, including the Neutrality Act, expressly prohibits participation in any military or naval expedition launched against a foreign nation from U.S. territory.

Fragment of the article "A Special Report" written by the terrorist Andrés Nazario Sargen, where responsibility is claimed for an attack launched from a "pirate" boat against a Cuban joint venture tourist hotel in May 1995. The article appeared in the Miami press and on the web site of the terrorist organization Alpha 66 in November 2000.

FOLLOWING THE ROUTE OF TERRORISM THROUGHOUT THE WORLD

Long before the U.S. terrorist Timothy McVeigh blew up the Alfred P. Murrah building in Oklahoma City on April 19, 1995, Cuban origin terrorists based in the United States were already using, with lethal consequences, ammonium nitrate, C-4, and other highly dangerous explosives.

On January 8, 1968, a bomb exploded in the warehouses of the Ministry of Communication in Havana; it was inside mailbag number 15 of Post Office 96, and was mailed in New York. The explosion injured several workers and caused substantial damage to the roof of the building, to the windows of the Postal Administration section and to the truck carrying the mailbags.

At approximately 11:45 p.m. on Monday, April 3, 1972, a violent explosion almost entirely destroyed the 12th floor of the Cuba Trade Mission in Montreal, Canada, causing the death of the official

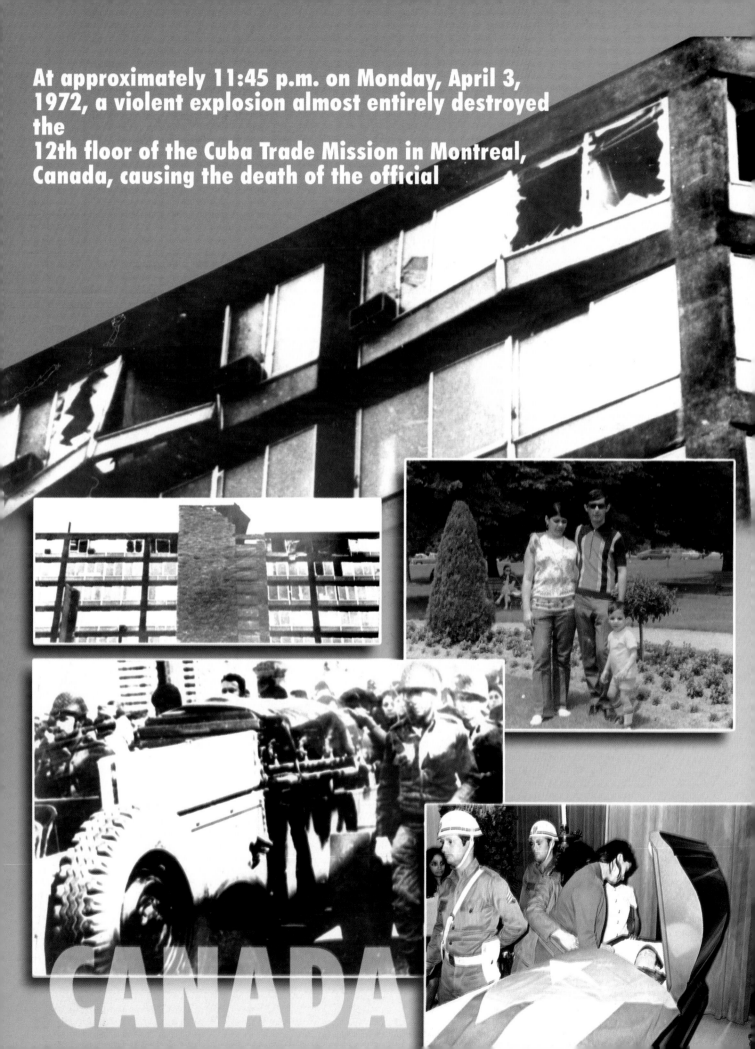

CANADA

On February 4, 1974, at around 4:45 in the afternoon, dynamite that had been placed inside a book sent to the Cuban embassy in Lima, Peru, exploded. As a consequence of the explosion the Cuban official Pilar Ramírez Vega was injured and suffered serious burns.

"It was a package the size of a book, with a red cover, by Aguilar, sent by Fernández Editores S.A. and with a postmark indicating that it had been sent from Chihuahua, Mexico. The wrapping paper was so tight that I had to use scissors to open it. When I tried to take it out there was a substantial explosion, which blew up the desk and the typewriter, and caused wounds to my abdomen, face, thigh and a breast. They told me it was plastic explosives, such as those used by counterrevolutionaries financed by the CIA. This package arrived contaminated by microorganisms, and a few days later I suffered from an infection they could not identify until they carried out analyses on the rest of the device and my body."

Testimony by Pilar Ramírez Vega

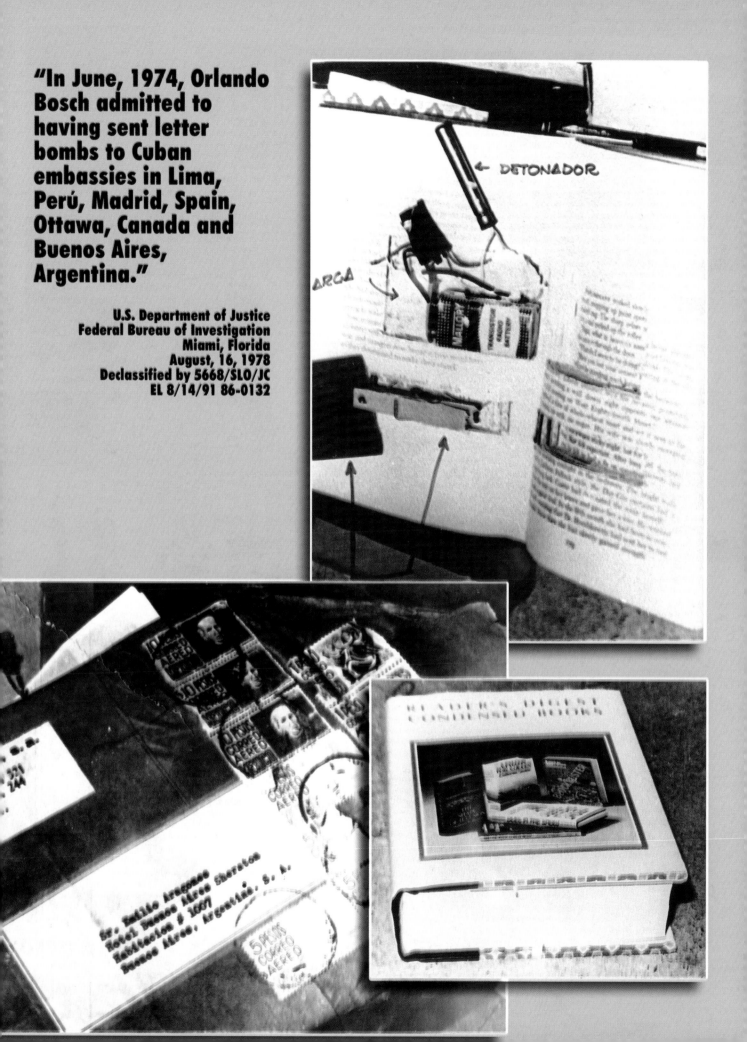

"In June, 1974, Orlando Bosch admitted to having sent letter bombs to Cuban embassies in Lima, Perú, Madrid, Spain, Ottawa, Canada and Buenos Aires, Argentina."

U.S. Department of Justice
Federal Bureau of Investigation
Miami, Florida
August, 16, 1978
Declassified by 5668/SLO/JC
EL 8/14/91 86-0132

On July 8, 1976, Cuban origin terrorists placed a bomb in the Cuban embassy in Madrid, which caused serious material damages.

On November 7, 1976, Cuban origin terrorists exploded a bomb in the office on the Cubana Aviation Company, in Madrid.

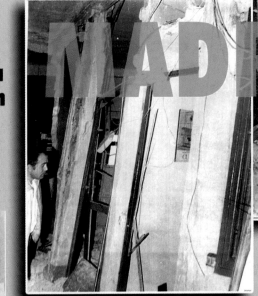

On June 6, 1976, a bomb exploded at the Cuban diplomatic repesentation to the United Nations, in New York, causing substantial material damage. Cuban origin terrorists resident in the United States claimed responsibility for the attack.

NUESTRA PRIMERA ACCION. EL ATENTADO AL EMBAJADOR DE CUBA EN LA ARGENTINA

On August 22, 1975, a moving car opened fire on the Cuban ambassador's vehicle in Argentina, just as it was entering the embassy garage.

CONSEJO REVOLUCIONARIO ANTICOMUNISTA LATINOAMERICANO

Los hombres revolucionarios de América, preocupados por el avance del comunismo en nuestros pueblos, hemos constituido un frente solidario, el cual se conocerá como *"Consejo Revolucionario Anti-Comunista Latinoamericano"* (CRAL). Nuestra meta es internacionalizar la guerra a niveles continentales, aplicando justicia a los traidores de la causa de la libertad.

Nuestras aspiraciones son las mismas que animaron a nuestros próceres: libertad y justicia. Por tanto hacemos un llamado a todos los hombres anti-comunistas de América para que se apresten a la lucha en cualquier parte donde radiquen.

Nuestra primera acción como Consejo Revolucionario Anti-

detengan la acción de los hombres que aman la libertad.

Por ser Cuba el único país de América donde impera un régimen comunista declarado y por ser este país el que más ha sufrido bajo este infra-humano sistema, hubimos de acordar que fuera *"Acción Cubana"* y su dirigente *Orlando Bosch*, quienes dirigieran y realizaran esta primer acción dentro de la nueva y prometedora etapa que comienza.

Las organizaciones que formamos parte del "Consejo Revolucionario Anti-Comunista Latinoamericano" y que firmamos este parte somos: *"Acción Cubana"* (A.C.), *"Trinchera Argentina"* (T.A.), *"Fuerzas Anti-Comunistas Ecuatorianas"* (F.A.E.), *"Acci-*

On February 21, 1975, in the parking lot of the Variety Children's Hospital in Miami, six caliber 45 shots ended the life of Luciano Nieves Mestre, a Cuban origin citizen who was known to support dialogue and family reunification.

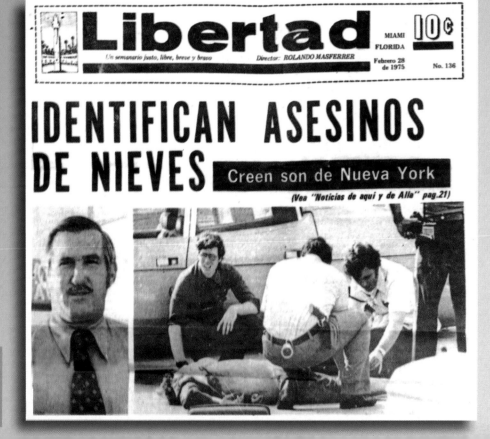

Libertad — MIAMI FLORIDA — 10¢

Un semanario justo, libre, breve y bravo — Director: ROLANDO MASFERRER — Febrero 28 de 1975 — No. 136

IDENTIFICAN ASESINOS DE NIEVES

Creen son de Nueva York

(Vea "Noticias de aquí y de Allá" pag.21)

MIAMI

On August 9, 1976, Cuban diplomats Jesús Cejas Arias and Crescencio Galañena Hernández, accredited to the Cuban embassy in Buenos Aires, Argentina, were apprehended in broad daylight and kidnapped by terrorist elements.

After being tortured and assassinated, the bodies of both officials disappeared. According to nonofficial sources, their remains are hidden in the foundations of one of the buildings that were being constructed in Buenos Aires at the time.

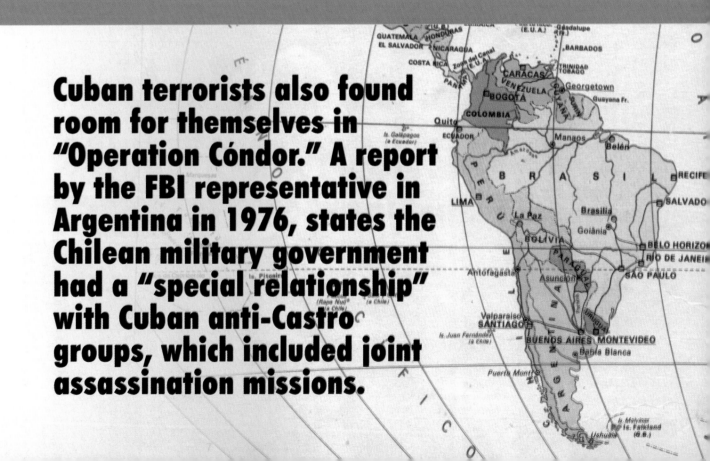

Cuban terrorists also found room for themselves in "Operation Cóndor." A report by the FBI representative in Argentina in 1976, states the Chilean military government had a "special relationship" with Cuban anti-Castro groups, which included joint assassination missions.

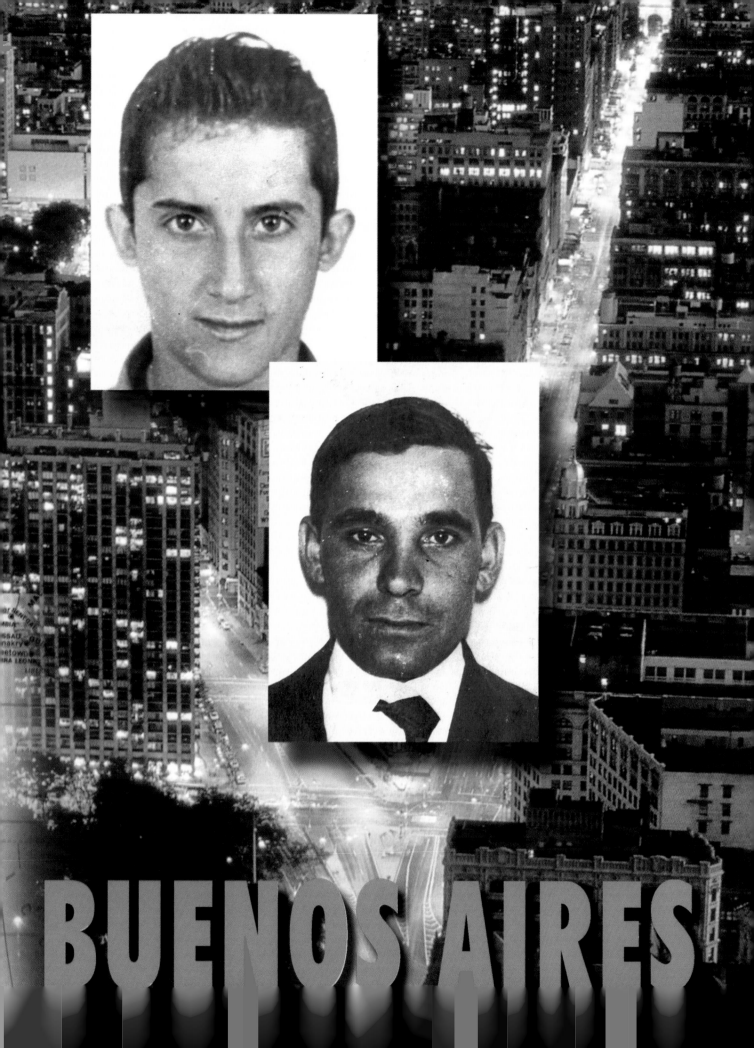

BUENOS AIRES

On March 25, 1979, Cuban origin terrorists placed a bomb in the office of the Cuban Program, directed by Eulalio José Negrín, in New Jersey.

On Sunday, November 25, 1979, in the presence of his 12-year-old son, the Cuban émigré Eulalio José Negrín Santos was assassinated in Union City, New Jersey. He had been working for the lifting of the blockade imposed on the island and for family reunification.

"... Arocena knew about and ordered the operation. ... He was subsequently informed about it by **PEDRO REMON** and **ANDRES GARCIA**, that the operation had been carried out and that **REMON** had been the one to **FIRE** the weapon.

"The MAC 10 machine gun was the same weapon used to kill Félix García later. The MAC 10 machine gun was under the control of **PEDRO REMON** and the gun itself was given to him by Arocena previously."

Federal Bureau of Investigations
11217-11221
Interview dated 9/25/82
9/28/82
In: Newark, New Jersey
Miami, Florida
Exp: NY 185-1009
(SUB-C)
By: Detective Robert Brandt and SA Larry E. Wack/Lew:mmb
Federal Bureau of Investigations
Date dictated: 9/30/82

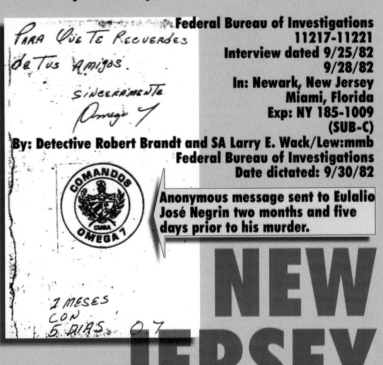

Anonymous message sent to Eulalio José Negrin two months and five days prior to his murder.

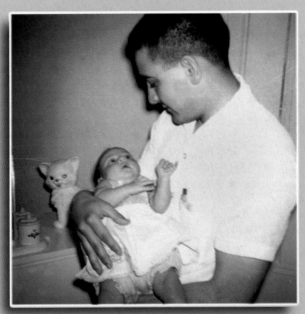

NEW JERSEY

NEW YORK

On September 11, 1980, the Cuban diplomat Félix García Rodríguez, protocol official of the Cuban Mission to the United Nations, was assassinated by several shots fired by Cuban origin terrorists while he was driving his car on the corner of Queens Boulevard and 55th Street in Queens, New York.

EMBASSY OF SWITZERLAND
United States of America Interests Section

No. 154

The United States of America Interests Section of the Embassy of Switzerland presents its compliments to the Ministry of Foreign Relations of the Republic of Cuba and has the honor to transmit to the Ministry the enclosed copy of a statement by the United States Attorney for the Southern District of New York, made on March 13, 1984.

The statement announces the 26-count indictment by a Federal Grand Jury, which charges Eduardo Arocena with participating in the first degree murder of Cuban United Nations Attache Felix Garcia, on September 11, 1980; the attempted murder of Cuban United Nations Ambassador Raul Roa on March 25, 1980; and other crimes for which responsibility has been publicly claimed by a group of Cuban exiles known as "Omega 7".

The United States of America Interests Section of the Embassy of Switzerland avails itself of this opportunity to renew to the Ministry of Foreign Relations of the Republic of Cuba the assurances of its highest and most distinguished consideration.

ENCLOSURE

Ministry of Foreign Relations
Havana, March 16, 1984

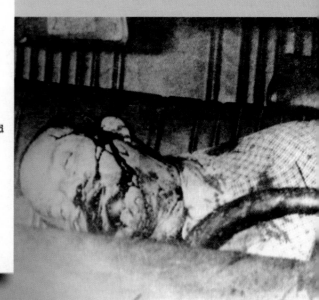

US ATTORNEY FOR SOUTHERN DISTRICT OF NEW YORK
MADE THE FOLLOWING STATEMENT LATE AFTERNOON OF MARCH
13, 1984:

BEGIN TEXT

-      A FEDERAL GRAND JURY IN MANHATTAN, IN A TWENTY-SIX
(26) COUNT SUPERSEDING INDICTMENT WHICH WAS FILED
TODAY, HAS CHARGED EDUARDO AROCENA, AGE 41, OF 10001
S.W. 14TH TERRACE, MIAMI, FLORIDA, WITH PARTICIPATING
IN THE FIRST DEGREE MURDER OF CUBAN UNITED NATIONS
ATTACHE FELIX GARCIA ON SEPTEMBER 11, 1980; THE
ATTEMPTED MURDER OF CUBAN UNITED NATIONS AMBASSADOR
RAUL ROA ON MARCH 25, 1980; THE BOMBING OF THF TRANS
WORLD AIRLINES TERMINAL AT JFK INTERNATIONAL AIRPORT
ON MARCH 25, 1979; THE BOMBING OF AVERY FISHER HALL
AT LINCOLN CENTER FOR THE PERFORMING ARTS ON DECEMBER
28-29, 1978; THE BOMBING OF THE SOVIET MISSION TO THE
UNITED NATIONS ON DECEMBER 11, 1979; AND OTHER
CRIMES FOR WHICH RESPONSIBILITY HAS PUBLICLY BEEN
CLAIMED BY AN ANTI-CASTRO GROUP OF CUBAN EXILES KNOWN
AS "OMEGA 7."

-      IN ANNOUNCING THIS INDICTMENT, RUDOLPH W.
GIULIANI, UNITED STATES ATTORNEY FOR THE SOUTHERN
DISTRICT OF NEW YORK, EXPLAINED THAT TODAY'S TWENTY-SIX

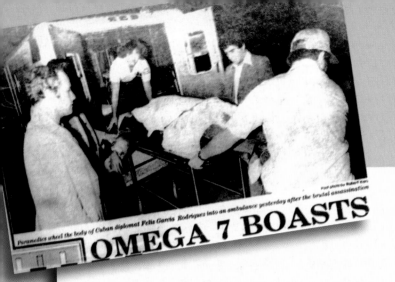

OMEGA 7 BOASTS

-2-

DISTRICT OF NEW YORK, EXPLAINED THAT TODAY'S TWENTY-SIX
(26) COUNT INDICTMENT SUPERSEDES A SEVEN (7) COUNT
INDICTMENT AGAINST AROCENA WHICH WAS PREVIOUSLY
RETURNED BY THE GRAND JURY AND MADE PUBLIC ON DECEMBER
28, 1983. MR. GIULIANI NOTED THAT AROCENA ALSO
REMAINS UNDER INDICTMENT IN THE SOUTHERN DISTRICT OF
FLORIDA ON CHARGES UNSEALED ON DECEMBER 28, 1983
WHICH ACCUSE AROCENA OF PARTICIPATING IN ELEVEN BOMBIN
OR ATTEMPTED BOMBINGS IN THE MIAMI AREA.

-      MICHAEL L. TABAK, THE ASSISTANT UNITED STATES
ATTORNEY WHO PRESENTED THE CASE TO THE GRAND JURY IN
NEW YORK, NOTED THAT TODAY'S SUPERSEDING INDICTMENT
CHARGES AROCENA WITH A SERIES OF BOMBINGS AND MURDERS
CARRIED OUT FROM 1975 THROUGH 1983. ACCORDING TO
MR. TABAK, THE GRAND JURY, THROUGH TODAY'S SUPERSEDING
INDICTMENT, HAS ACCUSED AROCENA OF CONSPIRACY OR
SUBSTANTIVE FELONY CHARGES RELATING TO:

(1) FEBRUARY 1, 1975 BOMBING OF THE VENEZUELAN
CONSULATE AT 7 EAST 51 STREET IN MANHATTAN (COUNT 8)

(2) SEPTEMBER 16, 1976 BOMBING OF THE SOVIET SHIP
"IVAN SHEPETKOV" AT PORT ELIZABEH, NEW JERSEY (COUNT 8)

(3) OCTOBER 5, 1978 BOMBING OF THE GERRY COSBY SPORTING
GOODS STORE NEAR MADISON SQUARE GARDEN IN MANHATTAN
(COUNT 8)

(4)   DECEMBER 28-29, 19
AT LINCOLN CENTER FOR T
MANHATTAN (COUNTS 8, 19

(5)   DECEMBER 28-29, 19
TO THE UNITED NATIONS

(6)   MARCH 25, 1979 BOM
TERMINAL AT JFK INTERNA

(7)   JUNE (OR PRIOR),
OCHOA, AT AROCENA'S DIR
ON A COMMERCIAL AIRLINE
(COUNT 8)

(8)   DECEMBER 7, 1978 B
THE UNITED NATIONS (COU

(9)   DECEMBER 11, 1979
TO THE UNITED NATIONS

(10) JANUARY 13, 1980 M
IN MIAMI, FLORIDA (COU

(11) JANUARY 13, 1980
TICKET OFFICES IN MANH

PUERTO RICO
NEW YORK

COMANDO

OMEGA 7

VENEZUELA
San Juan P.R

Arrestan al Presunto Director de la Organización Exiliada Omega 7

Los agentes habían estado buscando a Arocena dese Octubre de
1982 cuando él y cuatro personas
más fueron encausadas por
conspiración y transporte de armas entre estados. Los otros detenidos están encerrados desde octubre en la ciudad de New York.

Los agentes federales dijeron
que Arocena había logrado huir
de New Jersey a Miami donde él
había vivido a principios de la dé-
cada de los 70. Desde su fuga en
octubre Arocena era buscado por
más de 20 agentes federales que
sospechaban que él estaba es-
condido en alguna parte del suro-

reste de Miami, donde personas
que simpatizan con su causa po-
siblemente le habían dado asilo.

Este viernes, cuando compare-
ció ante el magistrado federal Pe-
ter Nimkoff, Arocena no dijo si se
opondrá al pedido de extradición
que hace New york de su persona.

En la operación contra Arocena
se ocuparon numerosas armas de
fuego y de otros tipos. Ahora el
FBI está buscando a un posible
depósito de explosivos, según in
formó el agente especial del F
encargado de la oficina en Miar
Joseph Corless.

Jurado de A
delibera 2 d
alcanzar ve

RESUMEN MENSUAL   SEPTIEMBRE,

Aroc
confiden

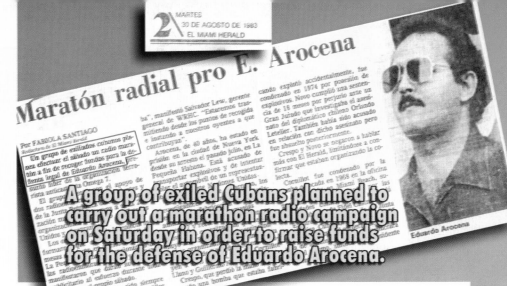

Maratón radial pro E. Arocena

Por FABIOLA SANTIAGO
Redactora de El Miami Herald

A group of exiled Cubans planned to carry out a marathon radio campaign on Saturday in order to raise funds for the defense of Eduardo Arocena.

Eduardo Arocena

—4—

BING OF AVERY FISHER HALL
RFORMING ARTS IN

BING OF THE CUBAN MISSION
HATTAN (COUNTS 8-10)

OF THE TRANS WORLD AIRLINES
L AIRPORT (COUNTS 8, 11-12)

RANSPORTATION BY EDUARDO
N, OF EXPLOSIVE MATERIALS
HT FROM FLORIDA TO NEW JERSEY

G OF THE CUBAN MISSION TO
, 13-15)

NG OF THE SOVIET MISSION
HATTAN (COUNTS 8, 16-18)

G OF PADRON TOBACCO COMPA

G OF AEROFLOT AIRLINES
(COUNTS 8, 19-20)

(11) JANUARY 13, 1980 BOMBING OF AEROFLOT AIRLINES
TICKET OFFICES IN MANHATTAN (COUNTS 8, 19-20)

(12) MARCH 25, 1980 ATTEMPTED MURDER, BY BOMBING, OF
CUBAN UNITED NATIONS AMBASSADOR RAUL ROA IN
MANHATTAN (COUNTS 1-5)

(13) SEPTEMBER 11, 1980 MURDER OF CUBAN UNITED NATIONS
ATTACHE FELIX GARCIA (COUNTS 6-7)

(14) SEPTEMBER 11, 1981 BOMBING OF THE MEXICAN
CONSULATE IN MIAMI, FLORIDA (COUNT 21)

(15) SEPTEMBER 11, 1981 ATTEMPTED ARSON OF THE OFFICES
OF REPLICA MAGAZINE IN MIAMI, FLORIDA (COUNT 21)

(16) SEPTEMBER 12, 1981 BOMBING OF THE MEXICAN CONSULATE
IN MANHATTAN (COUNTS 21-24)

(17) 1981-1982 CONSPIRACY TO KIDNAP AND MURDER LUIS
FUENTES PURSUANT TO AN ORAL CONTRACT WITH AN INDIVIDUAL
WHO AGREED TO GIVE MONEY TO AROCENA AND "OMEGA 7" IN
RETURN FOR THE KIDNAPPING AND MURDER OF FUENTES
(COUNT 21) (NOTE: FUENTES WAS NOT IN FACT KILLED)

(18) 1981-1982 CONSPIRACY TO EXTORT AND TO COMMIT ARSON
OF THE AUTOMOBILE OF HUGO ROMERO, IN RETURN FOR MONEY
FROM A DRUG DEALER (COUNT 21)

eiso
o de
na

a

n

cto

Arocena: sigue esperando

Si es declarado culpable, Arocena se enfrenta a una sentencia
obligatoria de cadena perpetua
por homicidio en primer grado
de un funcionario extranjero.
El jurado hizo saber al juez
Robert Ward que no existía la
posibilidad de alcanzar un vere-
dicto antes de las 2 P.M. del
sábado.

PAGINA: 110

a fue
de FBI

"The plot to assassinate Félix García, the Cuban attaché assigned to the Cuban Mission to the United Nations, involved a 50-day surveillance of the Cuban Mission to the United Nations, New York City, by AROCENA and members of PEDRO REMON´S cell.

"The original plan was to assassinate four individuals from the Cuban Mission to the United Nations. AROCENA, REMON, ANDRES GARCIA, AND EDUARDO LOSADA FERNANDEZ were all involved in the surveillance and the assassination.

"Pedro Remón made the credit call to the New York news media claiming responsibility for the murder in the name of Omega 7."

Federal Bureau of Investigations
11217-11221
Date of transcription: 10/6/82
Interview 9/25/82
9/28/82
In: Newark, New Jersey
Miami, Florida
Exp: NY 185-1009
(SUB-C)
By: Detective Robert Brandt and
SA Larry E. Wack/Lew:mmb
Date dictated 9/30/82

(19) 1981-1982 CONSPIRACY TO EXTORT OSCAR DARIO, IN RETURN FOR MONEY FROM A DRUG DEALER (COUNT 21)

(20) 1981-1982 CONSPIRACY TO MURDER RAYMOND VANYO PURSUANT TO AN ORAL CONTRACT WITH AN INDIVIDUAL WHO AGREED TO GIVE MONEY TO AROCENA AND "OMEGA 7" IN RETURN FOR THAT MURDER (COUNT 21) (NOTE: VANYO WAS NOT IN FACT KILLED)

(21) 1981-1982 SUPPLY ILLEGAL AND UNREGISTERED WEAPONS AND SILENCERS TO DRUG DEALERS (COUNT 21)

(22) SEPTEMBER 1, 1982 (TO THE PRESENT) OBSTRUCTION OF JUSTICE (COUNT 26)

(23) SEPTEMBER 2, 1982 PERJURY BY AROCENA BEFORE THE GRAND JURY IN MANHATTAN INVESTIGATING "OMEGA 7" CRIMES (COUNT 25)

(24) SEPTEMBER 2, 1982 BOMBINGS IN MIAMI (COUNT 26)

(25) JANUARY 11-12, 1983 BOMBINGS IN MIAMI (COUNT 26)

- MR. TABAK STATED THAT AROCENA'S TRIAL BEFORE JUDGE ROBERT J. WARD AND A JURY IS CURRENTLY SCHEDULED TO BEGIN ON APRIL 23, 1984. AROCENA IS BEING HELD AT THE FEDERAL CORRECTIONAL INSTITUTION IN OTISVILLE, NEW YORK IN LIEU OF $750,000 BAIL.

- MR. GIULIANI PRAISED THE FEDERAL BUREAU OF INVESTIGATION AND THE NEW YORK CITY AND MIAMI POLICE DEPARTMENTS FOR THEIR EXCEPTIONAL EFFORTS ON THIS CASE. MR. GIULIANI STATED THAT THE INVESTIGATIONS INTO MURDERS, BOMBINGS, AND OTHER CRIMES FOR WHICH RESPONSIBILITY HAS PUBLICLY BEEN CLAIMED BY "OMEGA 7" ARE BEING VIGOROUSLY PURSUED BOTH BY HIS OFFICE AND BY THE OFFICE OF STANLEY MARCUS, UNITED STATES ATTORNEY FOR THE SOURTHERN DISTRICT OF FLORIDA.

END TEXT.

On April 22, 1976, Cuban diplomats Adriana Corcho Calleja and Efrén Monteagudo Rodríguez were blown to pieces in a bomb explosion in Lisbon. Adriana had discovered the bomb and had gone to warn her colleagues of the danger they were in, but the explosion took them by surprise.

LISBON

"The suffering has been terrible, my sister was a 12-year-old girl and was left without a mother at that age. There were always parents meetings at the school with my father. My mother was never able to go again, I always wanted her to go, I was close to her; she couldn't attend my sixth grade, secondary school or high school graduations, or the birth of my daughter, major events in the life of a man."

Fragment of the testimony by Jorge Palenzuela Corcho

"I have always thought that I could have been different to the way I am, maybe happier, less responsible. And that doesn't mean that I don't like being responsible. My mother taught me, for the few years we were together, to be this way. . . .

"That bomb. . .it could have also put an end to the life of my father and two brothers, who used to arrive home from school at that time.

"It was Thursday, at around three or four in the afternoon. It had rained and that was why we were coming back from the countryside so early. I don't remember why I had cried so much that day. During those years I used to cry a lot, just like now when I remember everything that happened; I torture myself as if I were living it again, as if I were watching a horror movie that I can't walk away from.

"A teacher told me that some friends had come looking for me, that I should collect my things and go. . . .

"When I was almost home my grandparents told me that there had been an attack against the embassy in Portugal and that my mother had died there. I couldn't talk. To put it simply, I didn't believe them.

"My father alone was able to give me the answer that I didn't want to hear. And I had to listen to the terrible truth coming from him: that I was never again going to see the person who had given me life and who I most needed in the world.

"For many years I lived with the dream that my mother was still in Portugal. I couldn't accept that she was dead.

"What strikes me most is not so much the person who did the deed, what I think about most and what causes most hurt is the barbarity of the deed: that there are human beings in the world capable of killing innocent people in order to overthrow a government. We, my siblings and I, were not able to share the most important events in our lives with our mother.

"I know that my case is not unique. I met someone who had lost a loved one when the plane was blown up over Barbados. This is another crime that was committed the same year my mother was murdered. A huge vacuum in their lives unites that person's family, like mine. Sometimes words cannot convey the pain that we always carry inside ourselves. I, and my siblings, have lived longer than my mother lived and we still can't cope with everything I have just spoken about."

Fragments of the testimony by Betina Palenzuela Corcho, Havana, July, 2002

On July 23, 1976, in Mérida, Yucatan, Artaigñán Díaz Díaz, a Cuban fishing technician was murdered by two Cuban origin terrorists who then managed to escape.

That's where Artaigñán lay, in the middle of a pool of blood that flowed from his neck, abdomen and lumbar region. His widow and three orphaned children were waiting for him to return at his home in Havana, which he had left two days before.

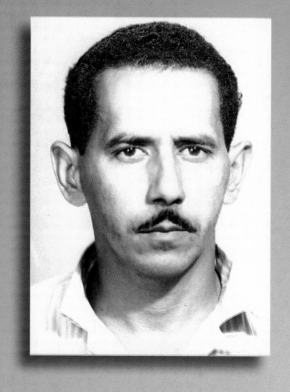

The Mexican authorities detained two renowned terrorists who admitted to being guilty. One of them, Gaspar Eugenio Jiménez Escobedo, managed to escape from prison in March, 1977. On November 17, 2000, he was detained in Panama while involved in the preparations for an attack against Cuban president Fidel Castro Ruz, in the auditorium of the university in Panama City.

They only had to see them before they would shout with joy, "Papá has arrived, Papá". Their father was not among the group of comrades returning that belonged to the Caribbean Shrimp Fleet. The father of Lissette, Esperanza and Enrique had been murdered in Mérida by a group of Cuban origin terrorists.

"Throughout these 24 years, my mother and my siblings have been waiting for the moment when justice would be done... One of those who shot my father, Eugenio Jiménez Escobedo, is in jail in Panama, together with Posada Carriles. No trial, however fair it might be, will bring my father back to life; but it would put an end to so many years of powerlessness, and would prevent macabre individuals, such as these, to continue leaving pain, suffering, and bloodshed in their wake... I am not asking for blood; I don't demand vengeance, I only ask for the support of honest people in the world, for solidarity, in this struggle against impunity and for justice."

Fragment of the testimony of Artainan's daughter

Detenido en la capital otro inodado en el fallido secuestro al cónsul de Cuba

El viernes por la noche, en el aeropuerto "Benito Juárez", de la capital de la República, fue detenido por elementos de la Policía Judicial Federal, Gaspar Jiménez, quien horas antes de su captura, acompañado de Orestes Ruiz Hernández y de Gustavo Castillo (a) Tabito, pretendieron secuestrar al cónsul de Cuba en esta ciudad, Sr. Daniel Ferrer. En el atentado, como oportunamente publicamos, murió Artagñan Díaz Díaz, acompañante del cónsul.

Gaspar Jiménez, célula del FLNC, dijo a sus captores, que los explosivos en

Gaspar Jiménez, detenido

auténti- sta y progra- para- amente el ani- miento

NOVEDADES DE YUCATAN

AÑO XII No. 4695

Mérida, Yuc., Sábado 24 de Julio de 1978

Acto de terrorismo en Mérida

El cónsul de Cuba escapa ileso de un atentado en que perece a balazos, frente a céntrica cantina, un acompañante suyo, cubano también. — Los pistoleros huyen en un automóvil que fue localizado en el aeropuerto — Versiones inexactas al

"Given the loss of support and financing for their activities, these groups have turned to attempted murders and extortion in an effort to obtain additional backing and funds for their cause. Some Cuban groups are apparently involved in terrorist attacks against the Cuban government, but in reality they are nothing other than delinquents who feed off the Cuban population and use funds raised for their own benefit."

Declaration by Thomas Lyons, Lieutenant in the Security Office in Dade County, Florida, testifying in a hearing of the Judicial Committee of the U.S. Senate, 94th Congress: "Terrorist Activity. Terrorism in the Miami Area," page 608.

Bosch's success has a simple explanation; it is the old Chicago gangster style. If you don't pay up, then he puts a bomb in your office, it is that simple. Bosch is an extortionist, not a patriot. In Miami everything has been reduced to criminal activity.

Jay Mallin, *Time* correspondent during the 1970s.

THE WARLIKE CONFLICT UNDERWAY
"We need to group 1 000 Cuban patriots who will be given a historic 100 dollar voucher."

Andrés Nazario Sargén, October, 2002.

On April 28, 1979, two 45-calibre bullets were fired by terrorists of Cuban origin from a moving vehicle. These bullets perforated the skull and spine of young Carlos Muñiz Varela.

A Miami-based terrorist group of Cuban origin claimed responsibility for the murder. "This is the first of the 75 traitors," said the communiqué released in the city by the terrorist group. The number of 75 referred to a committee of Cuban-Americans residing in Miami, New York and other U.S. cities who were working for family reunification and dialogue.

Organiza viajes a Cuba   plomos, aparentemente ca- ses.

Lo tirotean terroristas cubanos

Carlos Muñiz Varela, during the first visit (September 1976) he made to Cuba together with a large group of young Cuban-Americans who supported the lifting of the blockade, family reunification and the normalization of relationships between the two countries.

"When we told the child that his father had died, the initial reaction was to keep on staring straight ahead. He was so dumbstruck that both Damary and I were frightened because, as Damary explained to me, there is a period during which, if the child does not recover quickly, then psychological problems could arise; in other words, if the child doesn't react then he could be emotionally affected.

"When we saw that he was in a trance, that he wasn't speaking, that he had a faraway look in his eyes, wide open, Damary spoke to him, 'Listen, Carlitos, say something because your father is dead, but you are not going to be alone, you are with your mother.' Then he hugged me and began to cry. That was a terrible time for the child, he cried on me. He wanted to see him."

Fragments of the testimony by
Pilar Pérez Negrón,
widow of Carlos Muñiz Varela.

Terrorism "throughout the world" included U.S. territory.

Attacks of Cuban-American Terrorists:

February 4, 1975: Several bombs are placed in restaurants in Elizabeth, New Jersey.

August 1, 1975: A bomb is placed in the Pan-American Union premises, in Washington.

October 17, 1975: A bomb is placed in the Miami airport, which caused considerable material damage.

December 3, 1975: A bomb is placed in the offices of the FBI in Miami, Florida.

December 3, 1975: A bomb is placed in the post office of the Mail Department of Riverdale and Tamiami, in Miami, Florida.

December 3, 1975: Several bombs exploded in the Social Security offices at Flagger Bridge, in Barnet Bank, in the Department of Justice building and in the Police Headquarters in Miami, Florida.

April 6, 1976: Terrorists of Cuban origin place a bomb in the premises of the university, in Miami, Florida.

April 5, 1977: Terrorists of Cuban origin claim responsibility for a bomb placed in the Eastern Airlines Company, in Miami, Florida, which caused considerable material damage.

May 13, 1977: Terrorists of Cuban origin claim responsibility for a bomb placed in an airline company in Fort Lauderdale, Florida.

May 25, 1977: An explosion takes place in the offices of Mackey International Airlines Company, in Florida, which caused considerable damage. As a consequence of this terrorist act, the company decided to cancel plans to send flights to Cuba.

June 8, 1977: Terrorists of Cuban origin threaten the U.S. cruise line company Carras Lines, with placing bombs on their ships. For this reason the firm decides to cancel its business with Cuba.

December 20, 1977: An explosion occurs in a Miami warehouse from where packages to Cuba were dispatched. Substantial material damage is reported.

February 19, 1978: Terrorists of Cuban origin place a bomb in a pipeline in the state of Alaska, causing considerable damage.

October 22, 1978: Terrorists of Cuban origin place a bomb in the *La Prensa en New York* newspaper, due to research on activities of terrorist organizations carried out by some of its reporters.

November 18, 1978: Threats are made to place bombs on board TWA flights bound for Cuba.

March 25, 1979: Terrorists of Cuban origin place a bomb in the premises of the Almacén El Español company, in Union City, New Jersey, involved in sending packages to Cuba. The explosion causes considerable material damage.

March 25, 1979: A bomb explodes inside a suitcase, moments before it was carried on board a TWA flight, injuring four workers in John F. Kennedy airport in New York.

MIAMI BEACH CONVENTI

December 4, 1979: Terrorists of Cuban origin threat to place dynamite on board the aircraft in the John F. Kennedy, New York, and Newark, New Jersey, airports. Cubana de Aviación cancelled its charter flights between both cities and Havana.

December 4, 1979: Terrorists of Cuban origin threat to place a bomb in the airline company Butler Aviation, in the United States, which had plans to send flights to Cuba.

February 18, 1982: Terrorists of Cuban origin place a bomb in the premises of *Réplica* magazine and other in the cargo company TRASCUBA, in Miami, Florida, involved in sending medicines to Cuba.

February 21, 1982: Terrorists of Cuban origin open fire against the Hispana Freight Co., in Miami, Florida, which handled shipments to Cuba.

September 8, 1982: Terrorists of Cuban origin claim responsibility for placing a bomb in the city of Chicago, Illinois.

September 11, 1981: Terrorists of Cuban origin place a bomb in the Mexican consulate in Miami, Florida, causing serious material damage.

September 11, 1981: Terrorists of Cuban origin place a bomb in the Mexican consulate in New York and in the premises of the *Réplica* magazine, in Miami, Florida, set on fire.

September 3, 1982: Terrorists of Cuban origin place a bomb in the Venezuelan consulate in Miami as part of a campaign to push for the release of the terrorist Orlando Bosch Avila.

July 11, 1983: Terrorists of Cuban origin residents in Miami threaten to dynamite the musical instruments of the Cuban Aragón Orchestra, which was preparing to give a cha-cha-cha concert in New York.

July 9, 1976: A bomb explodes inside a suitcase, which will be on board the Cubana de Aviación aircraft, in Kingston, Jamaica, scheduled to have left forty minutes previously for Havana.

At the time scheduled for detonation, the plane would have been flying over the sea close to Montego Bay, off the north coast of Jamaica. The flight had on board the crew and 29 passengers of Cuban, Jamaican, Dominican, British, Argentine and U.S. origin.

The following day, the terrorist group CORU claimed responsibility for the attack in a communiqué released to different media in Miami.

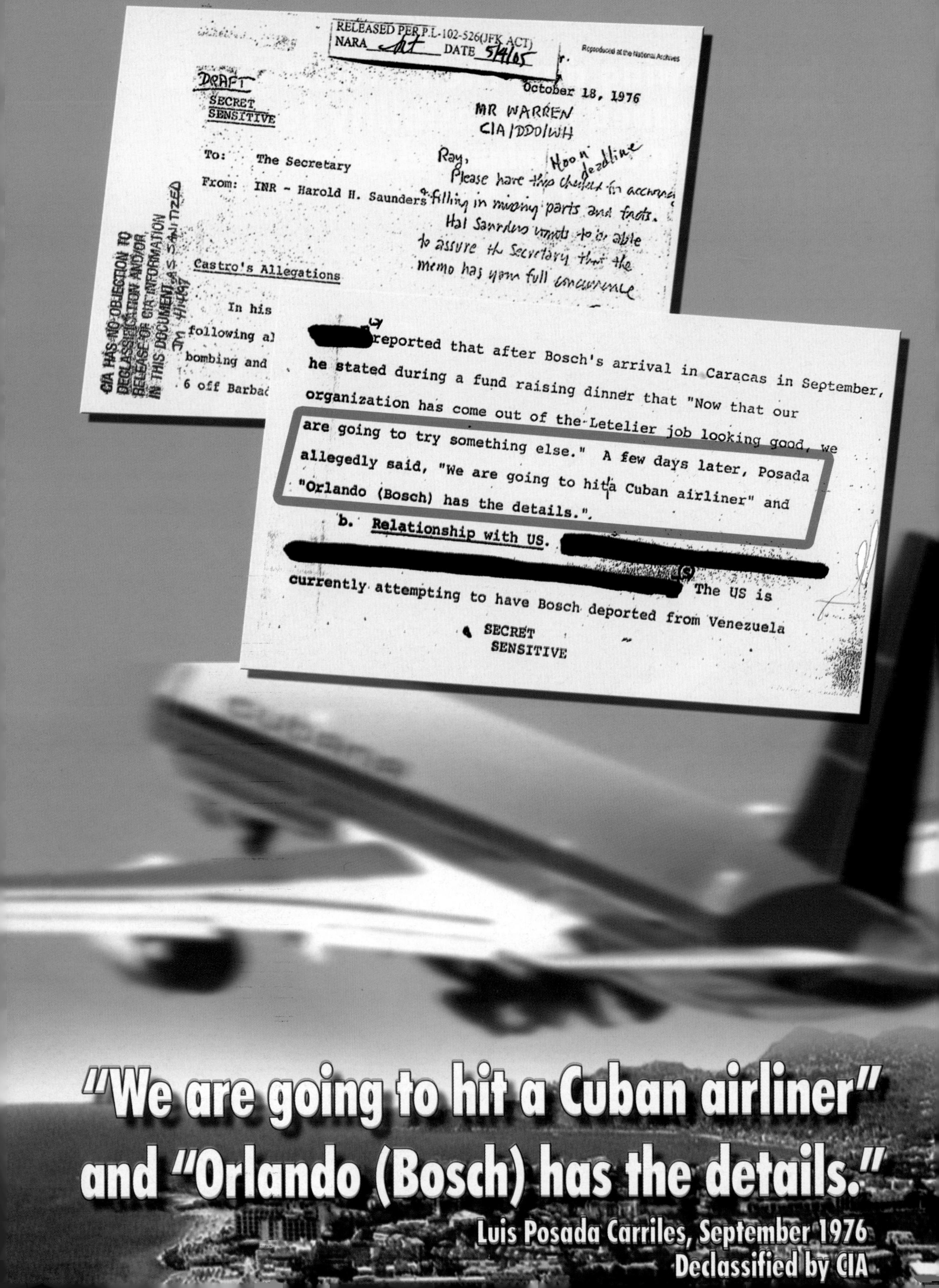

RELEASED PER P.L.102-526 (JFK ACT)
NARA ___ DATE 5/4/05

Reproduced at the National Archives

DRAFT
SECRET
SENSITIVE

October 18, 1976

MR WARREN
CIA/DDO/WH

To: The Secretary

From: INR - Harold H. Saunders

Ray,
Hoo'n deadline
Please have this checked for accuracy
filling in missing parts and facts.
Hal Saunders wants to be able
to assure the Secretary that the
memo has your full concurrence

Castro's Allegations

In his
following a[l]
bombing and
6 off Barba[dos]

reported that after Bosch's arrival in Caracas in September, he stated during a fund raising dinner that "Now that our organization has come out of the Letelier job looking good, we are going to try something else." A few days later, Posada allegedly said, "We are going to hit a Cuban airliner" and "Orlando (Bosch) has the details.".

b. **Relationship with US.**

The US is currently attempting to have Bosch deported from Venezuela

SECRET
SENSITIVE

"We are going to hit a Cuban airliner" and "Orlando (Bosch) has the details."

Luis Posada Carriles, September 1976
Declassified by CIA

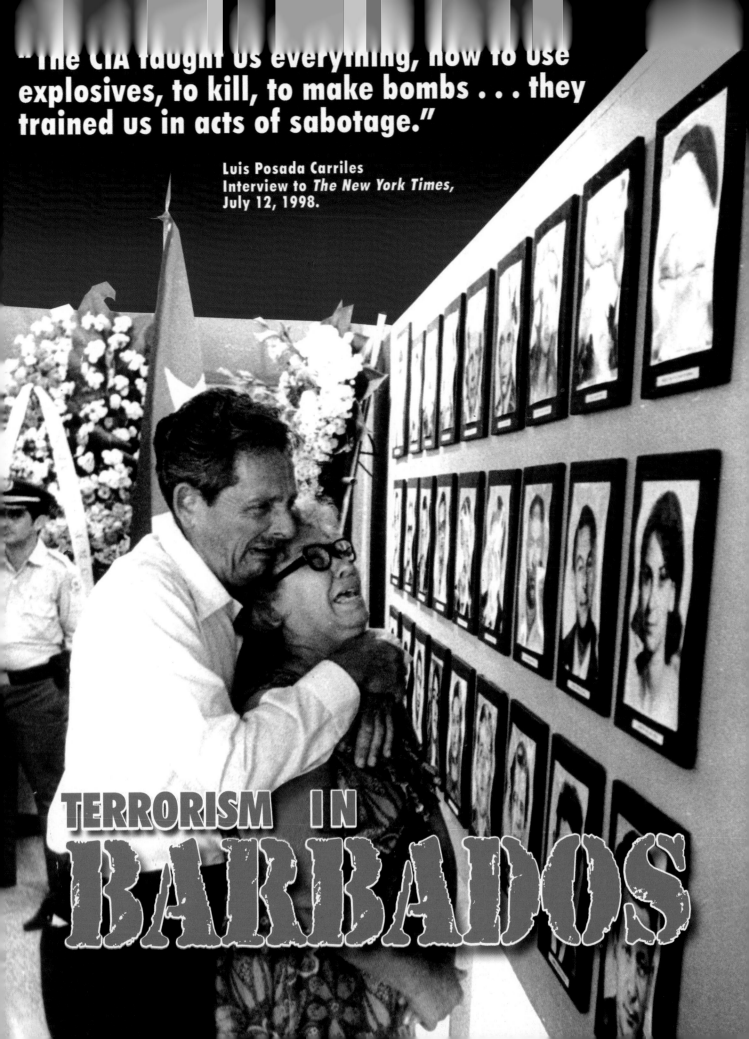

"The CIA taught us everything, how to use explosives, to kill, to make bombs . . . they trained us in acts of sabotage."

Luis Posada Carriles
Interview to *The New York Times*,
July 12, 1998.

TERRORISM IN
BARBADOS

BARBADOS

On October 6, 1976, a Cubana de Aviación DC-8 arrived at Seawell international airport in Barbados, as flight CU-455. It was 11:21 A.M. Fifty-four minutes later it departed for Jamaica. At 12:23 an explosion shook the aircraft, which caught fire and after five dramatic minutes fell to the sea. There were no survivors. Seventy-three people died (57 Cubans, 11 Guyaneses and 5 North Koreans). The Cuban youth fencing team, which had just won the Central America Championship in Caracas, were among the dead.

... ¡Seawell! ¡Seawell! ... CU-455...!

... CU-455 ... Seawell.

... We have had an explosion and we ar a fire on board!

... Close the door! Close the door!

... There is an intense fire on board!

... That's worse! Head toward the wate

... Cubana, this is Cariwest 650. How ca
... Cubana, this is Cariwest 650. How ca
... Cubana, this is Cariwest 650. How ca

ending immediately. We have

head toward the water!

of help?
of help?
of help?

Cubana

DW-455

"When Cuban pilots, diplomats or members of their families die, I am not sorry; the death of these people always makes me happy."

Guillermo Novo Sampoll, during an interview passed by mistake to the Soviet publication *Literaturnaya Gazeta*

CUARTEL GENERAL DE POLICIA
CALLE SAN VICENTE, PUERTO
ESPAÑA, TRINIDAD

Miercoles, 26 de Octubre de 1.976

DENNIS ELLIOTT RAMDWAR, declara:

Yo soy un Comisionado Adjunto del Servicio de Trinidad y Tobado. El jueves, 7 de oc-
tubre 1.976, dos (2) hombres quienes dijeron llamarse JOSE VASQUEZ GARCIA y FRE--
DDY LUGO fueron traídos al Cuartel General de Policía por el Comisionado Asistente -
BURROUGHS y un grupo de Oficiales de Policía. El Comisionado Asistente BURROUGHS
se reportó a mi. Como consecuencia de esto el señor BURROUGHS me dijo, a las 08:00
p.m. del día 8 de octuvre, 1.976 yo entrevisté un hombre que dijo llamarse JOSE VAS-
QUEZ GARCIA en la presencia del Superintendente Superior GORDON WATERMAN, -
Jefe del Departamento de Investigación Criminal; N° 6823 Cabo OSCAR KING del De-
partamento Especial y Miss JOY KELSHALL quienes actuaron como entérpretes. (sic)

que quería que me explicara lo que sabía sobre el asunto y le exigí una declaración
Me dió la declaración que va anexa y que está marcada D.R.I. para su identifica -
ción. Dicha declaración está fechada el 9 de Octubre de 1976. En esta declaración
JOSE VASQUEZ GARCIA me dijo que su nombre exacto era (correcto) HERNAN RI-
CARDO LOZANO, Cédula N° 3821507, que todo el resto en su Pasaporte era falso,
salvo su fotografía.

El sábado 9 de Octubre de 1976 entrevisté a FREDDY LUGO. Me identifiqué y le
informé que estaba investigando el accidente del vuelo CU-455 Cubana que ocurrió
alrededor...

"... I completely truste

Luis Posada Carril

Freddy Lug

SEDE PRINCIPAL D
CALLE SAN VICENTE PUERTO ES
TRINIDAD W.I.   27 de Octubre de 1.976.

OSCAR KING DECLARA:

Yo soy un Cabo, No. 6823, del Servicio de Policía de Trinidad y Tobago pe
teneciente a la Sede Principal, Puerto España. Soy igualmente interprete al español
del Servicio Policial.

Jueves 7 de Octubre de 1.976, alrededor de las 7:45 a.m. fuí citado ante
BURROUGHS en el Departamento de Investigación
...allí, el Comisionado
...ellos

STATEMENTS BY
FREDDY LUGO AND HERNÁN RICARDO

Police General Headquarters
Saint Vincent Street,
Port Spain, Trinidad.

Wednesday, October 26, 1976

DENNIS ELLIOTT RAMDWAR declares:

"I am the Adjutant Commissioner of the Trinidad
and Tobago Service. On Thursday, October 7,
1976, two (2) men who said they were called
JOSE VASQUEZ GARCIA and FREDDY LUGO were
brought to the General Headquarters of the Police
by Assistant Commissioner BURROUGHS and
a group of police officers.
Assistant Commissioner BURROUGHS reported to
me. As a consequence of what Mr. BURROUGHS
said to me, at 8:00 P.M. on October 8, 1976,
I interviewed a man called JOSE VASQUEZ
GARCIA in the presence of Chief Superintendent
GORDON WATERMAN, Head of the Criminal
Investigation Department; Sergeant No. 6823
OSCAR KING of the Special Department and Miss
JOY KELSHALL, who served as interpreters.

Hernán Ricardo."

os Caminos del Guerrero," page 210.

STATEMENTS BY
FREDDY LUGO AND HERNÁN RICARDO

"... that I wanted him to explain to me what he
knew about the matters and I demanded
a statement. I was given a statement which is
attached and marked D.R.I. for identification
purposes. The said statement is dated October 9,
1976. In this statement JOSE VASQUEZ GARCIA
told me his (correct) name was HERNÁN
RICARDO LOZANO, ID No. 3821507, and that the
rest of his passport was fake, except for the
photograph.

"On Saturday, October 9, 1976, I interviewed
FREDDY LUGO. I identified myself and informed
him that I was investigating the CU-455 Cubana
flight accident which took place. . . .

"Twenty minutes into the flight HERNÁN got up and went to the bathroom where he spent about four minutes. Then I saw that the flight attendant hurried past me and knocked on the door of the cockpit and then the pilot or copilot, I don't know which, came out and she said something to him, and then both went to the back of the plane. The pilot knocked on the door three times and on returning toward the seat HERNÁN pushed by me in a very nervous fashion, stepping on my toes, and then the pilot went past. HERNÁN said he had got locked into the bathroom and that the pilot had to open the door. I asked him how that had happened, that the door was easy to open, and he said he didn't know how because he had become nervous and I pointed out that he should have known how easy it was since they had been able to open it from the outside. He was very nervous for the rest of the flight and read a newspaper, hiding his face with its pages, and I started a conversation with a sportsperson who was on the plane. . . ."

What happened after they got off the said flight in Barbados?

"When the plane landed, they had not yet opened the door to let passengers off when HERNÁN got up and was the first to leave, passing by me. . . ."

STATEMENTS BY
FREDDY LUGO AND HERNÁN RICARDO

"At 3:15 P.M. on Saturday, October 16, 1976, FREDDY LUGO requested to see me in the presence of Chief Superintendent GORDON WATERMAN, Sergeant No. 5133 ANTHONY JACK, Sergeant No. 6823 OSCAR KING and Miss JOY KELSHALL. I attended LUGO in my office. He told me he had been rethinking the matter and wanted to tell me the truth about the Cuban flight accident. I took the appropriate measures in accordance with the judicial requirements in Trinidad and Tobago and he immediately made a statement which was put in written format. The said statement is attached, marked with D.R. 9. This statement is dated October 16, 1976. In this aforementioned statement LUGO said he was convinced that HERNÁN RICARDO was responsible for placing the bomb on the plane. He said that RICARDO had told him on the flight from Caracas to Trinidad that he (RICARDO) was going to blow up a Cubana flight. In the same statement he said that while they were in a Holiday Inn taxi at Piarco Trinidad Airport, RICARDO repeated, absolutely emphatically, that he was going to blow up a Cubana plane. . . ."

"On Sunday, October 17, 1976, at around 6:30 P.M. RICARDO asked to see me. This time I was accompanied by Chief Superintendent WATERMAN, Inspector HEADLEY, Sergeant JACK, Sergeant KING and Miss JOY KELSHALL. He said he wanted to speak to me confidentially and requested that Chief Superintendent WATERMAN, Inspector HEADLEY, JACK and KING leave the office. They left the office. Then he said:

(a) That he. . . .

(e) That the name 'El Cóndor' was a front for a group named CORU, which is an abbreviation for the Commando of United Revolutionary Organizations.

(f) That the head of CORU is ORLANDO BOSCH, also known as Señor ORLANDO and occasionally as Señor PANIAGUA.

(g) That LUIS POSADA CARRILES is the head of a company known as Commercial and Industrial Investigations C.A.

(h) That LUIS POSADA is the owner and boss of the said entity.

(i) And that LUIS POSADA. . . .

STATEMENTS BY
FREDDY LUGO AND HERNÁN RICARDO

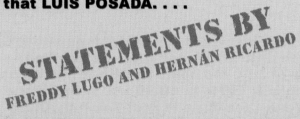

Luis Posada Carriles
(Luis or Gustavo)

Orlando Bosch Avila
(Orlando or Paniagua)

"He continued on and told me that if I used my police mentality it would become clear who was responsible for the bomb on the plane. I told him that I believed I knew who committed the crime. He hesitated for a few moments and then, addressing me, said, repeating it was in the strictest confidentiality, that Lugo had placed the bomb on board the plane. He asked for a sheet of paper and in his own handwriting described the steps that had to be followed before the bomb was placed on the plane and how a plastic bomb is detonated. This document is marked D.R. 12. On the reverse side of the document he drew the plan of the bomb and the detonator and described. . . .

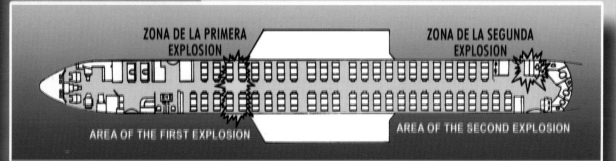

ZONA DE LA PRIMERA EXPLOSION

ZONA DE LA SEGUNDA EXPLOSION

AREA OF THE FIRST EXPLOSION

AREA OF THE SECOND EXPLOSION

STATEMENTS BY
FREDDY LUGO AND HERNÁN RICARDO

". . . as a type of pencil with chemical products that could be programmed for times of 8 minutes, 45 minutes, 1 hour, 2 hours, 3 hours, 8 hours and 24 hours. He said that the pencil-style detonators came in several colors, according to the time the bomb had been programmed to explode. He took a pencil from my desk and said that it was similar to one of the detonators he had just described. He told me that a certain chemical product is injected into a tube of Colgate toothpaste after the real paste had been removed. This pencil is in my possession. He continued by saying that he knew everything in relation to the organization CORU. He asked for another sheet of paper and on it he drew the structure of the organization. This document is marked D.R. 13. He told me that there. . . .

STATEMENTS BY
FREDDY LUGO AND HERNÁN RICARDO

"Afterwards he revealed some things about CIA operations. He continued giving a detailed account of how the bomb had been placed on September 1, 1976, at 10.00 A.M. in the office of the Guyana Consulate in Port Spain by OLEG GUITON RODRÍGUEZ DE LA SIERRA TRATAIKOEF and another member of the organization. He went on to say that a pound of C4 had been used on this job. . . . Then he said that ORLANDO BOSCH is the boss or head of CORU, also known as Señor ORLANDO or ORLANDO PANIAGUA, and that LUIS POSADA is the boss (big shot) in ICI (Commercial and Industrial Investigations). LOZANO also stipulated that he had three passports in his possession; one official U.S. passport, a fake Venezuelan passport, and an authentic Venezuelan passport.

STATEMENTS BY
FREDDY LUGO AND HERNÁN RICARDO

"On October 25, 1976, I went to see HERNÁN RICARDO LOZANO at his request. During the conversation he told me that they had been paid $25,000 USD for the job. He had received $16,000 USD and LUGO had been given $8000 USD. The other $1000 had been spent on miscellaneous expenses.

Trayectoria recorrida por el avión.

Trayectoria que debía continuar hasta Ciudad de La Habana.

Lugar aproximado donde ocurrió el siniestro.

BARBADOS
Bridgetown

Puerto España TRINIDAD-TOBAGO

Caracas

VENEZUELA

Georgetown

Examination of the remains recovered is testimony of the terrorist act and the horror these people experienced on board.

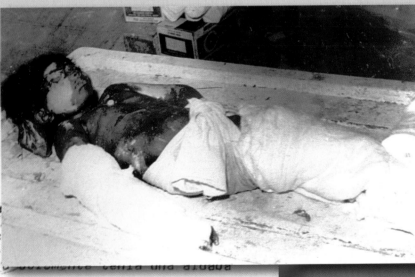

STATEMENTS BY
FREDDY LUGO AND HERNÁN RICARDO

"... he received a call from Caracas and answered saying, 'So LUIS what's up, here I am, man. I have got a problem, I don't know what to do, but the vermin went down and it seems that there are a lot of survivors and a total of seven stiffs (meaning deaths). Let the Boss PANIAGUA what's going on'. . . ."

STATEMENTS BY
FREDDY LUGO AND HERNÁN RICARDO

How many calls did HERNÁN RICARDO make from Barbados, who did he make them to and what did he say during the calls?
"He made several calls, one of them was to his girlfriend, he said he was going to call LUIS or GUSTAVO and that the **Bus with the dogs had gone down. . . .**"

Taken from official statements given by Hernán Ricardo Lozano and Freddy Lugo as recorded by the judicial files.

testándome de que se había queda

le dije que por qué le había súc

era fácil de abrirse, ya que ell

por dentro y que se la habían abierto desde fuera" . . Cuánta

"The sabotage was the most effective blow so far against Castro."

Luis Posada Carriles response to a question put to him by a journalist on the subject of the sabotage to the plane over Barbados. *The Miami Herald,* November 10, 1991.

llamadas, en una de esas llam

manifestó que llamara a LUIS o a GUSTAVO y que le d

ya el autobús con los perros se había caído, pero primeramen

te en el Hotel Holiday Inc de Barbados, él le había hecho -

una llamada a la novia que llamara a LUIS o a GUSTAVO y le di-

Due to the force of the explosion, the safety belt opened her stomach as if it had been a knife. The fire and lethal smoke did the rest. Of the fifteen corpses that surfaced, the girl from Guyana was the only one that could be identified without the help of forensic techniques. It was as if she were the accusing finger.

"My son was the greatest thing; I had a daughter of 7 years old, and a son of 11; and he was 20. He was my support and they took him away, he kept me going.

Martha Hernández Hernández

"They killed my couple for 20 years, my boyfriend for 20 years and the father of my children. No one can pay me for this; no one can ever compensate me for this because they mutilated my family, a completely happy family."

Iraida Malberti

"My father was not a soldier, a soldier on active duty; he was an ordinary worker, a completely innocent human being. That's why I can say, precisely together with all the people who are here, that we are very conscious of what happened to the U.S. people on September 11. The difference is that we have suffered it as family members since 25 years ago."

Carlos Cremata

"They murdered my father on the Barbados flight; my grandmother died with the pain of it as he was her favorite son; he was my counselor, the most important person in my life."

Josefina Ileana Alfonso

"... THE DEATH OF THESE PEOPLE ALWAYS MAKES ME HAPPY."

Guillermo Novo Sampol, Miami, December 19, 1976.

Two days before the end of 1976, the Soviet publication *Literaturnaya Gazeta* published an interview the terrorist of Cuban origin Guillermo Novo Sampol had given by mistake to two journalists of its staff.

The dialogue covered an entire page of the publication under the heading "Alpha, Omega and others." It gave an account of the terrorist activities of these groups throughout the United States and in different regions of Latin America and the Caribbean.

Some paragraphs are worth reproducing for the remarkable nature of their content:

"On 43rd Street, where 'Alpha-66' and 'Abdala'— whose terrorist activities are well known in the United States and other countries of the Americas— are based, they were notified that it was absolutely forbidden to give Novo's address. Nevertheless, they almost certainly find him at the Ford automobile store. Of course, the journalists appeared there as Guillermo's friends. When they asked for Novo, the sales assistant turned around and shouted, 'Bill, they are looking for you.' Bill came out to meet them, and thanks to the photo given to Andronov in the Solidarity with Chile Coordination Center, they immediately recognized Guillermo Novo.

"'Are you called Bill and not Guillermo?' they asked him while showing him a press card.
"'Translated into English Guillermo is William or simply Bill,' he replied with a smile, 'that's why I use your style now.'
He assumed I was American, I thought, I should let him talk, as he doesn't realize.
"'Have you had problems with the U.S. authorities?'
"'None.'
"'That's strange, taking into account the official investigation into the Letelier case in Washington.'
"'And so what?,' he laughed openly. 'They can investigate all they want; they sent me two summonses to appear before the Congress Commission and make a statement, but that doesn't worry me. They make a bit of a fuss and then they'll shut up. It has happened before.'
"'Why did you fire a bazooka against the UN?'
"'Yes, and I am sorry that we couldn't eliminate Che Guevara then.'
"'But during the explosions people of different political ideas perish, the elderly, children and women. How can you justify that?'
"'Victims are inevitable. When Cuban pilots, diplomats or members of their families die, I am not sorry, the death of these people always makes me happy. . . .'"

"I close my eyes and I remember it as if it were today. I knew my father was arriving that day. The one that came was Ortiz; he got out of the car and I saw him crying, he kissed me and said, 'Take good care of your mother, she has a bad heart. . . .' Then my mother broke the news to me, and I began to scream. Afterwards there was the funeral; I knew that he wasn't in any of the eight coffins. Everyone filed past, wherever I be, I couldn't hear the last post. So, as can be seen in this photo there were my mother and the three children. A few weeks later I started saying to my mother that he was going to return, that he was in an isle, and when I hear someone sounding a car horn, just in the same way that he used to do, I would run out and shout, 'Papá is coming!'"

*Odalys Pérez, daughter of the pilot
Wilfredo Pérez.*

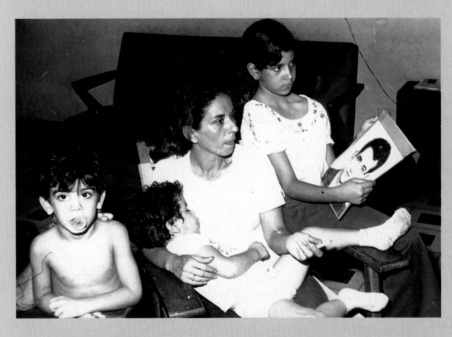

". . . Magaly was 33 years old when she died, and was the mother of two children of 12 and 2 years of age (Robertico and Abel Santiago), who left orphaned, it was a horrendous crime. . . ."

*William Grave de Peralta, father of Magaly Grave de Peralta,
flight attendant.*

". . . That horrendous crime in which my sister and 72 other human beings were murdered has been like a dagger embedded in my chest for 25 years. It was not a crime aimed at our people, I say this in the depth of my pain, but against humanity, and with all my strength I call for justice to be done. . . ."

*Nilda Esther Grave de Peralta, sister of Magaly, one of the flight
attendants murdered in the sabotaged plane.*

"It was an odyssey full of terrible times. The person who suffered most was Ninoska, the eldest daughter who was 13 years old at the time. She made an album of all the photos she had of her father and everything that appeared in the press. She is the one who spends the most time looking at the photos."

Nancy Cejas, widow of crewmember Ramón J. Ferrandiz Lefebre.

"I was the last one to find out. My mother was in the airport; she worked in international traffic, and that's where she met my father when she was 19 years old, and they fell in love. My brother also found out and, in spite of the fact that he was younger than me, he was 11 and I was 13, he didn't say anything to me. He kept quiet. He lay down on our parent's bed and I said, 'Come over here, if mom and dad arrive home they are going to wake you up.' But he didn't pay any attention to me. He stayed there waiting for mother. The house filled up with neighbors and I kept on sleeping. I wake up to go to school, and saw the house full of people. 'What happened?' 'Come here, I have to talk to you,' my mother said and she took me into the bedroom. The only thing that was left of my father was the cap of his uniform. My lifetime changed. Losing my father has become a lifetime trauma; I couldn't finish school, I had psychiatric help. When he left, I asked him what I had always asked him, 'When are you coming back?' 'Tomorrow afternoon,' he replied. And he never returned.

Ninoska Ferrandiz Cejas

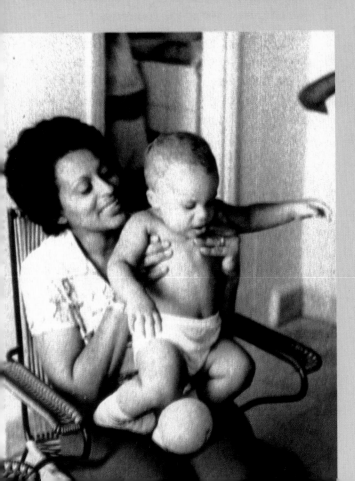

"We had a six-month-old baby boy, we were already planning to celebrate his first birthday. . . .

"It was not until Fidel talked in the mourning of the victims of that horrendous crime that I began to fully understand that I had lost Julio forever, the father of my son, the love of my life. I have never been able to forget him."

Martha Saudoral López, wife of Julio Herrera Aldona, member of the foil team.

"It is a brutal and cowardly act because that is what they have always wanted, as in the case of La Coubre. They are not brave enough for a face-to-face fight and so they attack innocent people, young people and workers who represented Cuba. The poor mother of my little son cannot be consoled. She was so looking forward to seeing him."

Carlos Leyva, father of Carlos Leyva, member of the foil team.

"... I often think about Virgen Filezala who wanted to be an architect; she was a flower that had hardly begun to bloom and was uprooted at 17 years old. And Carlos Miguel Leyva with his clean-shaven face and sweet gaze, as well as Nancy Uranga, the only married member of the young women's team, with those blue eyes that were forever smiling."

Irene Farbes, journalist and former fencer.

"It is not just the pain that I feel at the loss of my brother. The death of so many comrades has made it all so much more tragic."

Eloina Arencibia, sister of José R. Arencibia, member of the sword team.

"A quarter of a century has passed since then, but I always begin to feel really terrible around this time. I get so depressed particularly when I imagine the explosion of the plane in the air or I hear the interrupted communication with the air traffic control tower.

"... This is the most severe blow that has ever received my family. It traumatized my mother forever; I remember that she couldn't go on working after that. She claimed that she saw my brother in the door of her office just as he used to appear when he would go there to see her. At the end she died with all that pain of six years locked inside her, of a cerebral stroke. ...

"My father has been dead since 1979, three years after the sabotage he suffered a massive heart attack. He couldn't recover either. ..."

Maricela Leyva González, sister of Carlos Leyva González, member of the fencing team.

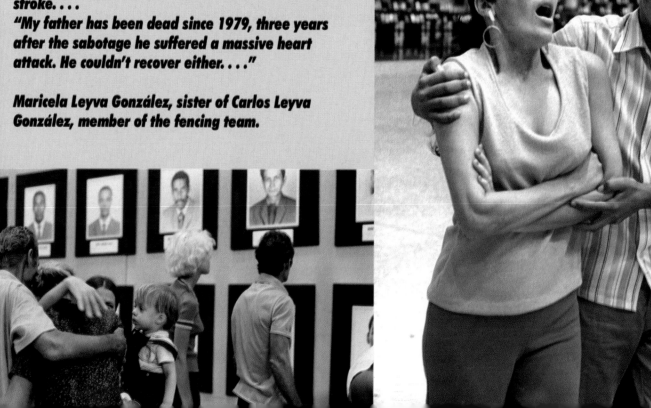

Six students from Guyana had been awarded scholarships to study medicine in Cuba.

ILLON DE PERSONAS RINDIERON HOMENAJE POSTUMO
LAS DEL AVION DE CUBANA DESTRUIDO POR LA CI

ESA M ITUD INABARCABLE

"When a strong and brave people cry, unjustice trembles."

"... the DC-8 plane brought down in Barbados was a war plane camouflaged with the Cubana de Aviación sign."

Orlando Bosch
Fragment of an article published in El Nuevo Herald, October 14, 2001.

Murieron 73 personas

Sabotaje
en el Avión Cuba
que Estalló en Barbad
se Atribuyen Exiliados Anticast

Fragments published in Venezuela press:
Ultimas noticias, El Universal, El Nacional, Meridiano,
October 1976.

Centroamericano de Esgrima

Arencibia de Cuba
Dominó en Florete

El cubano José Ramón Arencibia derrotó en un combate extra al venezolano Eliécer Gutiérrez y conquistó el título de florete individual masculino, correspondiente al cuarto campeonato centroamericano de esgrima que comenzó ayer en la pedana instalada en el Palacio de las Industrias. Arencibia y Gutiérrez había llegado empa-

Miami, Florida, EE.UU., 7 (EFE).

Una organización secreta de exiliados anticastristas se atribuyó hoy aquí el atentado que ayer causó la muerte a 73 personas que viajaban en un avión de la compañía "Cubana de Aviación".

Según el diario "The Miami Herald", una voz con marcado acento cubano llamó hoy a la redacción de este periódico para informar que había sido el grupo extremista de exiliados cubanos "El Cóndor", el autor del sabotaje que causó la caída al mar del avión cuba-

Esto está peor, esto está peor, pégate al agua", fue la última frase del piloto del avión de Cubana de Aviación que cayó ayer al mar escuchada por la torre de control del aeropuerto de Barbados.

Durante cuatro minutos, de las 13.24 a las 13.28 hora local de ayer, el capitán de la nave mantuvo repórticos diálogos con la torre de control del aeropuerto "Seawell" de esta capital, mientras el aparato perdía altura de manera dramática.

En su primera comunicación, el piloto expresó: "tuvimos una explosión aquí, y hay

según fue recogido por la grabación magnetofónica de la torre de control.

El aparato de Cubana de Aviación, un DC-8 procedente de Guyana y Trinidad-Tobago, despegó de aquí rumbo a Jamaica y La Habana, a las 13.16 hora local.

En el avión viajaban 73 personas, entre cubanos, guyaneses y coreanos, todos los cuales perecieron.

Pilotos de varios aviones que sobrevolaron el área informaron aquí que se ve perfectamente el avión a unos 200 pies de profundidad y considerando que no se puede rescatar.

Cuba se Llevó Todo
el Oro
del Centroamericano de
Esgrima

N.Uranga, campeona individual de florete.

La acción de las damas en el Florete por equipos es la última noche del campeonato.

Cuba Monopolizó
los Tres Puestos
en Sable Individual

Cuba prosiguió su dominio en el Centroamericano y del Caribe de esgrima cuando anoche ocupó los tres primeros lugares en la competencia de sable individual, especialidad para la que habían clasificado tres representantes cubanos, dos venezolanos y un colombiano.

Cuba aseguró la totalidad de medallas de oro en disputa manteniendo esta hazaña en su expresión en la región. Venezuela fue en la segunda competencia el mejor clasificado

extra y al ganar el título concluyó con cinco triunfos y un revés.

Otro cubano, José Fernández, quedó en el segundo lugar, y la medalla de bronce correspondió a Juan Duany, también de Cuba, con tres victorias y dos derrotas.

El venezolano José Ovalles fue el mejor clasificado de nuestro país, al ocupar la cuarta posición con dos triunfos y tres de derrotas.

clamó campeón de florete al derrotar espectacularmente al venezolano Eliécer Gutiérrez.

Hoy continuará el campeonato centroamericano de esgrima, efectuándose en horas de la noche competencia de florete por equipos.

La clasificación del sable individual fue la siguiente:

1) Alberto Drake (Cuba).

The Associate Attorney General

FILE: A28 851
             A11 861

IN THE MATTER OF:

ORLANDO BOSCH-AVIL

APPLICANT

Decision o

Pursuant to m
General, I have un
Naturalization Ser
concerning the appl
to the United Stat
consideration of th
and the Commission
Commissioner arguir
on his asylum appli
nonconfidential inf

As a result o
that it would be pr
United States to pr
concluded that he s
under 8 U.S.C. 1182
(29), and that his
deportation should

U.S. Department of Justice
Office of the Assistant
General Attorney

Washington, D.C. 20530

ARCHIVE: A28 851 622)
          A11 861 810) Procedure for inadmissibility by virtue of subsection
) c) of Article 235 in the presence of Assistant General Attorney
SUBJECT:) acting
)
ORLANDO BOSCH-AVILA,)
APPLICANT   )

Decision of the Acting Associate Attorney General

INTRODUCTION

Pursuant to by responsabilities as Acting Associate Attorney General, I have undertaken a review of the immigration and Naturalization Service's (INS) decision of May 19, 1989 concerning the applications of Orlando Bosch-Avila for admission to the United States and for asylum. This review has included consideration of the decision of the INS Regional Commisioner and the commisioner, the submission of Bosch to the Regional commissioner arguing against exclusion and requesting a hearing on his asylum application, and certain confidential and nonconfidential information respecting Bosch.

For 30 years Bosch has resolutely and perseveringly perpetrated acts of violence. He has threatened to carry out and has carried out violent acts of terrorism against numerous targets, including countries friendly to the United States and high-ranking officials of these countries. On repeated occasions he has expressed and demonstrated his desire to cause indiscriminate injury and death. His actions are those of a terrorist who does not respect the law or human decency, who threatens acts of violence and carries them out without any consideration for the identity of his victims.

The United States cannot tolerate the inherent use of terrorism as a means for resolving controversy. To give in to those who use force is nothing other than encouraging the appearance of more terrorists. We must consider terrorism as a universal evil, even when it is directed against those whose political sympathies we do not share. As a U.S. district court so eloquently pointed out in relation to this same case, "the evils of terrorism are no less in terms of those who perpetrate these acts or in terms of their cause." Orlando Bosch-Avila versus Perry Rivkind, 88-973-CIV-HOEVELER (S.D. Fla., June, 1, 1988. Ruling on a petition for a habeas corpus order). See also Rivero-Díaz case, 12 I & N Dec. 475 (BIA, 1967).

Annex

(Original: English)

U.S. Department of Justice

Office of the Associate Attorney General

Washington, D.C. 20530

In exclusion proceedings under
section 235(c) before the
Acting Associate Attorney
General

cting Associate Attorney General

INTRODUCTION

nsibilities as Acting Associate Attorney
n a review of the Immigration and
(INS) decision of May 19, 1989
ns of Orlando Bosch-Avila for admission
or asylum. This review has included
sions of the INS Regional Commissioner
submission of Bosch to the Regional
nst exclusion and requesting a hearing
, and certain confidential and
on respecting Bosch.

review, the conclusion is inescapable
dal to the public interest for the
a safe haven for Bosch. I have moreover
lien excludable from the United States
), (28)(ii), (28)(iii), (28)(iv) and
ations for asylum and withholding of
herein are denied.

EVIDENCE TO REFUSE ADMISSION

The information included in the archives indicates clearly and unequivocally that Bosch has personally promoted, encouraged and organized acts of violence in this country and several others and has taken part in them. . . .

CONFIDENTIAL

. . . INFORMATION INDICATING THE DETONATION OF A BOMB ON OCTOBER 6, 1976, ON A CUBANA AIRLINE FLIGHT, WAS A CORU OPERATION DIRECTED BY BOSCH.

CONCLUSION

For the reasons stated, on today's date, it hereby IS ORDERED that admission to Orlando Bosch-Avila be refused and that he be deported from the United States.

Likewise it IS ORDERED the refusal of his petition for assylum and the suspension of deportation, according to what is stipulated in 8 U.S.C., 1158 and 1253 h), respectively.

January 23, 1989

(Signed) Joe D. Whitley
Acting Associate Attorney General

"My government, and by the way all good-willed people, condemn this vile and senseless act. But Cuba's attempt to describe the United States as a defender of international terrorism and **backer of terrorists** is absurd."

Fragment from the reply by U.S. ambassador Mr. Perkins, during the session held on May 21, 1992, by the Security Council at the request of the Cuban government to debate the draft resolution presented by Cuba on the sabotage carried out on the plane over Barbados.

Ros mantiene viva campaña por Bosch

■ **El INS aseguró que decidirá el caso dentro de 60 días, aunque antes había prometido resolverlo antes del 12 de mayo.**

Por MIRTA OJITO
Redactora de El Nuevo Herald

La senadora estatal Ileana Ros-Lehtinen anunció el viernes que extenderá la campaña a favor de la libertad del médico y activista anti-castrista cubano Orlando Bosch hasta que las autoridades estadounidenses le concedan la libertad.

La senadora estatal Ileana Ros-Lehtinen anunció el viernes que extenderá la campaña a favor de la libertad del médico y activista anti-castrista cubano Orlando Bosch

"Orlando Bosch no ha violado... ció a la prensa hace una semana que... Servicio de Inmigración y Naturalización (INS) en Washington, anunció a la prensa hace una semana que... ese país, acusado de volar en 1976 un avión de la aerolínea Cubana de...

Aviación en el que perecieron más... las. La acusación nunca... en las cortes venezola... ...te mes, Ros-Lehtinen, ...Balart y otros legisla...Florida viajaron a Wa...tratar con represen...INS el caso de Bosch...istas Co...ll. Claude...solicitaron...el viernes pa...donde se suponía que Ro...pusiera fin a la campa...

mes, asistieron más de 100 personas.

Adriana Bosch, esposa del activista cubano, dijo que estaba muy contenta con el resultado de la campaña.

Ros-Lehtinen indicó que continuarán enviando telegramas y pla...

Just at the time of releasing Orlando Bosch

Las Américas daily, May 20, 1989.

Intercede el senador Connie Mack ante Bush por Orlando Bosch

D. LAS AMERICAS 30/6/18

(N. de la R.) El senador federal por el estado de la Florida, Connie Mack, le envió la siguiente carta a George Bush, Presidente de Estados, intercediendo por el doctor Orlando Bosch:

★ ★ ★

Honorable George Bush
La Casa Blanca,
Washington D.C. 20500

Estimado señor Presidente:

Le estoy escribiendo para solicitarle una entrevista suya con destacados líderes cubano-americanos de Miami a conveniencia de usted para discutir el caso de Orlando Bosch Avila.

En una opinión que deja mucho que desear el Departamento de Justicia el viernes de la semana anterior rechazó la petición de asilo político en Estados Unidos

CONNIE MACK

Señor presidente, este caso envuelve una pregunta fundamental: ¿Debe la tierra que re-

ORLANDO BOSCH'S ADDRESS:
11746 SW 11th St. MIAMI FL 33184

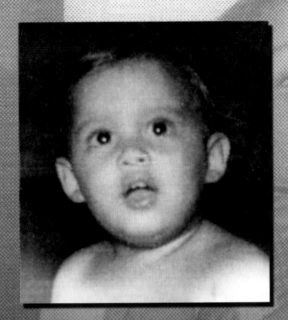

Octavio Borges
Aguilera

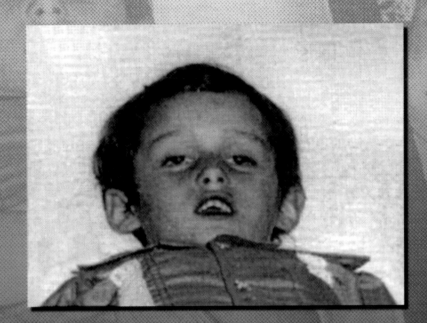

**Terrorist activity is consciously
directed against the civilian
population and its effectiveness
is related to its brutality.**

In 1981 an epidemic of hemorrhaging dengue broke out in Cuba, which in a matter of a few weeks cost the lives of 158 people, out of whom 101 were children. A total of 344,203 people were affected.

The first cases appeared at the same time in three different regions of the island, at a distance of over 300 km between them. There was no epidemiological explanation available to help understand these events as a natural infection.

The sudden appearance, without the prevalence of this epidemic in the Americas or in any of the countries with which Cuba was involved in major exchanges of personnel, in addition to the simultaneous appearance of the disease in different regions of the country, are pillars to the research carried out by renowned Cuban scientists in conjunction with their foreign counterparts. They all are highly qualified in the detection of and struggle against biological warfare.

Years later, during the trial held in New York to the Cuban terrorist Eduardo Arocena, a resident of that city, he confessed to having introduced the contagious virus into Cuba.

SUMMARY OF A TYPICAL MEDICAL RECORD

A five-year-old female patient, with a history of good health and well nourished, has been in a state of fever for three days associated to headache and suffering from "pain all over the body." She is vomiting and has a slight abdominal pain; on the day she was admitted red-colored marks appeared on her trunk and limbs, which the family presumed to be "blood stains."

Physical examination revealed petechias in the trunk and limbs, as well as ecchymosis on the right leg. Her state of consciousness was normal. Temperature: 38°C; blood pressure (BP): 90/60, cardiac frequency (CF): 120 per minute, respiratory frequency (RF): 28 per minute. On examination the respiratory apparatus and cardiovascular areas are found to be normal. Globulous abdomen, slightly painful in the epigastrium and right hypochondrium. Tactile examination of the liver reveals that it surpasses the rib edge by 1 cm. No splenomegalia. Laboratory results: reduced platelet level (thrombocytopenia) 80,000 x mm^3, leukogram normal for her age; hemoglobin: 12 g %; haematocrit: 34.

o Acevedo Martinez 3. Alain Veliz

s Barzaga Barzaga 6. Alexis García

an Nú Vall

arais és Col

olores López

Monzó ernán

en Ce Medr

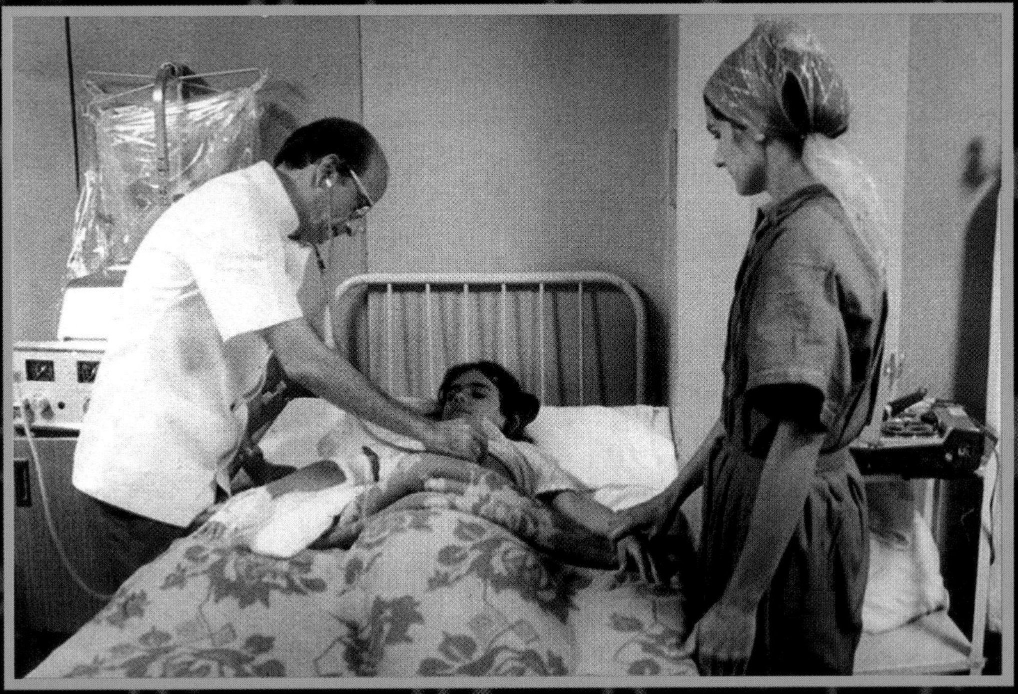

Núñez Perez 24. Daniel Gutiérrez

ardo Benítez Téllez 28. Elena Rodrígu

Herrera Bonet

Ros edo H

Estrada odrígue

l Velá Barr

emán H Araña

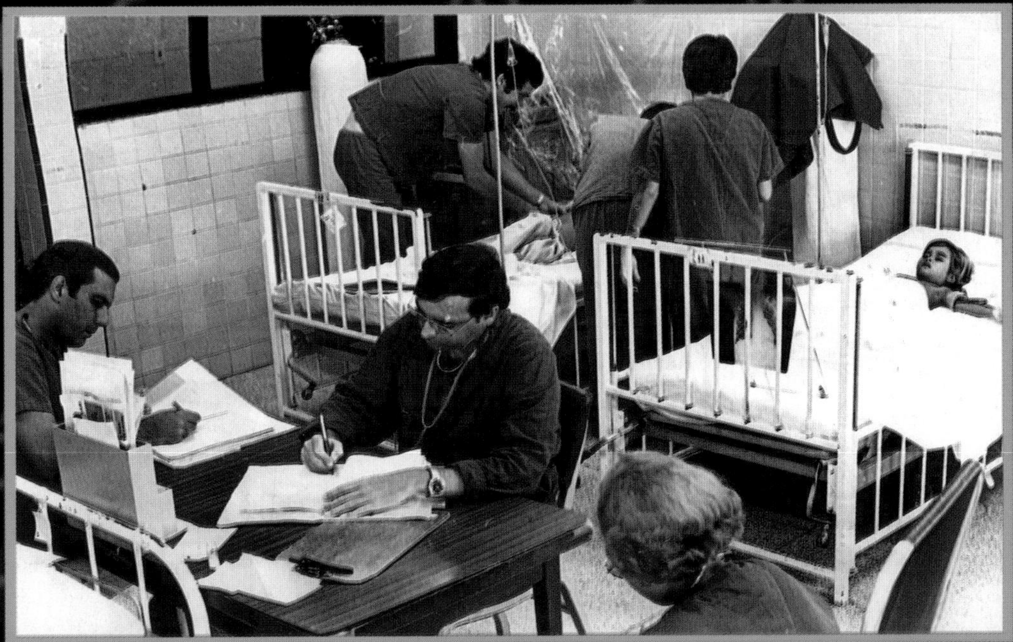

mar Riquems Rivera 46. Lissete Bacallao

ok 49. Marisela Cruz Cruz 50. Marilin Gon

Hospitals were completely full, to the extent that schools had to be opened and used as hospitals.

SUMMARY OF A TYPICAL MEDICAL RECORD

Six hours after being admitted to hospital, the marks on the skin had not changed, but the fever had suddenly dropped; she is sweating and crying because of intense abdominal pain in the epigastrium. The liver can be felt 3 cm under the rib edge and before auscultation there is a vesicular murmur at the base of the right lung (BP): 90/60, (CF): 128 x min, (RF): 32 x min. (RX) Thorax: pleural overflow on the right side.

She is on an intravenous drip (water and electrolytes in accordance with her age) and nothing is administered by mouth. Nevertheless, she has vomited three times, the last of which contained traces of blood. Her platelet count has reduced to 40,000 x mm³ and hematocrit has increased to 40.

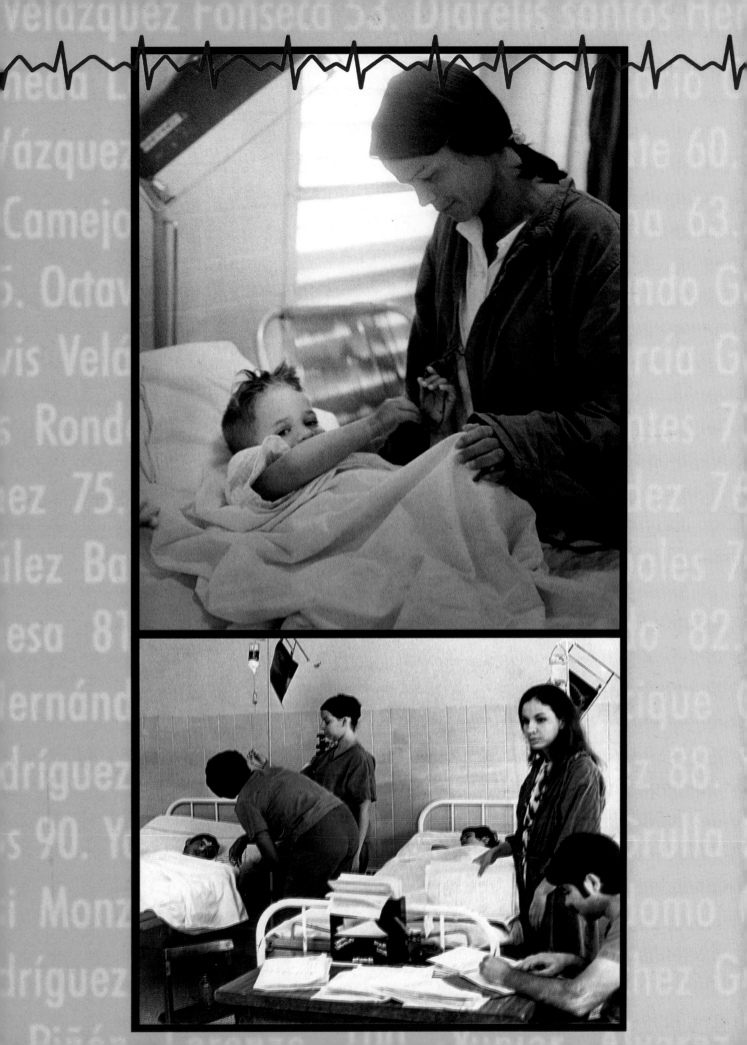

SUMMARY OF A TYPICAL MEDICAL RECORD

Her symptoms have been interpreted as a case of hemorrhaging dengue, with plasma extravasion (hydrothorax and upper hematocrit level). For this reason intravenous treatment with crystalloid solutions is being maintained and increased. New laboratory tests indicated coagulation disorders (prolonged prothrombin time, reduction of hepatic factors in coagulation).

Four hours later her symptoms included cold limbs, tachycardia of 160 per minute and 60/40 (B.P.), which are interpreted as signs of shock, she is vomiting blood (hematemesis). She is transferred to the Intensive Care Unit. Human albumen is administered together with platelet-rich plasma; she improves for a while and for two hours her blood pressure level is recovered. The thorax X-ray shows signs of bilateral pleural overflow and lungs with interstitial infiltrate.

She has dark defecation (semi-digested blood) and two sanguinolent vomits. Platelets dropped to 20,000 x mm³. Fresh blood, and oxygen have been indicated, and also liquids via intravenous until diuresis is obtained. However, maximum blood pressure has fallen again to 40 mmHg and she is just obnubilated.

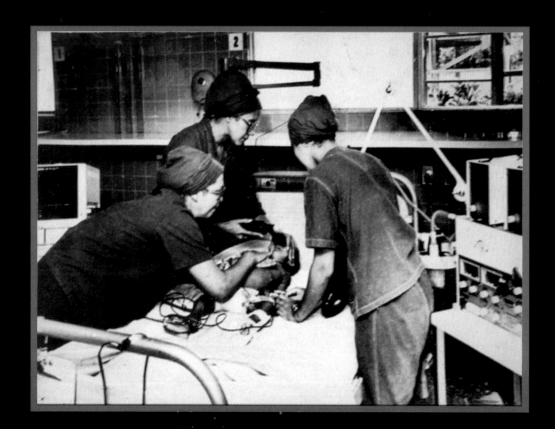

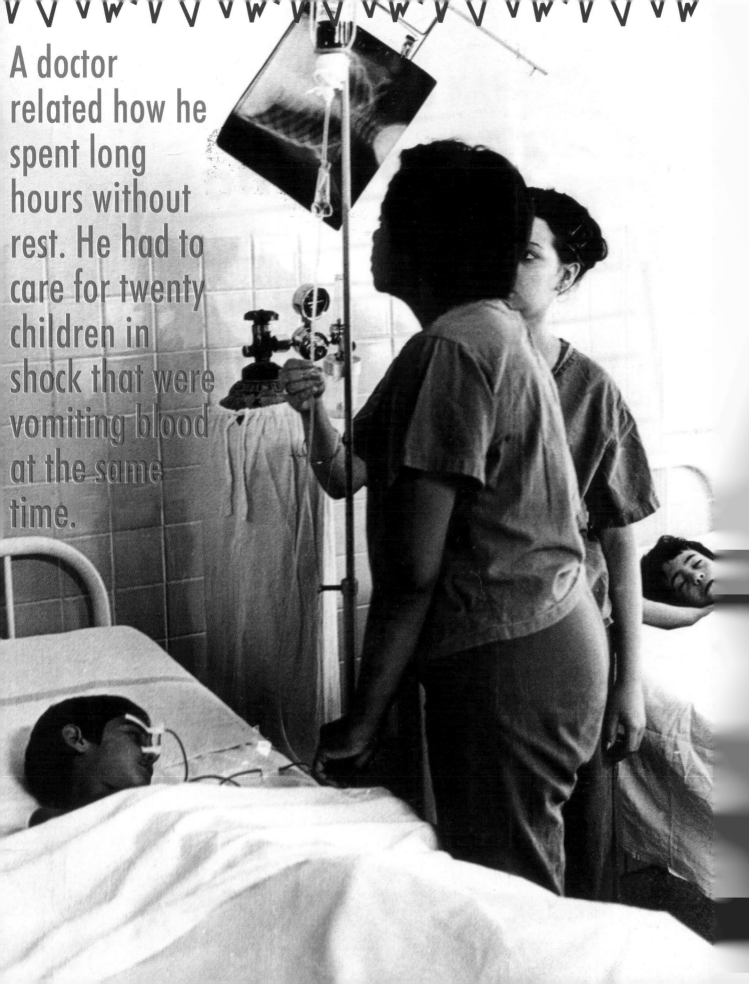

A doctor related how he spent long hours without rest. He had to care for twenty children in shock that were vomiting blood at the same time.

SUMMARY OF A TYPICAL MEDICAL RECORD

A few hours later she suffered from respiratory problems and signs of hypoxia and therefore pulmonar ventilation was applied. Blood pressure temporarily recovered with a new dose of human albumen but finally dropped to zero. Large amounts of blood appeared in the endotrachial tube, a sign of massive pulmonary hemorrhage, and she died.

Her time in the hospital was less than 27 hours and she died five days after the fever started, in spite of the family's concerns and the medical and nursing staff's care.

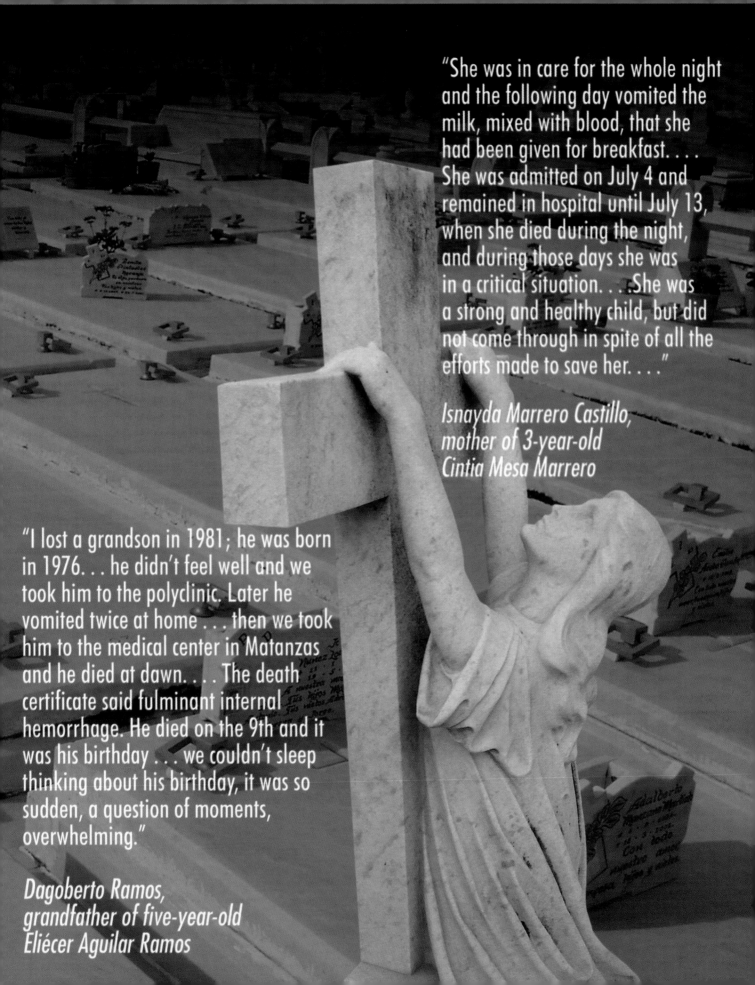

"She was in care for the whole night and the following day vomited the milk, mixed with blood, that she had been given for breakfast. . . . She was admitted on July 4 and remained in hospital until July 13, when she died during the night, and during those days she was in a critical situation. . . . She was a strong and healthy child, but did not come through in spite of all the efforts made to save her. . . ."

Isnayda Marrero Castillo, mother of 3-year-old Cintia Mesa Marrero

"I lost a grandson in 1981; he was born in 1976. . . he didn't feel well and we took him to the polyclinic. Later he vomited twice at home . . . then we took him to the medical center in Matanzas and he died at dawn. . . . The death certificate said fulminant internal hemorrhage. He died on the 9th and it was his birthday . . . we couldn't sleep thinking about his birthday, it was so sudden, a question of moments, overwhelming."

Dagoberto Ramos, grandfather of five-year-old Eliécer Aguilar Ramos

"My little girl said to me around noon, 'Mamita, I don't think I am going to live much longer, I am going to die.'. . . On the 19th at around two in the morning she was very agitated, the 20th she was taken to intensive care. . . . At seven in the evening they told a cousin of mine that she had died."

Zenaida J. Isla Romero, mother of 5-year-old Yamilé Villalonga

"She had Down's syndrome, but was not a chronic case. . . . She was healthy enough. . . . On June 20 she came down with a fever and I took her to the polyclinic . . . the pediatrician told me to bring samples of her feces and urine, but she fainted before I could do that. I called for a nurse: 'Miss, my little girl is dying' . . . on June 21, she died."

Inocencia M. Ledón Hernández, mother of Mailín Castañeda Ledón

"I lost my 13-year-old daughter and part of my life . . . She said to me, 'Mom, I am going to die, yes, I am going to die.' . . . A week later she was dead. . . . I am 64 years old and I am still working because I can't stay home; I seem to see her all the time beside me."

Casimira Camejo, mother of 13-year-old Nereida Carmona Camejo

"When we arrived home from the airport she vomited the breakfast. Shortly afterwards she said, 'I'm falling!' . . . At ten o'clock at night of that same day, she had nausea again and we come back to the hospital. . . . It was decided to admit her. . . . At midnight I told her to sleep but she answered no, that she was going to die. . . . Before closing her eyes she gave me a very cold kiss and asked me not to let go of her hand. . . . At around two in the morning she became increasingly weak and I felt her hand losing its grip on mine. When I looked at her she was purple colored . . . . And that was it. . . . Six months later, because of this, her father died; it affected his heart. . . ."

Silvia Torres,
mother of 12-year-old
Ernestina Oñate

"On July 7, 1981, my small son became a bit weak and I took him to see the pediatrician. He hold me that I should watch him; he continued to worsen and I took him back to the doctor. That's when they carried out an analysis and said that he was okay . . .the following day, at five in the afternoon, I was told that my son was off-color. I took him to the hospital and they took him straight into intensive care. I never saw him alive again."

Rosa M. Acuña,
mother of 10-year-old
Carlos A. Rodríguez Acuña

"I was with her when she died on the 13th . . .I have this grief for a time ago . . . they fought right up until the end, in the last few days the medicine Interferon arrived. . . .

Félix Mesa,
father of 3-year-old
Cintia Mesa Marrero

E 9 E
Lizet
Bacallao
del Llano
★ 16·4·19
✝ 1·7·19

During the epidemic the U.S. Treasury Department, applying the precepts of the blockade, delayed authorization for the sale and transportation to Cuba of the insecticides specified for combating the vector responsible for the disease, as well as the fumigation equipment that had to be used. Cuba had to purchase them from third countries at an additional cost of millions of dollars and with a vital delay in the arrival time in the country, which was, undoubtedly, a key factor in many of the deaths that took place.

Lizy:
tus padres,
hermanita,
abuela
   y familia
siempre te
recordaremos.

All the children that died were between 0 and 14 years old. Although the length of the illness varied between three and seven days, research carried out revealed on average: the third day of fever bleeding begins (in the skin, mouth and nose), as well as the alarm signals (intense abdominal pain, frequent vomiting, irritability or sleepiness); on the fourth day the patient goes into shock, shortly after the decline of the fever, sometimes this is followed by even heavier bleeding, such as hematemesis; and the fifth day is the day of death. Almost without exception, the children were healthy and well nourished.

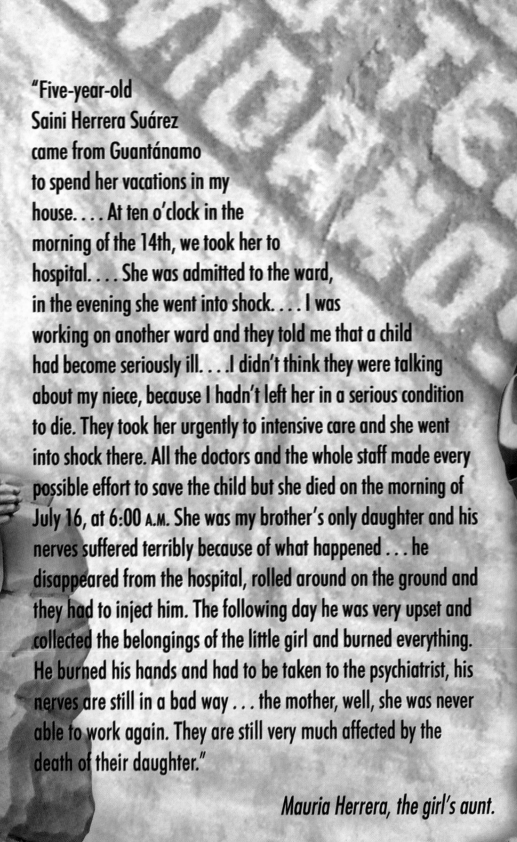

"Five-year-old
Saini Herrera Suárez
came from Guantánamo
to spend her vacations in my
house. . . . At ten o'clock in the
morning of the 14th, we took her to
hospital. . . . She was admitted to the ward,
in the evening she went into shock. . . . I was
working on another ward and they told me that a child
had become seriously ill. . . . I didn't think they were talking
about my niece, because I hadn't left her in a serious condition
to die. They took her urgently to intensive care and she went
into shock there. All the doctors and the whole staff made every
possible effort to save the child but she died on the morning of
July 16, at 6:00 A.M. She was my brother's only daughter and his
nerves suffered terribly because of what happened . . . he
disappeared from the hospital, rolled around on the ground and
they had to inject him. The following day he was very upset and
collected the belongings of the little girl and burned everything.
He burned his hands and had to be taken to the psychiatrist, his
nerves are still in a bad way . . . the mother, well, she was never
able to work again. They are still very much affected by the
death of their daughter."

Mauria Herrera, the girl's aunt.

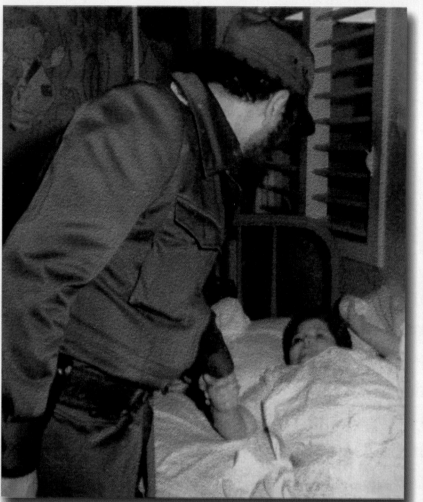

"No more children can die in Cuba."

Fidel Castro

Investments made to control the epidemic

Hospitalization	$ 38,796,316.00
Emergency care	1,290,854.00
Medicines used for ambulatory patients	1,021,673.00
Social Security expenses	4,724,040.00

"The mission of the group I led was to obtain certain types of germs and introduce them into Cuba. . . ."

Statement made by the Cuban-American terrorist Eduardo Arocena to the Federal Court in New York. Page 2189 of this statement, 1984. Exp. 2 FBINY 185-1009.

The terrorist Arocena was not tried because of this confession and the U.S. authorities did not carry out an investigation of any kind either.

The Miami Herald, September 1, 1981
WASHINGTON. The pompous statement by Fidel Castro that "harmful pests" which attack harvests and animals in Cuba, and that the dengue fever epidemic that had caused the death of over 100 people on the island are the work of the Central Intelligence Agency (CIA) does not appear to be inconceivable to the authors of a new book that will be published in autumn.
Former Federal Investigations Bureau (FBI) agent William W. Turner and the journalist Warren Hinckle claim that the United States used biological warfare in Cuba during the Nixon administration.
The authors allege that the CIA has involved the United States in a secret, undeclared and illegal war against Cuba for over 20 years. The so-called Project Cuba is the largest and least well-known CIA operation outside the legal limits of its statutes, they claim.

Anti-Cuban Congress members have initiated a campaign in the United States to free Eduardo Arocena from prison.

"It is not much to ask for justice to be carried out against professional terrorists who, from U.S. territory itself, have not ceased to apply their underhanded methods against our people to spread terror and destroy the economy of a blockaded and harassed country."

Fidel Castro Ruz

1. Aldaris Reyes Estrada
2. Alejandro Acevedo Martínez
3. Alaín Véliz Barreto
4. Alexander Céspedes Fonseca
5. Alexis Barzaga Barzaga
6. Alexis García Rodríguez
7. Alfredo Sánchez Villalobo
8. Aman Núñez Matos
9. Amarilis Valle Posada
10. Ana Milagros Gómez Parra
11. Anarais Machado Fleitas
12. Andrés Cobas Castro
13. Ángel M. Medina Vicario
14. Annia Dolores Pagán Padilla
15. Aramís López Cárdenas
16. Arquímides Delgado Zamora
17. Aslilie Monzón Rodríguez
18. Bárbaro Hernández García
19. Carlos Rodríguez Acuña
20. Carmen Cevallos Prieto
21. César Medrano Bello
22. Cintia Mesa Marrero
23. Danelys Núñez Pérez
24. Daniel Gutiérrez Balloga
25. Diorkis Salazar Betancourt
26. Eduardo Benítez Téllez
27. Elena Rodríguez López
28. Elieser Aguilar Ramos
29. Elison Herrera Carcore
30. Emiliana Bonet González
31. Emilio García Leonar
32. Eneida Ras Ladoy
33. Enrique Toledo Hernández
34. Ernestina Oñate Torres
34. Henri Estrada Martínez
36. Idalmis Rodríguez Cedeño
37. Inés Pérez Arruego
38. Ismael Velázquez Cena
39. Yoel Barnet Pérez
40. Jorge Luis Bocourt Brindis
41. José Alemán Hernández
42. José Antonio Araña Guerrero
43. José Lázaro González Varona
44. Leosmar Riquems Rivera
45. Lázaro Bacallao del Llano
46. Lissete Bolaños Suárez
47. Luz Rojas Speek
48. Maricela Cruz Cruz
49. Marilin González Yack
50. Danys Gutiérrez Hernández

51. Marilyn Velázquez Fonseca
52. Diarelis Santos Hernández
53. Martha Camacho Moy
54. Maylín Castañeda Ledón
55. Miguel de Jesús Osorio Canalero
56. Miguel Machado Ortega
57. Milvia Gin Vázquez
58. Mirelis Avello Carmenate
59. Mónica Caballero Tozanda
60. Nereida Carmona Camejo
61. Niurka Colás Quintana
62. Noemí Lamelas Miralles
63. Noemí Prieto Alonso
64. Octavio Borges Aguilera
65. Orlando González Gárgara
66. Osmany Gómez Ortega
67. Ovis Velázquez García
68. Pedro García González
69. Rafael Cardín Leyva
70. Raudel Rojas Rondón
71. Raúl Mustelier Fuentes
72. Rosa Carrazana Archel
73. Ruslán Mora Sánchez
74. Mario Fernández Fernández
75. Saini Herrera Suárez
76. Salvador Rafael González Batista
77. Silvia Olivera Nápoles
78. Tony Fernández Mayor
79. Walquis Romero Mesa
80. Yaima Cabrera Figueredo
81. Yaima Rodríguez Ferro
82. Yamila Covadonga Hernández Guerra
83. Yamilé Macique Caos
84. Yamilé Villalonga Isla
85. Yamilé Cobar Rodríguez
86. Yanet García Hernández
87. Yannete Chacón Caminero
88. Yannete Mendoza Burgos
89. Yaquelin Sosa Rey
90. Yasser Grulla Hidalgo
91. Yasmila Rodríguez Martínez
92. Yenesi Monzón González
93. Yoel Perdomo Cabrera
94. Yolanda Miralles Bodi
95. Yosvani Rodríguez Escalona
96. Yosvani Sánchez González
97. Yuleidis Cazaña Fuentes
98. Yunia Piñón Lorenzo
99. Yunior Alvarez Fleites
...

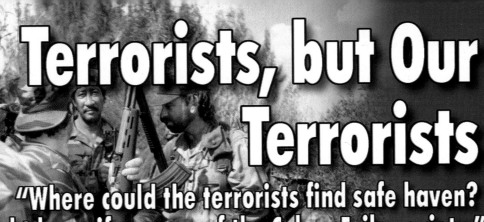

Terrorists, but Our Terrorists

"Where could the terrorists find safe haven? Right here, if you are of the Cuban Exile variety."

Kirk Nielsen
Miami New Times, December 20, 2001

TERRORISM UP TO THE PRESENT

In the nineties and up to the present day, terrorists of Cuban origin, residents in Miami, have carried out dozens of violent acts against Cuba. In spite of repeated reports made by the Cuban government, evidence sent to the U.S. government, declarations by the terrorists themselves in the press, on television and radio in the aforementioned city, they continue to act with impunity.

On October 14, 1990, the terrorists of Cuban origin Gustavo Rodríguez Sosa and Tomás Ramos Rodríguez, made their way from their Miami base and entered Cuban national territory via Santa Cruz del Norte, in Havana province.

. . . GUSTAVO RODRIGUEZ SOSA. . .occupant of 1231 30 Avenue, between 12th Street and 13th Street, South West, Miami, Florida, United States of America. . . .

He met the citizen of Cuban origin TOMAS RAMOS RODRIGUEZ in the United States of America. . . .

Their main objective was to carry out terrorist actions to overthrow the Cuban Revolution.

. . . NINO DIAZ asked if they were willing to take part in an incursion into Cuba with the aim of carrying out different terrorist activities and establish bases for future infiltration teams that would penetrate our national territory with different subversive goals and mainly with the mission of undertaking an attempt on the life of PRESIDENT FIDEL CASTRO. . . .

They received different types of training, both with weapons and explosives. . . .

They traveled to the area of Key West, Florida, United States of America, where they boarded the said vessel and left for Cuba. . . .

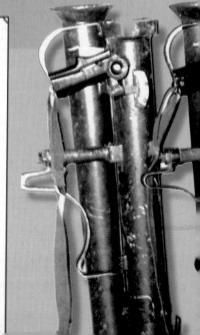

DECLARACION

----- En el local que ocupa el Organo de Instrucción del Departamento de la Seguridad del Estado, sito en San Miguel entre Anita y Golcuría, Municipio Diez de Octubre, Ciudad de la Habana, siendo las diez horas del día dieciseis de diciembre de mil novecientos noventa, "AÑO XXXII DE LA REVOLUCION", ante el Instructor actuante comparece el detenido que requerido de sus generales dice nombrarse GUSTAVO RODRIGUEZ SOSA, natural de Granma, hijo de Angel y María, de la tez blanca, de cuarenta y cuatro años de edad, por haber nacido el día dieciseis de diciembre de mil-novecientos cuarenta y seis, casado, desocupado, y vecino de la Treinta Avenida, número mil doscientos treinta y uno, entre Doce street y Trece street del South West, Miami, Florida, Estados -- Unidos de Norteamerica, y en Cuba en la calle Milagros, número-trescientos sesenta y tres apartamento treinta y dos, entre Octava y Porvenir, Lawton, Municipio Diez de Octubre, Ciudad de la-- Habana, quien impuesto del derecho que le concede la Ley de de-- clarar o abstenerse, opta por lo primero y manifiesta lo siguien te:-

----- Que abandonó ilegalmente el Territorio Nacional en el año--

Sergio González Rosquete, UNDP Secretary General, has declared that basic courses are given lasting for three months, during which time participants live and sleep within the training camps.

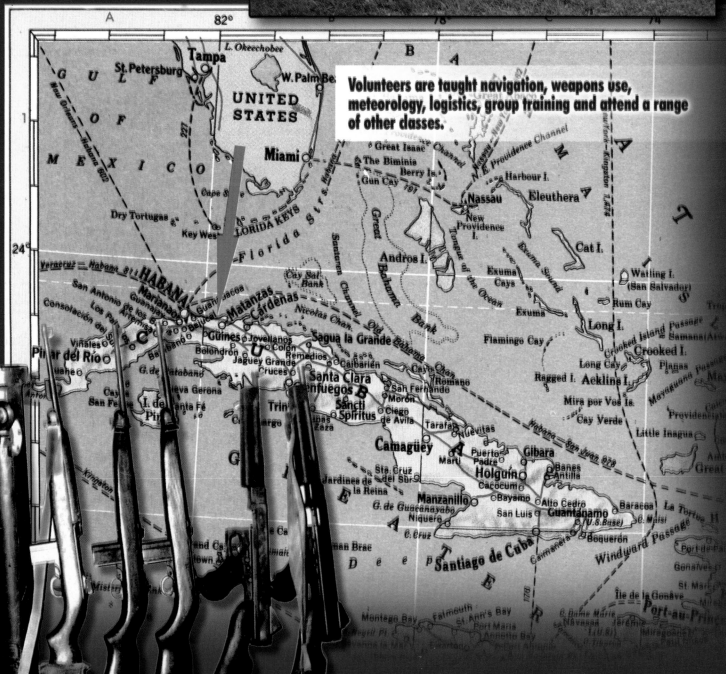

Volunteers are taught navigation, weapons use, meteorology, logistics, group training and attend a range of other classes.

e para dar--
n cantidad
cionaria, la que traerían a bordo de--
se infiltrarían en nuestro Territorio-

el dicente, que toda esta actividad es
civdadano norteamericano FRANK FIORINI
a organización contrarrevolucionaria y
IGENCIA (C.I.A.) de los Estados Unidos
ue las prácticas de explosivos les fue
tado elemento contrarrevolucionario RO
quien fuera preparador en épocas an-
infiltración a nuestro país, enviados
revolucionaria ALPHA-SESENTA Y SEIS y--
la CIA.--
---- Que después de varias reuniones con los principales dirigen-
tes de la organización contrarrevolucionaria se había logrado com-
prar por parte de los mismos, para su infiltración en Cuba, una-
pistola calibre cuarenta y cinco, una pistola Brownning de nueve-
milímetros, dos pistolas calibre veinticinco y un revólver treinta y ocho especial, una lancha rápida, dos equipos de comunicacio-
nes y varios miles de propagandas contrarrevolucionarias, todo lo-
cual había sido gestionado y comprado con los fondos de la organi
zación contrarrevolucionaria.--
---- Que llegado el domingo catorce de octubre de mil novecientos
noventa se trasladaron hacia la zona de Cayo Hueso, Florida, Esta
dos Unidos de Norteamérica, donde abordaron dicha embarcación y
partieron hacia Cuba, con todas las orientaciones de la organiza
ción anteriormente descrita.--
---- que ese mismo día en horas de la noche, desemb
zona de Santa Cruz del Norte, Provincia La Habana
jaron todos los medios conque contaban, menos la prop
ganda que habían botado al mar por la in   e había
hecho a TOMAS,   recer toda l   armamento-
para ese dicho   o las   verse despues
envueltos
---- se   tierra y cuando se-
encontra   ron detectados y detenido
en su c   atos de la Policía Nacional
Revolucion

On December 29, 1991, the terrorists Eduardo Díaz Betancourt, Daniel Candelario Santovenia Fernández and Pedro de La Caridad Álvarez Pedroso, set out from Miami, their place of residence, in the direction of a place known as La Sierrita, Cárdenas. Those who were captured declared that they had planned to carry out sabotage against a Matanzas paper mill, the Arrechavala rum factory, a Havana thermoelectric power station, leisure centers and public transportation means. Their statements were broadcast by Cuban television in January of 1992.

REPUBLICA DE CUBA
MINISTERIO DEL INTERIOR

000 104

"D E C L A R A C I O N"

-----En el local que ocupan las oficinas del Organo de Instrucción del Departamento de Seguridad del Estado, sito en la Calza
da de San Miguel, entre Anita y Goicuría, Víbora, Municipio -
Diez de Octubre, Ciudad de la Habana, y siendo las quince horas
del día once de enero de mil novecientos noventa y dos, "AÑO -
XXXIV DE LA REVOLUCION", ante el instructor actuante, comparece
el acusado que requerido de sus generales dijo nombrarse: DA-
NIEL CANDELARIO SANTOVENIA FERNANDEZ, natural de Cardenas, Pro
vincia de Matanzas, de la tez blanca, hijo de Daniel y Zoila, -
soltero, de treinta y seis años de edad por haber nacido el día
dos de febrero de mil novecientos cincuenta y cinco, con instrucción de sexto grado, de ocupación, chapista pintor por cuen
ta propia, y vecino de ciento ochenta y uno TERR. y once mil -
ochecientos diez SW Miami, Florida, Estados Unidos de Norteamerica, quien después de ser impuesto del derecho que le concede-

"resident at 11810 SW 181 Terr., Miami, Florida, United States of America. . . .

"That when they were willing to depart from the dock, in Key Marathon, Miami, Florida, United States of America. . . .

"their propaganda missions and the placing of explosive devices in different locations. . . ."

DANIEL C. SANTOVENIA FERNANDEZ. NACIDO EL 2 DE FEBRERO DE 1955 NATURAL DE CAR-DENAS, PROV. DE MATANZAS. ESTADO CIVIL : SOLTERO. NIVEL CULTURAL : 9no. GRADO.

On October 19, 1992, the Miami-based terrorists of Cuban origin Miguel Alfonso González, Eduardo González Torres and Gustavo David Torna Agudo entered the province of Sancti Spíritus via the beach of Playa Carbo and were detained.

The Bahamas authorities also arrested three other individuals of Cuban origin (Rubén Darío López Castro, Iván León Rojas and Jesús Morales García), who had links with the previously mentioned group. All six belonged to the crew of the yacht *Nautilus* and declared that Alfonso González, Torna Agudo and González Torres (detained in Cuba) had set out from the yacht in an inflatable rubber life raft for a destination unknown for them.

An investigation was carried out by the Bahamas authorities in Anguilla Key, where the *Nautilus* was found, and where the three terrorists were arrested. A MAC 10 machine gun with a silencer was discovered, together with a substantial amount of 45-caliber munitions, C-4 plastic explosive, an AKM loader with its cartridges and four more for machine guns, as well as electrical fuses and detonators.

REPORT ON CONVERSATIONS HELD IN THE BAHAMAS BY THE CUBAN DELEGATION IN RELATION TO THE "NAUTILUS" CASE.

INFORME SOB[...]
GACION CUBAN[...]

EL 4 DE NOVIEMBRE DE 1992, LA DELEGACION CUBANA QUE VISITO BAHAMAS-
CON MOTIVO DEL APRESAMIENTO POR AUTORIDADES DE ESE PAIS DE TRES IN-
DIVIDUOS DE ORIGEN CUBANO, EN CAYO ANGUILA, ENTRE EL 22 Y 23 DE OC-
TUBRE PASADO, SE TRASLADO A NASSAU, PARA SOSTENER UN INTERCAMBIO DE
INFORMACION RELACIONADO CON LA CAPTURA EN NUESTRO TERRITORIO DE ---
OTROS TRES SUJETOS, TAMBIEN CUBANOS, QUE PERTENI[...]
CION DEL "NAUTILUS", YATE EN QUE VIAJABAN LOS E[...]
EN BAHAMAS.

NUESTRA DELE[...]
CE-MINISTRO [...]
[...]O GONZALE[...]
[...]ES, FIS[...]

POLITICA DEL MINREX, -
[...]EFENSA, COMANDANTE ---

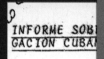

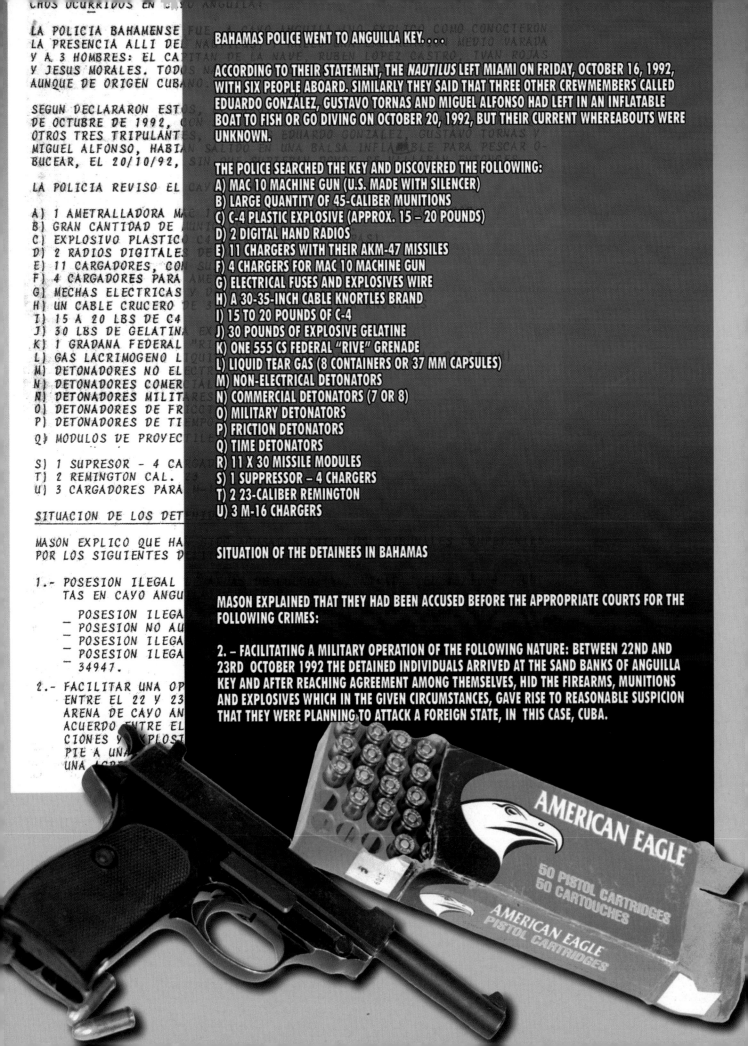

CHOS OCURRIDOS EN C.YO ANGUILA.

LA POLICIA BAHAMENSE ... FUE...
LA PRESENCIA ALLI DE... NA...
Y A 3 HOMBRES: EL CA.ITAN ...
Y JESUS MORALES. TODOS N...
AUNQUE DE ORIGEN CUBA...

SEGUN DECLARARON EST...
DE OCTUBRE DE 1992, CON...
OTROS TRES TRIPULANTES,...
MIGUEL ALFONSO, HABIAN ...
BUCEAR, EL 20/10/92, ...

LA POLICIA REVISO EL ...

A) 1 AMETRALLADORA M...
B) GRAN CANTIDAD DE ...
C) EXPLOSIVO PLASTICO ...
D) 2 RADIOS DIGITALES ...
E) 11 CARGADORES, CO...
F) 4 CARGADORES PARA ...
G) MECHAS ELECTRICAS ...
H) UN CABLE CRUCERO ...
I) 15 A 20 LBS DE C4 ...
J) 30 LBS DE GELATINA ...
K) 1 GRADANA FEDERAL ...
L) GAS LACRIMOGENO L...
M) DETONADORES NO EL...
N) DETONADORES COMER...
Ñ) DETONADORES MILIT...
O) DETONADORES DE FR...
P) DETONADORES DE TI...
Q) MODULOS DE PROYEC...

S) 1 SUPRESOR - 4 CA...
T) 2 REMINGTON CAL. ...
U) 3 CARGADORES PARA ...

SITUACION DE LOS DET...

MASON EXPLICO QUE HA...
POR LOS SIGUIENTES D...

1.- POSESION ILEGAL ...
    TAS EN CAYO ANGU...

    POSESION ILEGA...
  – POSESION NO AU...
  – POSESION ILEGA...
  – POSESION ILEGA...
  – 34947.

2.- FACILITAR UNA OP...
    ENTRE EL 22 Y 23...
    ARENA DE CAYO AN...
    ACUERDO ENTRE EL...
    CIONES Y XPLOSI...
    PIE A UNA...
    UNA...

BAHAMAS POLICE WENT TO ANGUILLA KEY....

ACCORDING TO THEIR STATEMENT, THE *NAUTILUS* LEFT MIAMI ON FRIDAY, OCTOBER 16, 1992, WITH SIX PEOPLE ABOARD. SIMILARLY THEY SAID THAT THREE OTHER CREWMEMBERS CALLED EDUARDO GONZALEZ, GUSTAVO TORNAS AND MIGUEL ALFONSO HAD LEFT IN AN INFLATABLE BOAT TO FISH OR GO DIVING ON OCTOBER 20, 1992, BUT THEIR CURRENT WHEREABOUTS WERE UNKNOWN.

THE POLICE SEARCHED THE KEY AND DISCOVERED THE FOLLOWING:
A) MAC 10 MACHINE GUN (U.S. MADE WITH SILENCER)
B) LARGE QUANTITY OF 45-CALIBER MUNITIONS
C) C-4 PLASTIC EXPLOSIVE (APPROX. 15 – 20 POUNDS)
D) 2 DIGITAL HAND RADIOS
E) 11 CHARGERS WITH THEIR AKM-47 MISSILES
F) 4 CHARGERS FOR MAC 10 MACHINE GUN
G) ELECTRICAL FUSES AND EXPLOSIVES WIRE
H) A 30-35-INCH CABLE KNORTLES BRAND
I) 15 TO 20 POUNDS OF C-4
J) 30 POUNDS OF EXPLOSIVE GELATINE
K) ONE 555 CS FEDERAL "RIVE" GRENADE
L) LIQUID TEAR GAS (8 CONTAINERS OR 37 MM CAPSULES)
M) NON-ELECTRICAL DETONATORS
N) COMMERCIAL DETONATORS (7 OR 8)
O) MILITARY DETONATORS
P) FRICTION DETONATORS
Q) TIME DETONATORS
R) 11 X 30 MISSILE MODULES
S) 1 SUPPRESSOR – 4 CHARGERS
T) 2 23-CALIBER REMINGTON
U) 3 M-16 CHARGERS

SITUATION OF THE DETAINEES IN BAHAMAS

MASON EXPLAINED THAT THEY HAD BEEN ACCUSED BEFORE THE APPROPRIATE COURTS FOR THE FOLLOWING CRIMES:

2. – FACILITATING A MILITARY OPERATION OF THE FOLLOWING NATURE: BETWEEN 22ND AND 23RD OCTOBER 1992 THE DETAINED INDIVIDUALS ARRIVED AT THE SAND BANKS OF ANGUILLA KEY AND AFTER REACHING AGREEMENT AMONG THEMSELVES, HID THE FIREARMS, MUNITIONS AND EXPLOSIVES WHICH IN THE GIVEN CIRCUMSTANCES, GAVE RISE TO REASONABLE SUSPICION THAT THEY WERE PLANNING TO ATTACK A FOREIGN STATE, IN THIS CASE, CUBA.

AMERICAN EAGLE
50 PISTOL CARTRIDGES
50 CARTOUCHES
AMERICAN EAGLE
PISTOL CARTRIDGES

On September 4, 1994, the terrorists of Cuban origin, residents in Miami, José Benito Menéndez del Valle and Irelio Marcelino Barroso Medina, entered the northern coast of the municipality of Caibarién via Cayo Palo Quemado. They were detained and their weapons confiscated.

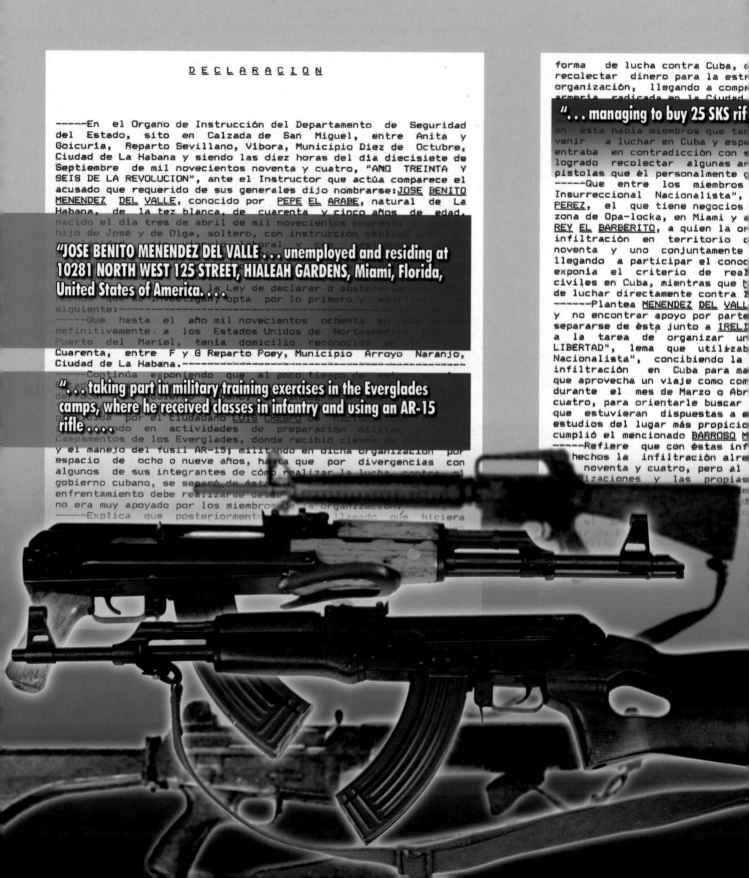

D E C L A R A C I O N

------En el Organo de Instrucción del Departamento de Seguridad del Estado, sito en Calzada de San Miguel, entre Anita y Goicuria, Reparto Sevillano, Vibora, Municipio Diez de Octubre, Ciudad de La Habana y siendo las diez horas del dia diecisiete de Septiembre de mil novecientos noventa y cuatro, "AÑO TREINTA Y SEIS DE LA REVOLUCION", ante el Instructor que actúa comparece el acusado que requerido de sus generales dijo nombrarse: JOSE BENITO MENENDEZ DEL VALLE, conocido por PEPE EL ARABE, natural de La Habana, de la tez blanca, de cuarenta y cinco años de edad, nacido el dia tres de abril de mil novecientos cuarenta, hijo de José y de Olga, soltero, con instrucción séptima grado,

"JOSE BENITO MENENDEZ DEL VALLE . . . unemployed and residing at 10281 NORTH WEST 125 STREET, HIALEAH GARDENS, Miami, Florida, United States of America. . . .

la Ley de declarar o abstenerse que se investigan, opta por lo primero y manifiesta lo siguiente:------
------Que hasta el año mil novecientos ochenta en que definitivamente. a los Estados Unidos de Norteamérica Puerto del Mariel, tenia domicilio reconocido en Cuarenta, entre F y G Reparto Poey, Municipio Arroyo Naranjo, Ciudad de La Habana.------
------Continúa exponiendo que al poco tiempo de

". . . taking part in military training exercises in the Everglades camps, where he received classes in infantry and using an AR-15 rifle. . . .

por el ciudadano LUIS CRESPO
do en actividades de preparación militar
Campamentos de los Everglades, donde recibió clases de infantería
y el manejo del fusil AR-15; militando en dicha organización por
espacio de ocho o nueve años, hasta que por divergencias con
algunos de sus integrantes de cómo realizar la lucha contra el
gobierno cubano, se separó de ésta
enfrentamiento debe realizarse desde
no era muy apoyado por los miembros de la organización
------Explica que posteriormente fue llamado que hiciera

forma de lucha contra Cuba, o
recolectar dinero para la estr
organización, llegando a compr
armería radicada en la Ciudad

". . . managing to buy 25 SKS rif

en ésta habia miembros que tan
venir a luchar en Cuba y espe
entraba en contradicción con su
logrado recolectar algunas ar
pistolas que él personalmente q
------Que entre los miembros
Insurreccional Nacionalista",
PEREZ, el que tiene negocios
zona de Opa-locka, en Miami y a
REY EL BARBERITO, a quien la or
infiltración en territorio d
noventa y uno conjuntamente
llegando a participar el conoc
exponia el criterio de real
civiles en Cuba, mientras que
de luchar directamente contra
------Plantea MENENDEZ DEL VALL
y no encontrar apoyo por parte
separarse de ésta junto a IRELI
a la tarea de organizar un
LIBERTAD", lema que utilizab
Nacionalista", concibiendo la
infiltración en Cuba para ma
que aprovecha un viaje como com
durante el mes de Marzo o Abr
cuatro, para orientarle buscar
que estuvieran dispuestas a e
estudios del lugar más propicio
cumplió el mencionado BARROSO M
------Refiere que con éstas inf
hechos la infiltración alre
noventa y cuatro, pero al
izaciones y las propias

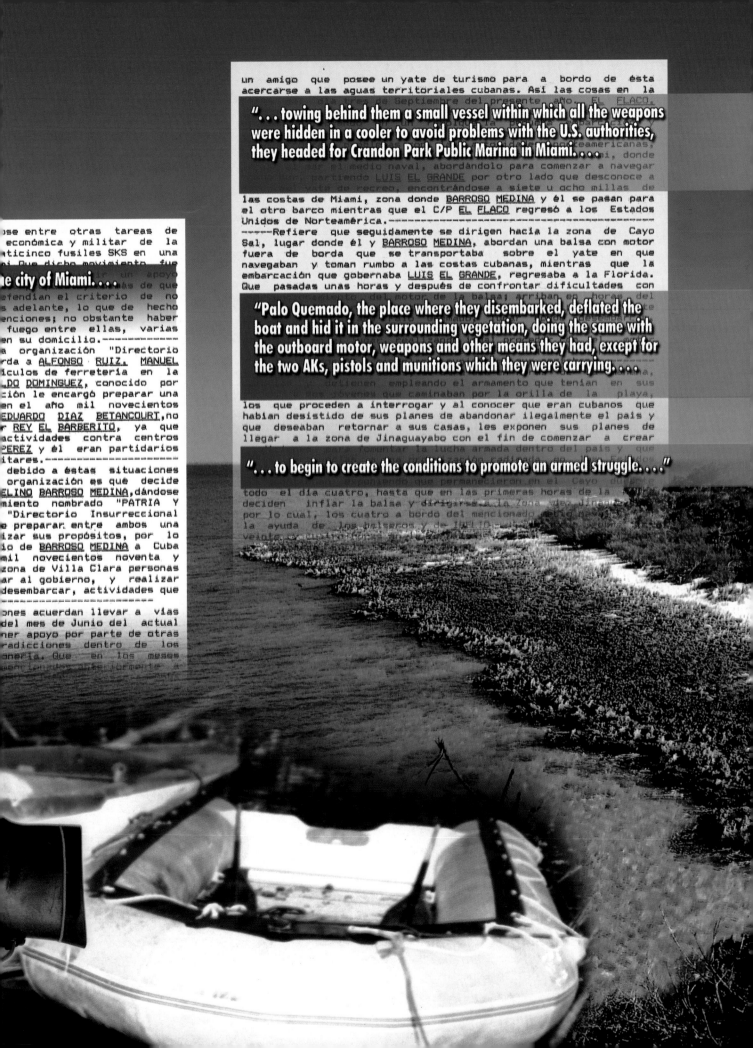

un amigo que posee un yate de turismo para a bordo de ésta
acercarse a las aguas territoriales cubanas. Así las cosas en la

"...towing behind them a small vessel within which all the weapons were hidden in a cooler to avoid problems with the U.S. authorities, they headed for Crandon Park Public Marina in Miami...."

el medio naval, abordándolo para comenzar a navegar
partiendo LUIS EL GRANDE por otro lado que desconoce a
de recreo, encontrándose a siete u ocho millas de
las costas de Miami, zona donde BARROSO MEDINA y él se pasan para
el otro barco mientras que el C/P EL FLACO regresó a los Estados
Unidos de Norteamérica.————————————————————————
————Refiere que seguidamente se dirigen hacia la zona de Cayo
Sal, lugar donde él y BARROSO MEDINA, abordan una balsa con motor
fuera de borda que se transportaba sobre el yate en que
navegaban y toman rumbo a las costas cubanas, mientras que la
embarcación que gobernaba LUIS EL GRANDE, regresaba a la Florida.
Que pasadas unas horas y después de confrontar dificultades con

"Palo Quemado, the place where they disembarked, deflated the boat and hid it in the surrounding vegetation, doing the same with the outboard motor, weapons and other means they had, except for the two AKs, pistols and munitions which they were carrying...."

detienen empleando el armamento que tenían en sus
que caminaban por la orilla de la playa,
los que proceden a interrogar y al conocer que eran cubanos que
habían desistido de sus planes de abandonar ilegalmente el país y
que deseaban retornar a sus casas, les exponen sus planes de
llegar a la zona de Jinaguayabo con el fin de comenzar a crear
fomentar la lucha armada dentro del país y que

"...to begin to create the conditions to promote an armed struggle...."

poniendo que permanecieron en el Cayo durante
todo el día cuatro, hasta que en las primeras horas de la
deciden inflar la balsa y dirigirse a la zona de Jina
por lo cual, los cuatro a bordo del mencionado medio
la ayuda de los balseros y de JULIO
veinte y cuatro

ose entre otras tareas de
económica y militar de la
ticinco fusiles SKS en una
Que dicho movimiento fue
un apoyo
de que
efendían el criterio de no
s adelante, lo que de hecho
enciones; no obstante haber
fuego entre ellas, varias
en su domicilio.————————
a organización "Directorio
rda a ALFONSO RUIZ, MANUEL
ículos de ferretería en la
LDO DOMINGUEZ, conocido por
ción le encargó preparar una
en el año mil novecientos
EDUARDO DIAZ BETANCOURT, no
r REY EL BARBERITO, ya que
actividades contra centros
PEREZ y él eran partidarios
itares.————————————————————
debido a éstas situaciones
organización es que decide
ELINO BARROSO MEDINA, dándose
miento nombrado "PATRIA Y
"Directorio Insurreccional
e preparar entre ambos una
izar sus propósitos, por lo
io de BARROSO MEDINA a Cuba
mil novecientos noventa y
zona de Villa Clara personas
ar al gobierno, y realizar
desembarcar, actividades que

ones acuerdan llevar a vias
del mes de Junio del actual
ner apoyo por parte de otras
radicciones dentro de los
onería. Que en los meses

e city of Miami....

On April 2, 1993, the tanker *Mikonos*, bearing a Maltese flag, with a Cuban-Cypriot crew, was machine-gunned seven miles to the north of the coast of Matanzas while transporting oil to the island. The attack was carried out by Rigoberto Acosta Díaz, José Méndez Mirabal, Guillermo Casasús Toledo and Rafael Carrera Manso, members of the terrorist organization Secret Armed Army.

The Cuban Foreign Ministry **MINREX** dispatched its Note No. 311 to the U.S. Interests Section informing them of the attack against the *Mikonos*. The Note stipulated that the tanker had been fired at from a small powerboat, which, after numerous shots, headed north toward the United States. The attackers used 7.62-caliber guns, which left numerous bullet holes in the tanker, and although the damage was not substantial, the lives of the crew members had been in serious danger. Furthermore, the bullets could have caused a fire on board the vessel.

"According to sources in the Cuban administration and within the United States, Llamera financed a machine-gun attack on a Cypriot flag-bearing tanker, the *Mikonos*. Commandos L opened fire on the ship when it was heading toward the Cuban port of Carúpano. **Charges were never presented by the U.S. authorities in this case or in the case of subsequent attacks.**"

"Terrorists, but Our Terrorists"
by Kirk Nielsen
Miami New Times, December 21, 2001.

On October 15, 1994, the Miami-based terrorists of Cuban origin Armando Sosa Fortuny, Lázaro González Caraballo, Pedro Guisao Peña, José Ramón Falcón González, Jesús Manuel Rojas Pineda, Miguel Díaz Bouza and Humberto Real Suárez were assigned the mission of establishing themselves in the Escambray mountains. From there they would carry out violent attacks against the local population and the economy. As soon as they disembarked they murdered the Cuban citizen Arcilio Rodríguez García, who was fishing in the area.

"He liked sport, particularly swimming and fishing. He loved going fishing in the rivers. He wore a T-shirt with number 19 from his baseball team, Villa Clara. He was an affectionate and loving young man. He adored his sister, as she adored him. He was always looking after her, in the same way that he cared for me and his father.

"On the 14th he called by my home and left me a bottle of rum. He told me that he was going with his father to harvest a small rice plantation that they had and the following day they planned to kill a piglet to eat it with me, and drink some rum together."

Marta García, Arcilio's mother

"At six o'clock in the morning of the 15th, someone knocked on the door; I thought it was him, as that was the plan. When I opened it was Pedro Rodríguez, his uncle, who said, 'Get ready to leave as Tati has had an accident,' and he left immediately. I got dressed and headed off on my bicycle for my son's house. As I was arriving at his house in Caibarién, I saw a huge crowd had gathered round, at the same time as his friend Israel told me, 'They have killed him, Marta, they've killed him.'

"I threw my bicycle down and ran in; I asked Juan Carlos to take me to see him, but he replied that he couldn't as an investigation was being carried out on the scene of the crime. When I came back to reality, that same day, I felt as if I had been emptied from inside out . . . and although time has passed since then I still can't accept what happened.

"Normita, his sister, had given him a present of some very nice clothing. When Arcilio received it he said, 'Sister, this is beautiful, I am going to keep it for a special occasion, for something important.' That's why, when Noel asked me, 'Marta, what are we going to dress him in?' I answered, 'The clothes that his sister gave him as a present for a special occasion.' "

Marta García, Arcilio's mother

"We were a happy family. Arcilio was a wonderful father, husband and son, very much loved by those who knew him."

Xiomara Barnet Fernández, Arcilio's widow

DECLARACION.-

------ En el local que ocupa el Organo de Instrucción del Departamento de Seguridad del Estado, sito en San Miguel entre Anita y Goicuría, - Sevillano, Diez de Octubre y siendo las dieciocho Horas del día veinte y uno de octubre de mil novecientos noventa y cuatro, "AÑO XXXVI DE - LA REVOLUCION", ante el Instructor actuante comparece el acusado que requerido de sus generales dice ser: HUMBERTO ELADIO REAL SUAREZ, natural de Matanzas, Cuba, de la tez blanca, hijo de Humberto Andrés y -- Graciela, con veinte y seis años de edad, nacido el dieciocho de febrero de mil novecientos sesenta y ocho, con noveno grado de escolaridad soltero, que labora como ensamblador en la carpintería "Ihosvany Furniture", sita en Miami, Florida, Estados Unidos y vecino de dos mil cuarenta North West dieciseis Avenida Miami, Florida, Estados Unidos;

CONT. H/II

continúa explicando que para subir a la embarcac ostas de los Estados Unidos, todos los participan os de civil y se cambiaron despues en la traves iformes de camuflajes, debido a que en caso de si eran detectados podian ser detenidos. Esta tre las cero dos o las cero tres horas de la ma de octubre, estando sobre la lancha los siete ltración, incluyendo al acusado que declara. -- ue a poco tiempo de estar navegando, es decir o acusado que declara, quien venía sentado en la de la embarcación con todo su equipo, tomó el la lancha durante aproximad sal, haciendo tambien durante ar la misma, lo que hizo tir misma area estuvieron perdid participantes que alegaron no lo tenian en realidad, rientación incluso tratando aron nunca, llegando en hor ostas de Cuba, comenzando a

"REAL SUAREZ . . . occupant at 2040 North West 17th Avenue, Miami, Florida, United States. . . .

"... and he was immediately taken to a military training camp in the Everglades where he was taught how to shoot a Chinese semi-automatic AK rifle and given physical training. The training lasted three months and he subsequently resumed his daily lifestyle. . . .

"... that they would infiltrate via the Caibarien coast, in Villa Clara, to attempt to reach the Escambray mountains in the same region. . . .

"They were assigned military teams, knapsaks and weapons and they moved toward the boat they were to travel in, they boarded in and took charge of the weapon they were given. . . .

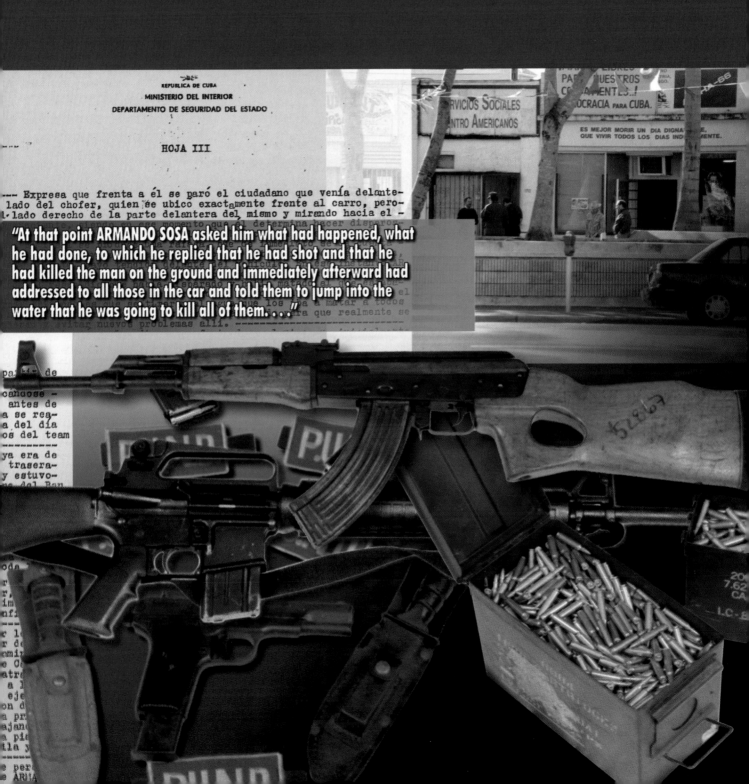

"I only want to say that terrorism must be fought so that there aren't as many mothers and fathers feeling the pain we feel; that there aren't as many children left orphans by terrorism, that homes are not destroyed."

Marta García, Arcilio's mother

REPUBLICA DE CUBA
MINISTERIO DEL INTERIOR
DEPARTAMENTO DE SEGURIDAD DEL ESTADO

HOJA III

---- Expresa que frenta a él se paró el ciudadano que venía delante-
lado del chofer, quien se ubico exactamente frente al carro, pero-
l·lado derecho de la parte delantera del mismo y mirando hacia el -

"At that point ARMANDO SOSA asked him what had happened, what he had done, to which he replied that he had shot and that he had killed the man on the ground and immediately afterward had addressed to all those in the car and told them to jump into the water that he was going to kill all of them...."

Hermanita Linda:

Me disculpas lo informal de este papelito pero sé que esto hace falta, lo más importante es que estén bien y yo sé que aunque tienen una situación difícil ustedes y nosotros no estamos tan mal.

Me disculpas por que el día de las madres no te mandé ni siquiera una postal, pero no tenía para nadie, de todas formas tú estás, entre las 3 mamás más lindas del mundo. Le das un beso grande a Cindy; y que, para la próxima sea más cariñosa con su tío, me saludas a Jorge y para ti, toda la felicidad del mundo un beso grandote de tú hermano que te quiere mucho.

Tati.

FRUSTRADO
FAILED

"I took the rifle from my back and pretended I was going to hand it over to him. ...desvie un poco la punta de la arma. Esa fue la fracción de segundo que aproveché para rastrillar mi M-52, al tiempo que de un...

"The burst of gunfire aimed at me was enough to make me to respond by firing six times. The back windscreen shattered, I injured the driver in the arm and the other in the head. ...zan hacia el costado del camión. Uno intenta escapar pero de un gaznatón lo pone en "nuestra patia", posición que...

"'Do you want my watch? I will give it to you, man.'
'I don't need a watch to live.'
'Listen, we are part of a thousand-strong invasion.'
'Don't be an asshole. A hundred thousand men on their feet wouldn't fit on this causeway. ...' ...quitarles todo lo que traen y desbaratarles los planes.

—Hasta que no veo caras no conozco a nadie, así que dale, bien arrimao a la lomita.

Reconocido Macana, Juan José le alcanza un R-1 de los abandonados dentro del carro. Minutos después llegan en una camioneta Raúl, el chofer y Osmel, otro CVP.

"Es maravilloso cómo en nada se formó una especie de milicia popular. Yo no sé qué piensa esa gente. Aquí...

"'To take my weapon away from me you'd have to kill me and make sure I was dead,' said Juan José."

EPÍLOGO

Pronto la cantera Guajabana se convirtió en un hervidero. Policías, bomberos, guardafronteras y gente de pueblo, llegaron en las primeras horas del día. A los tres infiltrados capturados por Juan José se les ocuparon dos fusiles AKM de fabricación china, una pistola Makarov moderna y otra P-38, un cuchillo comando y otros artículos para este tipo de operación: linternas, mochilas, alimentos enlatados y un envase con veneno líquido.

On March 20, 1995, the terrorists Santos Armando Martínez Rueda and José Enríquez Ramírez Oro, U.S. residents, were detained in the José Martí International Airport. They had entered Cuba with fake passports as Costa Rican tourists. These same individuals had previously entered the country via the coast of the municipality of Puerto Padre in Las Tunas bringing explosive materials with them, part of which was used to construct a bomb that was desactivated on time.

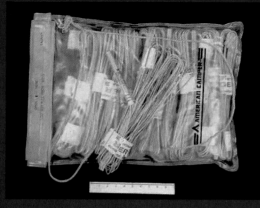

DECLARACION

EN EL LOCAL QUE OCUPA EL ORGANO DE INSTRUCCION DEL DEPARTAMENTO DE SEGURIDAD DEL ESTADO, SITO EN SAN MIGUEL ENTRE ANITA Y GOICURIA, VIBORA, 10 DE OCTUBRE, CIUDAD DE LA HABANA, SIENDO LAS 08.00 HORAS DEL DIA 26 DE NOVIEMBRE DE MIL NOVECIENTOS NOVENTA Y CINCO. "AÑO DEL CENTENARIO DE LA CAIDA DE JOSE MARTI", ANTE EL INSTRUCTOR ACTUANTE COMPARECE EL CIUDADANO QUE REQUERIDO DE SUS

"SANTOS ARMANDO MARTINEZ RUEDA ... MOVED TO THE UNITED STATES, WHERE HE CURRENTLY LIVES AT 2326 SW, 9th ST., MIAMI, FLORIDA....

"NUMEROUS MEETINGS ... IN A THREE-STORY BUILDING CLOSE TO 97TH AVENUE AND 20TH OR 30TH STREET, NORTH WEST, MIAMI, A BUILDING WHICH APPEARS TO BE AN INSURANCE AGENCY ACCORDING TO A SIGN. THEY SAID THEY BELONGED TO AN ASSOCIATION OF CUBAN VETERAN MEMBERS OF THE U.S. ARMY, IDENTIFIED BY THE LETTERS "CAVA" AND CONSIDERED THEMSELVES TO BE THE ARMED WING OF CUBAN EXILES. THEIR MEMBERS HAD DEVISED AMONG THEIR PLANS AGGRESSIVE INCURSIONS AGAINST CUBA WITH COASTAL ATTACKS USING SPEEDBOATS, INTRODUCING COMMANDOS, THE CREATION OF CLANDESTINE CELLS WITHIN THE COUNTRY TO CARRY OUT TERRORIST ACTIVITIES AMONGST OTHER SUBVERSIVE GOALS AIMED AT CHANGING CUBAN REALITY.

"... PRACTICAL AND THEORETICAL CLASSES ... EXPLOSIVES HANDLING AND TRAINING ... PRACTICE WITH DETONATORS AND SMALL C-4 CHARGES IN THE SUGAR CANE PLANTATIONS OF WEST PALM BEACH."

AÑADE QUE LA PREPARACION DE LOS CONOCIDOS POR **ALEXIS** Y **MARINO** INCLUYO EL MANEJO DEL SISTEMA DE POSICIONAMIENTO GLOBAL (GPS) LA FORMA DE OPERAR UNA PLANTA DE RADIO AFICIONADO, EL FUNCIONAMIENTO DE EQUIPOS DE NAVEGACION Y AUNQUE LE ABORDARON ESTA MATERIA, NO LE INSISTIERON EN EL TRABAJO CON LAS CARTAS NAUTICAS AL DEMOSTRARLES TENER ALGUN CONOCIMIENTO DE ELLO. AÑADIO

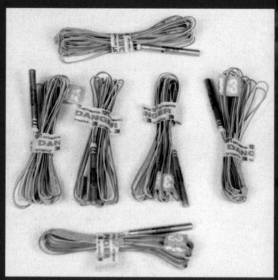

January 1993. Five terrorists on board a vessel armed with heavy machine guns and other weapons were detained by the U.S. coastguard service while heading for the Cuban coast. They were set free.

November 1994. The terrorist Luis Posada Carriles and five of his accomplices smuggled weapons into Cartagena, Colombia, during the 4th Ibero-American Summit, in order to carry out an attack against President Fidel Castro. Posada Carriles would later declare to *The New York Times*: "I was standing behind some journalists and I saw Fidel Castro's friend, García Márquez, but I only managed to see Castro from a distance."

"ALBERTO MONZON . . . 'CHIQUITICO.' . . . 'ARNOLD STORE OWNED BY MONZON,' FOR WHICH REASON IT IS PRESUMED THAT THE LATTER IS REALLY CALLED ARNALDO . . . CUBAN AMERICAN NATIONAL FOUNDATION.

"IT MEANT THAT MONZON HAD A LOT TO DO WITH THE SUPPLY OF FINANCIAL RESOURCES FOR CAVA'S ACTIVITIES, PROVIDING MONEY . . . FOR SUBVERSIVE PLANS. HE SAID GOODBYE TO THEM AT THE MIAMI RIVER WHEN THEY CARRIED OUT THE INCURSION AND SUBSEQUENTLY IN THE AIRPORT AT MIAMI WHEN THEY DEPARTED FOR CANCUN.

"... USING THE IDENTITY OF *WILIAN ORTEGA CALDERON* FOR HIMSELF AND *RAFAEL ANTONIO ORAMUNDO BLANCO* FOR *RAMIREZ ORO* WITH THEIR RESPECTIVE DRIVING LICENCES AND WITH TEMPORARY RESIDENCE IN THE UNITED STATES, AS WELL AS A MOTOROLA BEEPER, WHICH HAD TO BE TESTED IN CUBA AND A CELL PHONE THAT WAS PERSONALLY HANDED TO HIM BY *NOVO SAMPOLL* SO THAT HE COULD PROVIDE ONGOING INFORMATION THIS WAY. . . .

"AROUND FEBRUARY TWENTY SEVEN HE LEFT FROM MIAMI RIVER IN A 'OPERVICHER' SPEED BOAT WITH TWO 200-HORSEPOWER OUTBOARD MOTORS, TWENTY TWO FEET LENGTH AND SIX FEET WIDE, WHILE *JOSÉ ENRIQUE* LEFT WITH LIGHTWEIGHT TERRORIST EQUIPMENT INSIDE A BRIEFCASE IN A YACHT WITH A CREW OF THREE OTHERS WHICH THEY TOWED UNTIL THEY APPROACHED CUBAN JURISDICTIONAL WATERS. DURING THE CROSSING, A THIRD VESSEL TRANSSHIPED IN OPEN SEA A PLASTIC CONTAINER WITH AROUND FIFTY POUNDS OF C-4 EXPLOSIVE.

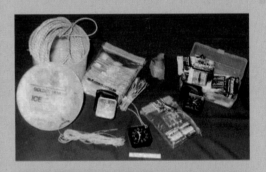

"... ONCE THIS FIRST OPERATION WAS CARRIED OUT SUCCESSFULLY, TWO THOUSAND DOLLARS WERE HANDED TO *JOSÉ ENRIQUE* AND FOUR THOUSAND TO HIM, IN ADDITION TO TWO THOUSAND THAT THEY HAD GIVEN HIM VIA CREDIT CARD, MONEY WHICH WAS TO GUARANTEE THE REST OF THE OPERATION INSIDE CUBA PASSING AS COSTA RICAN TOURISTS.

July 12, 1995. Three terrorist elements were detained in the United States when they attempted to infiltrate Cuba. In spite of carrying weapons and explosives, they were set free by U.S. authorities.

"ON MARCH FIFTH OF THE CURRENT YEAR *RAMIREZ ORO* AND HE DEPARTED FROM MIAMI FOR CANCUN WHERE THEY WERE HELPED BY SOMEONE KNOWN AS *JULIO PEREZ*, A CUBAN WHO HAD BEEN INTRODUCED BY *GULLERMO NOVO SAMPOLL* AS HAVING LINKS WITH AND KNOWLEDGE OF THE 'FOUNDATION.' "

December 16, 1995. Two individuals were detained in the United States in the attempt to infiltrate Cuba to engage in terrorist activities. In spite of carrying weapons and explosives, they were set free by U.S. authorities.

January 23, 1996. U.S. authorities intercepted a vessel at Key Marathon with five armed terrorists on board heading for Cuba. They were set free the same day by the FBI.

November 1996. Channel 23 of Miami television broadcast a live interview with Luis Posada Carriles and Orlando Bosch. They emphasized their intentions to continue with their terrorist activities against Cuba.

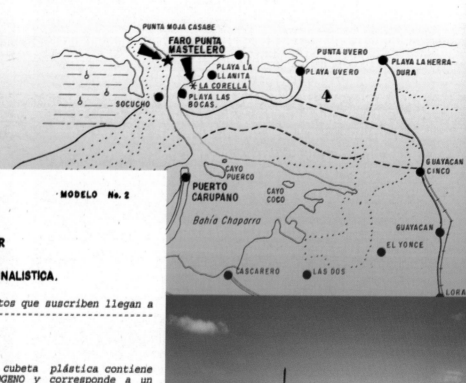

PLACES WHERE EXPLOSIVE MATERIALS AND DEVICES WERE BURIED IN THE AREA OF PUERTO PADRE, TUNAS, BY PERSONS INFILTRATING CUBA ON MARCH 2, 1995 AND MARCH 14, 1995.

MODELO No. 2

REPUBLICA DE CUBA

MINISTERIO DEL INTERIOR

LABORATORIO CENTRAL DE CRIMINALISTICA.

Que por todo lo antes expuesto los peritos que suscriben llegan a las siguientes:--

CONCLUSIONES

PRIMERA- Que el producto ocupado en la cubeta plástica contiene como sustancia explosiva HEXOGENO y corresponde a un explosivo de tipo plástico de composición C-4, clasificado como rompedor de alta potencia y utilizado con fines militares.------------------------------

SEGUNDA- Que el producto explosivo de composición C-4 investigado posee características semejantes al producido en los Estados Unidos (USA), según los análisis practicados y la bibliografía especializada consultada.------------

TERCERA- Que el cordón detonante investigado es producido con fines militares e industriales y contiene como sustancia explosiva PENTRITA.--------------------------

On May 28, 1998, the terrorists Ernestino Abreu Horta and Vicente Marcelino Martínez Rodríguez disembarked on the coast of Pinar del Río from Miami. They were assigned the mission, among other directives, of carrying out subversive activities that would sow panic amongst the population.

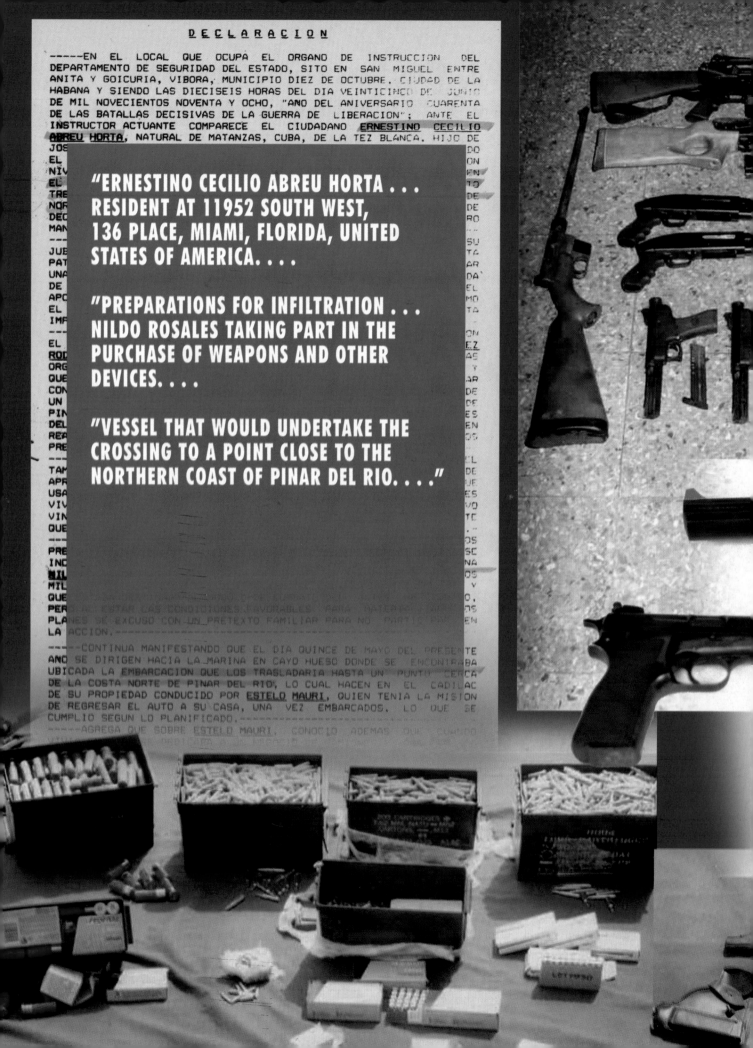

DECLARACION

-----EN EL LOCAL QUE OCUPA EL ORGANO DE INSTRUCCION DEL DEPARTAMENTO DE SEGURIDAD DEL ESTADO, SITO EN SAN MIGUEL ENTRE ANITA Y GOICURIA, VIBORA, MUNICIPIO DIEZ DE OCTUBRE, CIUDAD DE LA HABANA Y SIENDO LAS DIECISEIS HORAS DEL DIA VEINTICINCO DE JUNIO DE MIL NOVECIENTOS NOVENTA Y OCHO, "AÑO DEL ANIVERSARIO CUARENTA DE LAS BATALLAS DECISIVAS DE LA GUERRA DE LIBERACION"; ANTE EL INSTRUCTOR ACTUANTE COMPARECE EL CIUDADANO **ERNESTINO CECILIO ABREU HORTA**, NATURAL DE MATANZAS, CUBA, DE LA TEZ BLANCA, HIJO DE JOS...

"ERNESTINO CECILIO ABREU HORTA . . .
RESIDENT AT 11952 SOUTH WEST,
136 PLACE, MIAMI, FLORIDA, UNITED
STATES OF AMERICA. . . .

"PREPARATIONS FOR INFILTRATION . . .
NILDO ROSALES TAKING PART IN THE
PURCHASE OF WEAPONS AND OTHER
DEVICES. . . .

"VESSEL THAT WOULD UNDERTAKE THE
CROSSING TO A POINT CLOSE TO THE
NORTHERN COAST OF PINAR DEL RIO. . . ."

PER AL ESTAR LAS CONDICIONES FAVORABLES PARA MATERIALIZAR... PLANES SE EXCUSO CON UN PRETEXTO FAMILIAR PARA NO PARTICIPAR EN LA ACCION.

-----CONTINUA MANIFESTANDO QUE EL DIA QUINCE DE MAYO DEL PRESENTE AÑO SE DIRIGEN HACIA LA MARINA EN CAYO HUESO DONDE SE ENCONTRABA UBICADA LA EMBARCACION QUE LOS TRASLADARIA HASTA UN PUNTO CERCA DE LA COSTA NORTE DE PINAR DEL RIO, LO CUAL HACEN EN EL CADILAC DE SU PROPIEDAD CONDUCIDO POR **ESTELO MAURI**, QUIEN TENIA LA MISION DE REGRESAR EL AUTO A SU CASA, UNA VEZ EMBARCADOS, LO QUE SE CUMPLIO SEGUN LO PLANIFICADO.

-----AGREGA QUE SOBRE **ESTELO MAURI**, CONOCIO ADEMAS QUE CUANDO...

October 27, 1997. The U.S. coastguard detained a vessel west of Puerto Rico, which had two high precision weapons on board. One of the crewmembers claimed that they were planning to assassinate President Fidel Castro when he arrived at Isla Margarita in Venezuela, to attend the Ibero-American Summit on November 7, 1997.

The U.S. authorities specified that the powerboat was registered to a Florida company, the president of which is a board member of the Cuban American National Foundation. One of the weapons was registered in the name of the Foundation's president, who was not even charged. The powerboat's four crewmembers were identified as active members of terrorist groups operating out of U.S. territory against Cuba. In spite of confessions made and proof of illegal possession of weapons, false statements and arms trafficking, after an entangled legal trial, a Federal Court absolved them in December 1999.

The Cuban government had done everything in its power to ensure that the U.S. authorities fulfilled their obligation to put an end to these illegal activities being carried out from within its territory. For this purpose it had supplied precise information and documentary proof on facts, plans and the perpetrators. For example, on June 16 and 17, a delegation that included two senior FBI members was passed detailed information in Havana on *forty terrorists*. All of them continue to operate with impunity.

September 4, 1997: detonations of explosive devices in the Tritón, Chateau-Miramar and Copacabana hotels. A young Italian tourist, Fabio Di Celmo, died as a result of the explosion in the Copacabana. The same day another bomb went off in La Bodeguita del Medio restaurant.

REPUBLICA DE CUBA
MINISTERIO DEL INTERIOR

D E C L A R A C I O N

EN EL LOCAL QUE OCUPA EL ORGANO DE INSTRUCCION DEL DEPARTAMENTO DE SEGURIDAD DEL ESTADO, SITO EN SAN MIGUEL ENTRE ANITA Y GOICURIA, SEVILLANO, DIEZ DE OCTUBRE Y SIENDO LAS DIEZ HORAS DEL SEIS DE FEBRERO DE MIL NOVECIENTOS NOVENTA Y OCHO, "AÑO DEL ANIVERSARIO CUARENTA DE LAS BATALLAS DECISIVAS DE LA GUERRA DE LIBERACION", ANTE EL INSTRUCTOR ACTUANTE COMPARECE **RAUL ERNESTO CRUZ LEON**, NATURAL DE SAN SALVADOR, REPUBLICA DE EL SALVADOR,

"RAUL ERNESTO CRUZ LEON, CITIZEN OF SAN SALVADOR, REPUBLIC OF SAN SALVADOR, WITH PASSPORT NUMBER 350888. . . .

"TO A SUBJECT NAMED FRANCISCO ANTONIO CHAVEZ ABARCA, NICKNAMED EL PANZON, BECAUSE HE WAS OVERWEIGHT, ASSIDUOUS VISITOR OF. . . .

"FOR THE SAKE OF OBTAINING MONEY, AT APPROXIMATELY THE END OF LAST YEAR HE WAS OFFERED THE OPPORTUNITY TO CARRY OUT ATTACKS USING EXPLOSIVES. . . .

"THE ACCUSED ACKNOWLEDGES THAT FROM THE OUTSET HE ACCEPTED IMMEDIATE RECRUITMENT, WITHOUT HAVING BEEN TOLD THE DETAILS OF THE OPERATION HE WAS TO CARRY OUT. FOR THE PURPOSES OF THIS OPERATION HE WAS SHOWN A PACKAGE IN DECEMBER 1996, APPARENTLY A FACTORY PACKAGE, SAYING THAT IT CONTAINED C-4 PLASTIC EXPLOSIVE AND BOTH HEADED FOR A BEACH ON THE OUTSKIRTS OF SAN SALVADOR WHERE CHAVEZ ABARCA, USING THIS EXPLOSIVE, A CALCULATOR, A BATTERY, A CIRCUIT, A DETONATING CAPSULE AND A VOLTIMETER OR TESTER TO TEST THE DEVICE BEFOREHAND, PREPARED THE BOMB AND BLEW IT UP BESIDE SOME STONES. . . ."

CANF
CAN
ENCA
ENCA

On September 4, 1997, the mercenary Raúl Ernesto Cruz León, a Salvadorean citizen and resident of El Salvador, was detained as the person responsible for causing explosions in the Capri, Nacional, Tritón, Chateau-Miramar and Copacabana hotels, as well as in the Bodeguita del Medio restaurant. On June 12, 1997, he had been recruited and trained by Francisco Chávez Abarca, a Salvadorean and resident in El Salvador, under the guidance and with the financial support of Luis Clemente Posada Carriles.

"HE ALSO STATED THAT IN THE MONTH OF MAY, ALTHOUGH HE COULDN'T REMEMBER THE EXACT DATE, *CHAVEZ ABARCA* CONTACTED HIM AGAIN AND PUT IT TO HIM THAT HE CARRY OUT A MISSION INVOLVING PLACING TWO EXPLOSIVE DEVICES IN ANOTHER COUNTRY, WITHOUT STATING WHERE, AND THEN, WITH THE APPROVAL OF THE ACCUSED, IN THE MONTH OF JUNE LAST CHAVEZ TOLD HIM THAT THE COUNTRY WAS CUBA, WHICH SURPRISED THE ACCUSED BECAUSE HE . . . .

"FOR THE SAKE OF BOOSTING HIS MORALE *CHAVEZ ABARCA* TOLD HIM THAT HE HAD BLOWN UP A BOMB IN A HOTEL IN CUBA AND HE HADN'T HAD ANY PROBLEMS. HE REITERATED THE PROPOSAL THAT FOR COMING TO CUBA AND CARRYING OUT TWO ATTACKS OF THIS KIND HE WOULD RECEIVE THIRTY THOUSAND COLONES, WHICH IS A LITTLE OVER THREE THOUSAND DOLLARS OUT OF . . . .
THEY HAD TO WAIT FOR INSTRUCTIONS ON HIS FINAL DEPARTURE, WHICH MADE HIM REALIZE THAT THERE WERE OTHER PEOPLE GIVING ORDERS TO *CHAVEZ ABARCA* . . . THAT ON AROUND JULY 4TH LAST *CHAVEZ ABARCA* REQUESTED HIS PASSPORT TO INITIATE PROCEDURES FOR ACQUIRING A VISA AND TICKET TO CUBA, HELPING THE ACCUSED IN THE AGENCY . . . .

"HE ADDED THAT ON THE NIGHT OF JULY 8TH *CHAVEZ ABARCA* ARRIVED AT HIS HOME WITH THE MATERIALS FOR THE . . . .

"IN RELATION TO HIS TRIP TO THE COUNTRY *CHAVEZ ABARCA* INDICATED THAT HE WOULD ARRIVE VIA COSTA RICA AND RETURN VIA GUATEMALA, ARRIVING IN CUBA IN LATE EVENING. . . .
AND FINALLY HE HANDED HIM FIVE HUNDRED DOLLARS . . . ."

"HE EXPLAINED THAT ON THAT SAME NIGHT HE SET ABOUT PREPARING THE BOMBS IN HIS ROOM, STARTING TO CONNECT THE CIRCUITS OF THE CALCULATORS ON THE BEDSIDE TABLE, HE TESTED THE . . . ."

The New York Times

"Mas financed activities against the Cuban government," says Posada Carriles.

Published in *El Nuevo Herald*, Sunday, July 12, 1998.

"In an interview given to The *New York Times* on the condition that no photographs be taken and his whereabouts were not revealed, the Cuban exiled Luis Posada Carriles made it clear that the deceased leader of the Cuban American National Foundation, Jorge Mas Canosa, 'controlled everything' in reference to money sent to finance his activities against Fidel Castro's government."

Ann Louise Bardach and Larry Rother
The New York Times, July 12, 1998.

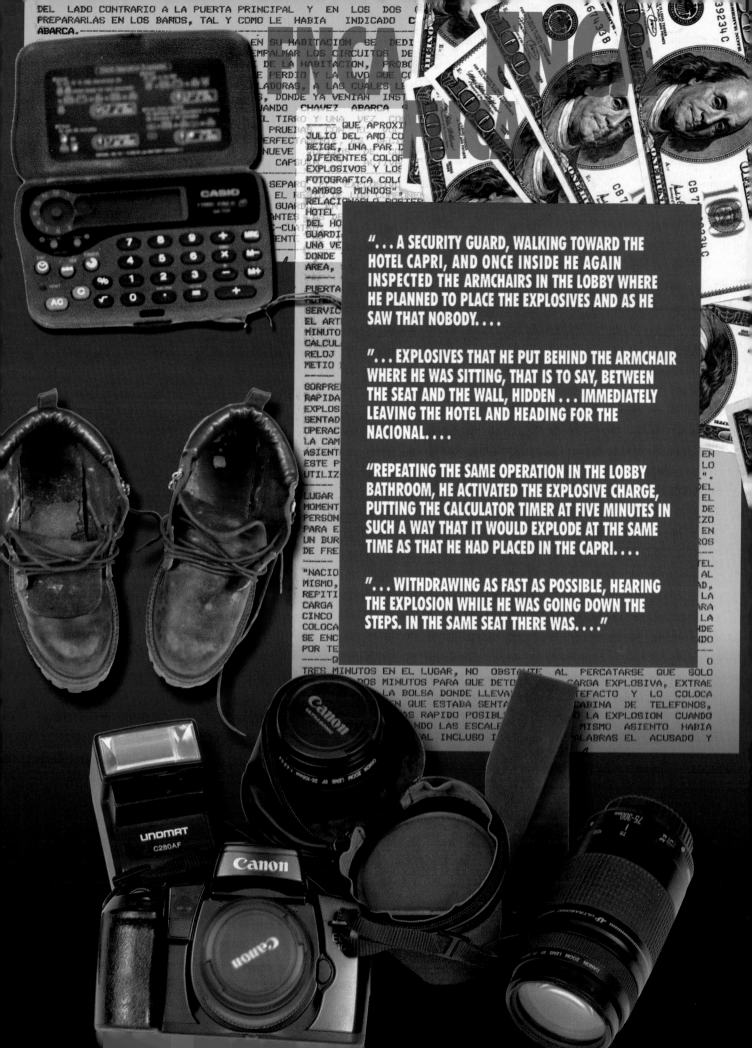

"... A SECURITY GUARD, WALKING TOWARD THE HOTEL CAPRI, AND ONCE INSIDE HE AGAIN INSPECTED THE ARMCHAIRS IN THE LOBBY WHERE HE PLANNED TO PLACE THE EXPLOSIVES AND AS HE SAW THAT NOBODY. . . .

"... EXPLOSIVES THAT HE PUT BEHIND THE ARMCHAIR WHERE HE WAS SITTING, THAT IS TO SAY, BETWEEN THE SEAT AND THE WALL, HIDDEN . . . IMMEDIATELY LEAVING THE HOTEL AND HEADING FOR THE NACIONAL. . . .

"REPEATING THE SAME OPERATION IN THE LOBBY BATHROOM, HE ACTIVATED THE EXPLOSIVE CHARGE, PUTTING THE CALCULATOR TIMER AT FIVE MINUTES IN SUCH A WAY THAT IT WOULD EXPLODE AT THE SAME TIME AS THAT HE HAD PLACED IN THE CAPRI. . . .

"... WITHDRAWING AS FAST AS POSSIBLE, HEARING THE EXPLOSION WHILE HE WAS GOING DOWN THE STEPS. IN THE SAME SEAT THERE WAS. . . ."

"'Jorge controlled everything,' said Posada. 'Whenever I needed money, he used to say that he would send me $5,000, $10,000, $15,000, and he would send it.'

"Posada calculates that over the year Mas sent him more than $200,000. 'He never said that this was the Foundation's money,' he commented laughing. 'The money would arrive with a message: This is for the Church.'

"*The New York Times* cited Posada saying that Mas Canosa had given him money for several of his terrorist activities, and according to the newspaper version he linked it with the wave of bomb attacks that took place in Cuba last summer."

By Rui Ferreira, *El Nuevo Herald*

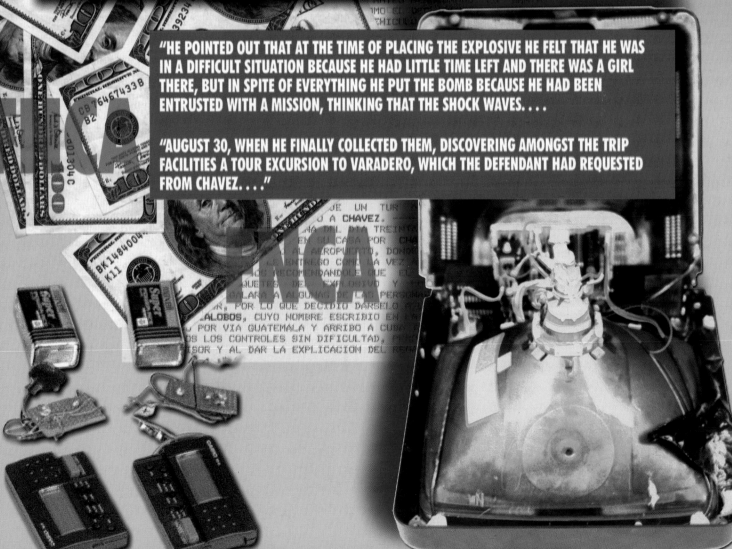

"HE POINTED OUT THAT AT THE TIME OF PLACING THE EXPLOSIVE HE FELT THAT HE WAS IN A DIFFICULT SITUATION BECAUSE HE HAD LITTLE TIME LEFT AND THERE WAS A GIRL THERE, BUT IN SPITE OF EVERYTHING HE PUT THE BOMB BECAUSE HE HAD BEEN ENTRUSTED WITH A MISSION, THINKING THAT THE SHOCK WAVES. . . .

"AUGUST 30, WHEN HE FINALLY COLLECTED THEM, DISCOVERING AMONGST THE TRIP FACILITIES A TOUR EXCURSION TO VARADERO, WHICH THE DEFENDANT HAD REQUESTED FROM CHAVEZ. . . ."

> "While the police in Cuba were arresting Raúl Ernesto Cruz León, one of the Salvadoreans, last September, Posada and two other conspirators in Guatemala were trying to introduce more explosives into Havana, according to two people with deep knowledge of the affair."

> "THE MEANS OF TERRORIST ACTIVITY. HE OPENED UP THE BACK PART OF THE TELEVISION WITH A TOOL THAT HAD BEEN GIVEN TO HIM FOR THIS PURPOSE, TOOK OUT THE TWO PACKAGES OF EXPLOSIVES, WHICH SPLIT AT SEVERAL POINTS ON BEING EXTRACTED, AND THE ELECTRICAL CIRCUITS PACKAGE, ALL WRAPPED IN BLACK PLASTIC AND INSULATING TAPE OF THE SAME COLOR. HE SEARCHED THE ROOM FOR A PLACE TO HIDE THE EXPLOSIVE DUE TO. . . .

> "LIKEWISE, HE STATES THAT HE HEADED TOWARD THE HOTEL CHATEAU-MIRAMAR, TAKING MORE OR LESS FIVE MINUTES TO GET THERE FROM THE COPACABANA AND HE ENTERED AROUND ELEVEN AND FORTY. . . .

> "DIRECT TO THE BATHROOM TO PREPARE THE EXPLOSIVES, ALTHOUGH THE DEVICE IN THE COPACABANA HAD NOT YET BLOWN UP. . . .

> "THAT HE SAT DOWN IN THE LOBBY WHERE HE WAS TO PUT THE BOMB, TO HIS RIGHT THERE WAS A DESK WITH SOME PEOPLE AROUND IT AND TO THE OTHER SIDE WERE PEOPLE WHO WATCHED HIM SIT DOWN. . . .

> "HE RELATED HOW HE WALKED OUT AND HEADED FOR THE TRITON CALCULATING THAT IT SHOULD TAKE BETWEEN TEN AND FIFTEEN MINUTES TO COVER THE ROUTE. . . .

> "INSIDE THE BATHROOM HE ACTED THE SAME WAY AS THE PREVIOUS CASES, BUT IN THIS TIME HE GAVE ONLY NINE MINUTES TO BLOW UP. . . ."

CORDE A
EN S
UALMENT
AL HOTE

URISTIC
BIENDO
OCULTA
ERA DE
EFECTO
VARIOS
, TODO
R. BUSC
O A L
NDOSE
BALCON
EL AIR
NO SE

EN LOS
A COMOD
SITIO
PERSONA
UE NO L
E TENI
DE SU
"MELI
R ERROR
RISTICA
E. Y L
EMA DE
Y DEJ
DEMAS E
CLOSET
HILA D
A Y H

CONTINUA EXPONIENDO QUE EL DIA SIGUIENTE DESPUES D
DESAYUNAR PROBO EL FUNCIONAMIENTO DE LAS CALCULADORAS CON E
LOS COMPARTIMENTOS DE LA
EN UN CENICERO, LE COLOCAB
, RESETEANDOLAS CON LA PUNT
LA CALCULADORA AL INICIO D
COMENZARLAS, HACIENDO UN
ESULTADOS POSITIVOS, FASAND
ELECTRICO, IDENTIFICAD
"ARAÑITAS".
BLAJE DEL ARTEFACTO UTILIZ
ETA DE TELEFONOS, DEBIDO
E BASABA EN LOS COLORES D
ESTOS ULTIMOS UN POCO MA
DE FORRO DE CABLE, LO QU
O, QUE INCLUSO DESCARGAB
TUAR, REALIZABA LA PRUEB
NUEVE VOLTIOS, DANDO U

"... THEY SAT DOWN ON THE SOFA TO HIS LEFT AND THEN A CHILD OF BETWEEN TWELVE AND FIFTEEN YEARS OLD SAT DOWN OPPOSITE THE DEFENDANT, WHILE TWO OTHER SLIGHTLY OLDER GIRLS DID THE SAME ON ANOTHER SOFA TO HIS RIGHT. . . .

"HE ADMITS THAT IN SPITE OF EVERYTHING HE TOOK THE DECISION TO PLACE IT RIGHT THERE AND THEN AFTER CARRYING OUT SOME MANEUVERS WITH. . . .

"HE TOOK A PRIVATE TAXI FROM THE DOOR OF THIS TOURIST VENUE AND ASKED THE DRIVER TO TAKE HIM TO THE RIVIERA HOTEL WITH THE AIM OF CONFUSING HIM TOO . . . . THAT WHEN THEY REACHED THE WIDE AVENUE CLOSE TO THE TRITON HOTEL THE EXPLOSION WAS HEARD. . . .

"A PRIVATE CAR LEFT HIM IN EL FLORIDITA RESTAURANT, FROM WHERE HE HEADED TO LA BODEGUITA DEL MEDIO BECAUSE HE HAD PLANNED TO PLACE THE REMAINING EXPLOSIVE DEVICE THERE. . . ."

Cruz León declared to the Special Rapporteur for the United Nations Commission for Human Rights that he had acted for money and that he had felt like a movie hero fulfilling a mission. Chávez Abarca's instruction had been simply to cause as much chaos as possible. Recently imprisoned, the accused had grasped the full significance of what he had done and asked for forgiveness from the victims and their families, and from the Cuban people. He believed that he did not deserve to be executed for his activities.

"The responsibility of agents operating outside of Cuba is clear. In the course of a statement to *The New York Times* and during an interview with CBS, while the Salvadorean Cruz León was being tried, Luis Posada Carriles admitted that through his agent he had paid money to Cruz León to carry out the attacks and that plans for further attacks that would cause serious problems in Cuba were under way."

From the Special Rapporteur's report on Mercenaries for the UN Human Rights Commission

No state can legitimately consent to or authorize the use of its territory to form or hide organizations that have as their goal to plan or carry out activities leading to hostility against another country or its government. The Special Rapporteur must state that it represents in itself an injustice that while the culprits involved in the attacks have been severely punished, those who recruited, trained and contracted them, who provided the material and explosives, the fake documents and who paid them, are at large and enjoying impunity in those countries where they are currently located. They are perhaps even more guilty that those who actually carried out the attacks, of ongoing criminal behavior. The organizations on whose behalf the detainees acted are guilty.

From the Special Rapporteur's report on Mercenaries for the UN Human Rights Commission during his visit to Cuba from September 12 to 17, 1999.

On Monday, November 22, 1999, fourteen illegal emigrants capsized in a fragile vessel just a few miles off the coast of Florida, and a five-year old Cuban boy was discovered clinging to the inner tube of a car tire, not far from Miami.

For six months, against the will of his father, relatives who were manipulated by the Cuban American National Foundation kidnapped him.

Following a legal process that reached the U.S. Supreme Court and with the support of eighty per cent of the population, according to polls, the child was able to return to Cuba.

During the months in which his father fought for the return of his son, the name of the child appeared day in and day out on the pages of the world press and on international TV news reports. His name is Elián González.

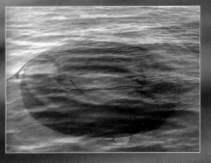

The Cuban Adjustment Act

It is the cause that such a delicate problem was created with a child kept back in that country that was given for his care to a person who did not have the minimum ethical requirements for that task.

Law to adjust the status of Cuban refugees to that of lawful permanent residents in the United States and for other purposes.

"... Without prejudice to that stipulated in section 245 of the Immigration and Naturalization Act ... the status of any foreign native or Cuban citizen ... inspected and accepted ... after January 1, 1959 ... may be adjusted ... in accordance with the regulations prescribing that a foreigner legally admitted to reside permanently ... will be applied to their spouse and children...

... admitted legally ... to reside permanently....

Clinging to a stretcher, as he had done to the inner tube of a car tire, his dehydrated gaze cancelled the interest of the world in any other event.

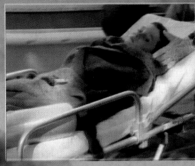
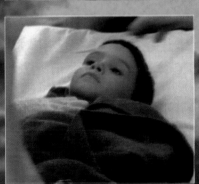
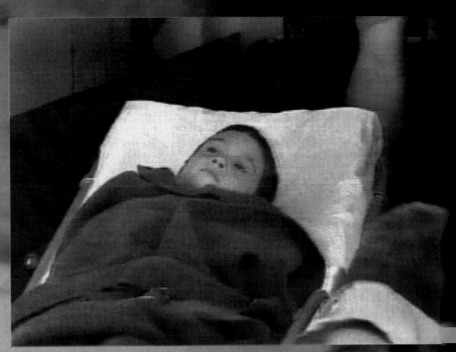

Cárdenas, November 28, 1999
40th Anniversary of the Revolution

Comrade Felipe Pérez Roque
Minister of Foreign Affairs

Dear Felipe:

I, Eleodora Raquel Rodríguez Rodríguez, mother of Elizabeth Brotons Rodríguez, write to ask you to do all that is humanly possible to ensure that my little grandchild Eliancito González Brotón return to our family . . . my husband and the paternal grandparents, who are also suffering . . . he has had with us attention, love and everything he has needed. . . .

Eleodora Raquel Rodríguez Rodríguez

Immigration authorities handed the boy over to distant relatives who have been living in the United States for fifteen years, nine years prior to the birth of Elián. The authorities did not demand any documentary proof of the distant family relationship. Subsequently, a Miami judge, Rosa Rodríguez, awarded the great uncle, who had seen the child only once before in his life, the custody of the boy.

Violated articles of the Convention on the Rights of the Child:

- Right to retain nationality.
- Right not to be separated from the parents.
- Right to remain in the child's cultural context.

UNICEF

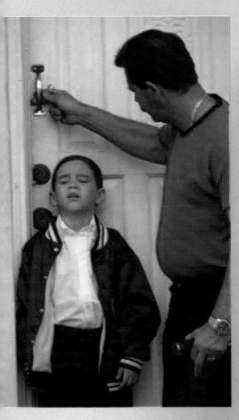

The note continued by saying that Juan Miguel González, born in Cárdenas, and father of the five-year-old child, Elián González, had contacted the Foreign Ministry, requesting that procedures be initiated for reclaiming his son. Elián had miraculous survived the disaster at open sea after being illegally taken out of the country, without prior consultation, by his stepfather and Juan Miguel's former wife, who had the custody of the boy, both of whom died at sea.

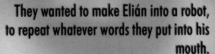

They wanted to make Elián into a robot, to repeat whatever words they put into his mouth.

The Cuban-American extremists were intent on putting Juan Miguel under strong pressure. They offered him two million dollars if he traveled to Miami and remained in the United States with the child.

Elián's relatives closed him off in a house in Little Havana. Terrorists belonging to the Cuban American National Foundation, led by Jorge Mas Santos, Ninoska Pérez, Congress members Ileana Ross Lehtinen, Lincoln Díaz Balart, José Basulto, and the Miami mayors Alex Penelas and Joe Carollo, and other individuals from the Cuban-American Mafia world and the U.S. far right wing were the main figures behind the abduction.

A simple case of acknowledging the parental authority of a loving father would have been resolved in any other part of the world, except for the United States, in relation to Cuba. A routine procedure became a nightmare for Elián, and a political, commercial and publicity show for his captors in Miami.

The kidnappers bedazzled him with expensive toys, clothes and jewelry; he was given a new bicycle and a huge Mickey Mouse cartoon figure but the child showed an astonishing ability to resist and became increasingly aggressive.

One evening, while he was playing in the kidnapper's garden, he heard the sound of an aircraft flying over the place. He lifted his arms to the sky and cried out, "I WANT YOU TO TAKE ME BACK TO CUBA."

To attempt to uproot a child, to try to buy him off with toys, to make him forget his mother tongue, the love of his father, his little brother, cousins and grandparents, to wrench his identity away from him and to paw his innocence is an outrageous crime, committed right in front of the television cameras. The U.S. people reacted immediately: The child must be returned to his father and the rest of his family.

"There is no question that Mr. González is in fact Elián's father. Furthermore, Mr. González has maintained a close paternal and ongoing relationship with his son. During interviews with the INS, Elián's father provided clear details about his paternal relationship with his son and about the nature of their father-son tie. He gave abundant information about Elián's education, about his health record, and showed photos of him, and other family members, together with Elián frequently taking part in different activities. This atmosphere and the level of details provided by Mr. González helped the INS to understand the nature and the closeness of the relationship between Mr. González and his son Elián."

This was the INS conclusion after several of its officials traveled to Cuba and interviewed Elián's father, Juan Miguel González.

Elián's grandmothers met in Washington with Janet Reno and Doris Meissner, district attorney and Immigration and Naturalization Service Commissioner respectively, on Saturday, January 22, 2000. They informed both officials that they wanted to see the boy for a few hours at least, while they were waiting for U.S. government to take the logical decision.

. . . He hardly spoke, he wasn't expressive and he had never been like that. He was always very affectionate; he used to kiss me, hug me and tease me all day long. . . .

. . . They have changed him completely; he has to be saved, saved right away and taken back to his father and his family. . .

. . . I feel really terrible because the reason for the visit was to see the boy and take him back with us. . . .

Our grandchild is entirely different. He has changed utterly; we have got to save him as quickly as possible.

. . . The farewell was very sad. When we went to say goodbye to him, they came and told us that the visit was over. Put yourselves in our place, imagine you go to see a family member who was being kept prisoner and you are told: the visit is over, you have to go; they took the child and led him away. . . .

But eyes are sightless. You have to seek with your heart.
Antoine de Saint-Exupéry.

Elián Is Undergoing Psychological Treatment

The harassment, the manipulations, the pressure and invasion of privacy and innocence must cease.

My son is being harmed in such a way that, unfortunately, could have life-long consequences. Every day that passes, the damage grows. Those who can prevent it are under the moral obligation to act with extreme urgency.

The boy's distorted face, bloodcurdling grimaces and a vacant look in the direction of a home video camera, were the diabolical prelude to images of the boy who was to say, "Dad, I don't want to go to Cuba, if you want, stay here. I am not going to Cuba. Dad, you saw, that old woman who went to the nun's house wants to take me to Cuba. I tell her, and I am telling you, that you are all saying I want to go to Cuba, but I am saying now that I don't want to go to Cuba. If you want to tire yourselves out that's up to you, but I don't want to go to Cuba."

"On Friday, when Juan Miguel González went to the school to collect his son Elián to spend the weekend together, he was told that Elizabeth Brotons, his former wife and the mother of the boy, had taken him away at mid-day and not returned him in the afternoon. This seemed normal to Juan Miguel in his divorced lifestyle. Since he and Elizabeth had separated on the best of terms, two years previously, the child had lived with his father and spent his days between his father and mother's homes. However, given that Elizabeth's door was padlocked, not just the whole weekend, but on Monday too, Juan Miguel began to

investigate the matter. That was how he got the bad news that had begun to become public knowledge in the town of Cárdenas: Elian's mother had taken him to Miami, together with 12 other people, in an aluminum vessel of 5.5 m length with a decrepit engine that had been repeatedly repaired, and without life preservers.

"It was November 22, 1999. 'That day my life was over,' said Juan Miguel four months later. Since their divorce he had maintained a stable and cordial relationship with Elizabeth, that was, however, somewhat unusual, as they continued to live under the same roof and share dreams in the same bed, in the hope that, as lovers, they would have the child that they had never been able to have while married. It seemed impossible; Elizabeth conceived but miscarried continuously in the first four months of the pregnancy. After seven miscarriages, and with the help of medical specialists, the much longed-for child was born, for whom a unique name had

"It should be pointed out to those who are mistaken about the name of the boy: it does not come from the Bible nor was it a discovery by Rubén Darío. Far from thinking about the lives of the saints, the couple did what so many others do in Cuba: they linked the first three letters of the mother's name and the last two of the father's name.

"Elizabeth was 28 years old when she took the boy to Miami. She had been a good student for hotel waitress and was always friendly and helpful as a first-class waitress in the hotel Paradiso-Punta Arenas in Varadero. In love with Juan Miguel since she was 14 years old, she married him when she was eighteen. 'We were like brother and sister,' said Juan Miguel, a calm and good-natured man who also worked in Varadero as a cashier in Josone Park. Following the divorce, and with the child . . . they continued living in Cárdenas, with the brother-sister relationship he mentioned still intact . . . until she fell in love with a man who cost her her life, Lázaro Rafael Munero, an unemployed flashy type, a womanizer who learned judo not as part

of a physical education program, but rather to fight. He had been sentenced to two years imprisonment for robbery with violence at the Hotel Siboney in Varadero. In the meantime, Juan Miguel married Nelsy Carmenate, with whom he currently has a six-month old son, who was the center of Elián's life until Elizabeth took him to Miami.

". . . the one who was behind it and led the whole operation was Lázaro Munero, who had taken part in two clandestine trips to the United States to make the preparations. In this way he had the right contacts and a lot of pluck to take not just Elizabeth with her son but also a younger brother, his own father, who was over seventy, and his mother, still recovering from a heart attack. His partner in the operation took his entire family: his wife, his parents and his brother, and a neighbor that lived opposite, whose husband was waiting for her in the United States. At the last minute, via a payment of a thousand dollars per person, a young woman of twenty-two, Arianne Horta, her five-year old daughter, Esthefany, and Nivaldo Vladimir Fernández, a friend's husband, boarded the vessel.

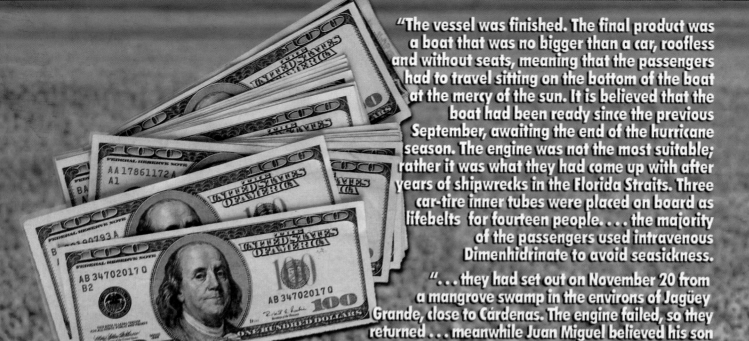

"The vessel was finished. The final product was a boat that was no bigger than a car, roofless and without seats, meaning that the passengers had to travel sitting on the bottom of the boat at the mercy of the sun. It is believed that the boat had been ready since the previous September, awaiting the end of the hurricane season. The engine was not the most suitable; rather it was what they had come up with after years of shipwrecks in the Florida Straits. Three car-tire inner tubes were placed on board as lifebelts for fourteen people.... the majority of the passengers used intravenous Dimenhidrinate to avoid seasickness.

"... they had set out on November 20 from a mangrove swamp in the environs of Jagüey Grande, close to Cárdenas. The engine failed, so they returned ... meanwhile Juan Miguel believed his son was already in Miami....

"While they were repairing the engine, Arianne Horta decided to leave her daughter with the family; she did not know that this would save her life. It is said that Elián also became aware then of the dangers of the crossing and he cried out loud to be left behind. Munero, fearing that the boy's cries would be heard, threatened his wife, 'Either you shut him up, or I will.'

"Finally, they set out at dawn on the 22nd, with a calm sea but a troublesome engine. This was the end for them, in a black night and a nightmare of panic. The older people that did not know how to swim should have drowned immediately. A factor that sealed the fate of the majority was the Dimenhidrinate, which in effect prevents seasickness, but causes drowsiness and slows down reflexes.

"Arianne and Nivaldo clung to one of the inner tubes; Elián, and perhaps his mother too, held on to another. No one knew what happened to the third inner tube. Elián knew how to swim, but Elizabeth didn't, and probably let go in the midst of confusion and terror. 'I saw Mom when she got lost at sea,' the child would later say to his father by phone.

"November 25. Juan Miguel received a call from a doctor in Miami to find out what illnesses Elián had suffered from, which medicines he could not take, and whether he had ever been operated

on. . . . The castaway child had given the name of his father, and his address and phone number while in hospital. . . . The following day, the child and his father talked by phone, during which time Elián spoke of how he had seen his mother die. He was concerned about his knapsack and school uniform . . . days later, when he spoke to his teacher by phone he asked her, "Take care of my desk."

"The mobilization of the Cuban people and the outpouring of ideas within the country demanding the return of the abducted child were spontaneous and spectacular. There was a novel aspect to this new development: massive participation on the part of young people and children. The Catholic poet Cintio Vitier, astonished by the clumsiness of the United States, wrote in a poem for Elián, "What fools! They have united us forever."

Fragments from the article "Castaway in Terra Firma" by Nobel Prizewinner for Literature Gabriel García Márquez.

The kidnappers played for time so that their allies in the Chamber of Representatives and the Senate could present a draft bill awarding U.S. citizenship to the child.

On March 21, 2000, U.S. Attorney General Janet Reno indicated that it is time that this little child who has suffered so much be returned to live with his father.

The Attorney General and the Director of the Immigration and Naturalization Service remained steadfast . . . the position of the president of the United States with respect toward those who have the true and inalienable right to parental authority over this tormented child has not changed.

On April 22, Janet Reno ordered that use of force be employed to carry out the rescue and on the morning of that day the much longed-for reunion between the child and his father took place in Washington.

... At that moment his mind registered and recorded an affectionate voice, certainly unknown to him until then, a voice that when, in his adolescence, he puts together the jigsaw puzzle of those days, he will recall as that of a policewoman. Maybe he will even get to know her when time has passed, a woman who in those minutes of expectation, violence and fear, when he was freed from his captors, in the key moment of the rescue, carried Elián out and, hugging him tightly to her, said with tenderness "It's okay, we are going to see your father. Don't cry, don't cry, we're going to see your father .... You're going to see your father, your father, your father. I am taking you to see your father. Now you are going to see your father, your father."

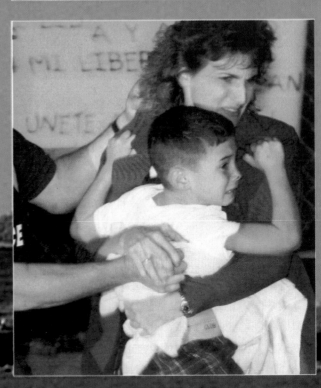

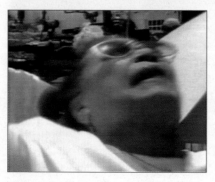

But the time to return to Cuba had not arrived. Extremists stamped their feet on the U.S. flag in Miami and provoked rioting.

On June 28, the Supreme Court decided that Elián should return to Cuba. Over seven months had gone by since the child had arrived in the United States. The nightmare was over.

U.S. television showed the world an image that puzzled viewers. Looking up to the sky, this Cuban-American woman, resident in Miami, shouted out, while the aircraft that was taking the child home flew over the city, "FATHER ABOVE, CRASH THAT PLANE, CRASH THAT PLANE!"

"Cuba has never offended a U.S. national symbol."

The most publicized terrorist kidnapping of a child in the world had come to an end.

"Other consequences of the

Between 1959 and 2001 a total of 51 Cuban planes were hijacked, and the majority were forced to fly to the United States. Many of the planes still remain there in the United States, shamelessly stolen by the Miami Mafia. More than a few pilots, guards and other people have been murdered or injured in the course of these hijackings. The U.S. government has never punished any of the hijackers involved.

On the other hand, between 1968 and 1984, a total of 71 planes were hijacked in the United States and forced to fly to Cuba. A total of 69 participants in these actions have been tried and imprisoned in Cuba. The vast majority of them have left the country after finishing their sentence.

On September 18, 1980, the Cuban government returned two hijackers to the United States, putting them in the hands of the U.S. Justice, after making a public warning that it would act the same way in future cases.

With these measures Cuba put an end to hijacking planes and diverting them to its territory.

Cuban Adjustment Act"

Marine vessels have also been hijacked and those who have murdered for their own ends have not been put on trial nor punished; they are free within the United States.

August 6, 2002

Five people hijacked the vessel *Plastico 16*, based at La Coloma, Pinar del Río.

August 27, 2002

Cuban authorities made an official presentation, via Note 1428, of a request for the hijackers to be returned to Cuba. Months later they were given their freedom in the United States.

January 29, 2003

The vessel *Cabo Corriente* is hijacked from the Isle of Youth and taken to the United States. Cuban authorities presented a diplomatic note calling for the return of the four hijackers and of the aforementioned vessel. The United States authorities have not replied, but it freed the hijackers immediately.

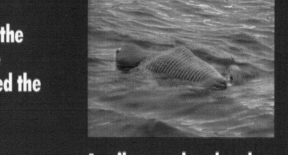

A sailor murdered and thrown into the water by the hijacker of a passenger boat.

The murderer reaches Miami. He was not returned, tried or punished.

March 19, 2003

7:24 P.M. A DC-3 plane belonging to the National Company of Air Services, covering the Nueva Gerona-Havana route, is hijacked. Ten miles south of the Boyeros airport, when the plane was ready to land, the captain of the plane informed Air Traffic Control at Boyeros that he had problems on board and that he was heading north; for this reason he requested the coordinates for the most direct route because he had a fuel shortage, and would head for Key West.

March 20, 2003

The head of the U.S. Interests Section in Havana is contacted and a diplomatic note is handed to him demanding the return of the passengers and crew, the hijackers and of the plane itself. A similar note is handed to the Department of State in Washington.

April 10, 2003

A U.S. federal judge ratified the decision of a Florida magistrate to release on bail the six Cubans accused of hijacking and diverting the Cuban DC-3 plane on last March 19 with 31 passengers on board.

Why do they go? Because they are absolutely certain of impunity. Because in more than a few cases they would be considered inadmissible for residing in the United States if they were to follow legal departure procedures, due to their criminal records.

The total certainty of impunity and of the privileges and advantages offered to them by this act are a powerful incentive to engage in terrorism.

How is it possible to ignore the seriousness of carrying out a hijacking with ferocious knives put to the throat of pilots?

When these hijackings take place, involving children, women and the elderly –honest Cubans–, they are subjected to maltreatment on their arrival in Florida, handcuffed and detained for several days against their will.

March 31, 2003

An AN-24 plane, with 46 people on board, including 6 children, traveling from the Isle of Youth to the José Martí airport in Havana, was hijacked by an individual who carried a grenade in his hand and threatened to blow up the plane if he were not supplied with sufficient fuel to continue to the United States.

April 2, 2003

The *Baraguá* ferry was leaving the mouth of the bay carrying an unknown number of passengers; everything seemed to indicate that it had been hijacked.

The group that took over the vessel was comprised of 11 people and they made the 29 passengers their captives. Included among the captives were children and four young tourist women (two French and two Nordics) who were the first to be threatened with death as their captors were aware of the damage that this would cause to the country's economy.

Only 40 hours after the hijacking, with the cooperation of the captives themselves, who jumped into the water, all hostages were rescued unharmed.

The main man behind the hijacking had been involved in 15 judicial cases or criminal incidents of a common delinquency nature. On several occasions he was sentenced to prison; on 28 occasions he was officially warned for harassing tourists and 119 times he was taken to police stations for different reasons.

Those who travel illegally are people who would never receive a visa due to their lack of educational or technical qualifications and because of their social and criminal records. They choose very carefully who they award visas to from a long list that they compile . . . . So those who travel illegally are those who do not receive the visa there. The latter are the most violent and dangerous.

GOOD TERRORISTS?

(Film footage taken during the hijacking.)

"CUBA NEEDS EYES AND

EARS IN FLORIDA"

Major General retired Edward Atkenson, former Director of Military Intelligence of the CIA and senior fellow at the Institute of Land Warfare

Early on the morning of September 12, 1998, the FBI informed Ileana Ros-Lehtinen and Lincoln Díaz Balart, supporters of the Batista terrorist Mafia in Miami, that they had just arrested Fernando González Llort, Antonio Guerrero Rodríguez, Gerardo Hernández Nordelo, Ramón Labañino Salazar and René González Sehwerert, as presumed "agents" resident there. At that time the FBI was unaware of the identity of three of the detainees and knew only that the other two had U.S. citizenship.

Although the Florida congressional delegation is composed of 25 members, the only ones who were given prior warning by the investigators were the aforementioned "legislators," who did not hold positions in Congress related to security or intelligence matters. Why were they privileged to this information? Why did they reveal to them an "investigation" which had not yet been publicized?

The formal accusation would not be made for four days, but from the very outset it was clear that the operation was of a political-repressive nature, the outcome of which was none other than to please the most aggressive and violent sector that

Federal Attorney Thomas Scott points to a supposed network of Cuban spies that had been uncovered.

Antonio, Fernando, Gerardo, Ramón and René were born on different dates and in different homes as a result of loving relationships. Many years later, some of them got to know each other on the difficult mission of infiltrating terrorist groups in Miami. Others identified themselves in the midst of the dangers and severity of an unjust imprisonment, to which they were brought in September 1998 for figthing terrorism. Since then, they have considered each other as brothers.

Antonio Guerrero Rodríguez

YOU ARE
To my son

You are my hand
if faraway friends I cannot greet.
You are my voice
if in the tribunes of ideas I cannot denounce.
You are my smile
if in the hours most pure I cannot console.
You are my dream
if the moment arrives I cannot dream.

June 30, 2001

I WILL NOT DEFRAUD YOU (Fragment)
To my father

I attend on this day to your name
on this singular day of summer
Austere, resolved, clear, faraway.
If I am so firm, father, do not be surprised.

I am not that one, but today I am the man
that your dreams lead by the hand.
I am not a child, but clean and sane,
to my firmness I put your renown.

"Papá will return.

"He always showed concern for my health and my school work. There was a lot of love and affection between us. I feel pride, admiration and respect for him. I know he will return because he is innocent, dignified and a patriot . . . he is an educated person, highly trained, intelligent, good fun, tells good stories, laughs. When he is annoyed he speaks in short sentences and is sometimes cutting, but is always honest . . . he doesn't know how to be spiteful and never forgets those who do him a favor."

Tonito, Antonio's son.

"My dear son:

"I woke up very early in the morning thinking about you. I always think about you, about how you are and how your schoolwork is coming along. I felt so happy when you wrote in your letter and said on the phone that things are going well, or rather very well. Happy birthday!

"Don't lose heart, always remember that you can achieve and you will achieve what you want. . . . When you are tired think about the love that surrounds you, think how much I love you and what I would want you to be, remember that you can always give more and you will be able to. Read all you can, tales and stories that inspire you, which will be an example for you. Take care. It is certain that we will see each other again, although we will have to wait a little while for that. With all my love. Your father, Tony."

Fragment of a letter written to his son Gabriel, October 16, 2001.

"We do not have the freedom that we all desire, although in our hearts and thoughts we are entirely free, but we have sufficient bravery and dignity to compensate for the lack of liberty. . . . We are here to triumph. We have every reason in the world to look ahead to the future, certain of better times to come. . . ."

Fragment of a letter to his mother, October 20, 2001.

Fernando González Llort

"My dear niece:

"I believe you when you say that if your maturity depends on this situation, you would prefer to carry on with your idle thoughts. . . . This is a sign of your affection for me and of how painful this situation is for you . . . from this situation a more mature and stronger Laura will emerge, as you say. Of course, I would prefer not to see you go through this and that your maturity come about as a result of a less traumatic course of events. . . .

"A big kiss from your uncle who loves you a lot,

"Fernando."

"Fernan is passionate about reading and prefers books about history. This is particularly the case right now when he spends a great deal of time reading, thanks to books sent to him from all over the world, he shares reading with me, we study each book and the context in which it was written."

Rosa Aurora Freijanes, Fernando's wife.

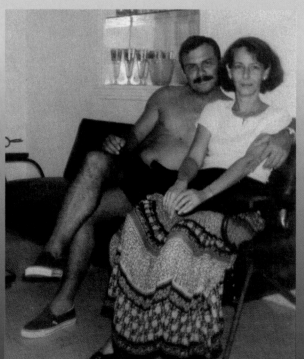

"Always trust in victory and keep your spirits as high as I can see they are in your letter. Together with this letter I enclose all the affection and love of a son who proudly sees your bravery and strength during these difficult times. . . ."

Fragment of the first handwritten letter received by his mother on February 4, 2001, after several years without receiving any handwritten letters by Fernando.

"The title of Heroes of the Republic of Cuba that has been awarded to us is an immense honor and a huge morale boaster. At the same time, it is a commitment to continue with this and with any other task or struggle that has to be waged. . . .

"I am so fortunate to receive from you not just maternal love, unconditional and tender, but also the permanent motivation of an attitude I admire and I am proud of. . . ."

Fragment of a dedication written on a birthday card to his mother.

"Today, three years on from being taken prisoner and at the point of being sentenced, after having gone through situations that you know about, I am not going to reiterate something I have already said in this letter, I just want to use a phrase by Silvio Rodríguez in his song 'El Necio' which has meant so much to us: I DIE AS I HAVE LIVED. . . ."

Fragment of a letter Fernando wrote to Rosa Aurora when they were taken for the second time to the "hole."

Gerardo Hernández Nordelo

Letter to my children that are to be born

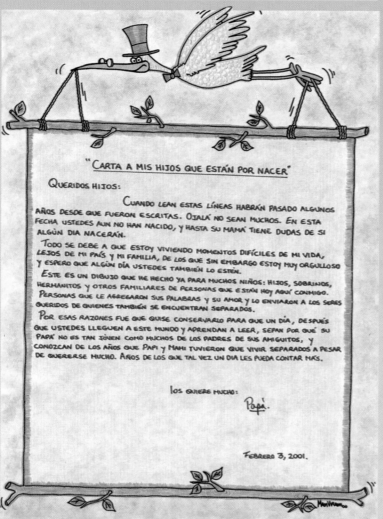

YEARNING

I will say how much I appreciate your years of
        devotion,
your infinite silence and your immense bravery,
and you will know how much I yearn for returning
        to your land,
to be reborn in your arms and feel your warmth.

It will arrive with tears of passion and joy
because, hidden in my heart, it will await
        the return,
and how much I would yearn, meanwhile
        that day arrives,
that you, Mother, could read these verses.

Fragment of a poem that Gerardo wrote in the "hole,"
        dedicated to his mother.

"We have a very beautiful love story which is impossible to write in these lines, but the years will go by and our love will grow. I have been, and I am, happy to share my life with an extraordinary man who is today part of this country's history. A man blessed with enviable qualities and who knows how to enrich and expand this wonderful feeling of love. . . . Thank you for so much happiness and for loving me so much. I miss you terribly. . . ."

Fragment of the letter written by Adriana to Gerardo on the occasion of their thirteenth wedding anniversary, July 11, 2001.

"No memory that I can recall today is more painful, no image in my mind is more bitter than that of the tear running down your cheek. Those tears that I have caused and have not seen I also regret . . . I regret the times that I walked, although it was only a few steps beside you, without taking your hand. I regret all the times I looked at you thinking, 'My God, how beautiful she is' and didn't say it to you. . . .

"I love you and my greatest desire, the one that is always in my mind, the one that is with me every moment of every day and night, is that all of this will come to an end and I will have enough time left to give you what until now I have not given you. . . .

"I love you, my bonsai"

Fragment of a letter from Gerardo to Adriana on their thirteenth wedding anniversary.

Ramón Labañino Salazar

"My beloved Laurita:

"When you receive this letter, on touching it, I want you feel I am in every letter, and that every comma, period and sigh, is a huge kiss from me to you. And it says I love you, a lot, infinitely, my darling, my little girl, my little daughter, my treasure, mine, mine. . . .

". . . but I promise to erase all this time apart, without your affection or mine, without being able to bring you up, teach you how to read and write, and so many other things life has to offer, that I want you to learn about. . . .

"Your dad. I love you."

DEBT

I dedicate my devotion, my absence to her
and all my sacrifices.
My silence was in honor of her
. . . .
Today I am happy to see you multiplicated in a thousand mothers and flags.

Fragment of the poem dedicated by Ramón to his dead mother.

"I love you and I believe that thanks to this love everything is so much more beautiful. Thanks to this love, victory is closer every day. With every day that goes by I know that it is one day less here, and one day closer to our final reunion to loving each other eternally. . . . Therefore, every day that passes is also a more beautiful day in this love story. . . ."

Fragment of a letter from Ramón to Elizabeth, his wife.

"You are 15 years old today. . . .

"I could write you a beautiful poem today. . . . But I prefer, today, to talk about you and me, of our lives and our love. And perhaps this is the most beautiful poem that I have ever written for you. . . .

"Right at that moment—when I heard about the birth—I knew what it meant to be a father, you have given me the happiness of being a father for the first time in my life. . . .

"Love always overcomes!
my daughter,

love has overcome.
And then fifteen white roses fell away from the sun. . . .

"I love you forever!"

"Your father
"Ramón Labañino Salazar"

Fragment of a letter by Ramón to Ailí.

"Letter to my daughters

"My beloved daughters,

Now you will be able to understand why your father cannot spend time with you or enjoy so many happy and joyful occasions that all fathers experience with their children. . . .

"Fo the time I have been absent, because I couldn't be with mom when she was pregnant, because I didn't see you being born, because I couldn't be there when you opened your lives, because I couldn't change your diapers, or help you to take your first tiny steps . . . and even for the reason that the youngest hardly knows me. . . .

"But I want you to know that I went away because of the love I have for you and for everyone. That wherever I have been, and wherever I will be, you will always be with me. . . .

"I will return, have no doubts about that . . . and when I return we will rebuild all the dreams and aspirations that have had to wait. . . .

"See you soon,
"Papá Ramón"

Fragment of a letter from Ramón to his daughters.

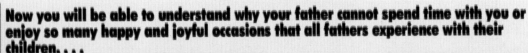

René González Sehwerert

For Irmita on her fifteenth birthday

Fly high butterfly. Break lances, harvesting joy. And the chimeras would be the legacy of your fifteen springtimes, the pedestal on which you raise your universe, a solid base of love, to which we proudly dedicate this verse. And with confidence!

September 15, 1999.

"For my darling baby:

"On the date I was arrested, September 12, 1998, you were hardly four and a half months old. On the previous night your mother had gone to work and I stayed home to look after you. When I gave you your milk you fell into a deep sleep and I decided to let you sleep on me while I lay face up on the bed watching television. When your mother arrived she was so amused to see you sleeping like that, with your limbs spread out and a look of satisfaction on your face, that she couldn't resist taking a photo of us. That was the last one in which we appeared together."

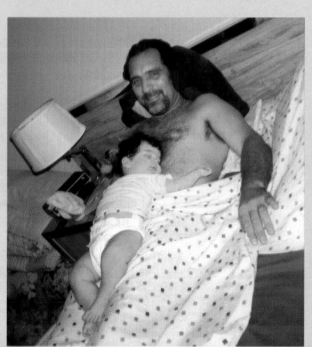

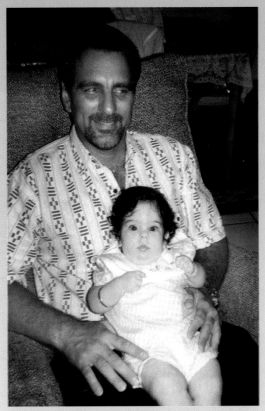

"René is the kind of person that people call —in Cuban slang— 'Feliciano' (happy man) . . . is one of the few people that I have known who is unaware of the value of material things; he is one of those friends who would give you everything without expecting anything in exchange . . . ."

Fragment of a letter by Liván, René's young brother.

XVI

Don't be afraid, that from seeds of nobility a cowardice bile sprout putridly for the vileness of this world is not enough to crush the firm seed of nobleness.

Fragment of a poem by René to his parents.

"Be happy whatever the price. Don't allow pessimistic thoughts or unpleasant memories, or even the trace of a vile action that some time gave you a bad moment. Think that you overcame all those things, inside and outside the jail by means of sheer force of personality, morale and principles. . . ."

Fragment of a letter by René to his wife.

Period prior to the trial

Necessary cooperation

"In the face of increased terrorist activities with the United States as the base during the 90s, in an endeavor to work jointly against this scourge, the authorities of the Cuban Ministry of the Interior provided the Federal Bureau of Investigation with detailed information about violent plots being hatched in Miami, together with video and audio tapes, and in-depth personal information related to the organizers of these criminal activities.

"The report did not state, although it was obvious, that the only way of obtaining this information was via infiltration of these terrorist groups."

Confidencial

REPUBLICA DE CUBA
Ministerio del Interior

ACTA DE ENTREGA DE EVIDENCIAS

Entre los días 16 y 17 de junio de 1998, una delegación de los Estados Unidos de América visitó la Ciudad de La Habana, Cuba, para conocer las investigaciones y evidencias que la parte cubana posee en relación con acciones terroristas que se han desarrollado contra la República de Cuba, la mayor parte de cuyos autores directos e indirectos residen y actúan desde territorio estadounidense.

La delegación norteamericana estuvo presidida por el Sr. Augustine Rodríguez, en representación del Departamento de Justicia de los Estados Unidos, e integrada además por los funcionarios: José F. Orihuela y Luis O. Rodríguez, Especialistas del FBI en Miami; Daniel M. Hickey y Thomas J. Mohnal, Peritos; Coronel Héctor Vela, Oficial de Enlace Internacional del Departamento de Transporte de Estados Unidos, y Michael George Kozak y Charles Burgess, Jefe y Funcionario, respectivamente, de la Sección de Intereses Norteamericanos en La Habana.

Después del análisis de las pruebas documentales y periciales sobre los casos que fueron puestos a disposición de la delegación visitante, la parte cubana accedió a entregar al Representante del Gobierno de los Estados Unidos, Sr. Augustine Rodríguez, las evidencias siguientes:

Carpeta Nº. 1 : "Informe Sobre las Actividades Terroristas contra Cuba", Folios
Confidencial   1-64.

Carpeta Nº. 2 : "A   Operations", Folios 1-51.
Confidencial

Carpeta Nº. 3 "Ele
Confidencial

Carpeta Nº. 4 "Inf
Ter

Muestra Nº. 1 Dos
: en

Muestra Nº. 2 Dos
: en

Confidencial
Hoja Nº. 2

Muestra Nº. 3 : Dos (2) gramos de sustancia explosiva del artefacto que se le ocupara a los ciudadanos guatemaltecos Nader Kamal Musalam Barakat y María Elena González Meza, el 4.3.98.

Cassette video : Fragmentos de las declaraciones del detenido Santos Armando
Nº. 1.   Martínez Rueda.
Confidencial

Cassette video : Fragmentos de las declaraciones del detenido Cecilio Reinoso
Nº. 2.   Sánchez.
Confidencial

Cassette video : Reconstrucción de los actos terroristas realizados en
Nº. 3.   instalaciones turísticas por Raúl Ernesto Cruz León.
Confidencial

Cassette video : Entrevistas a los mercenarios guatemaltecos María Elena
Nº. 4.   González Meza y Nader Kamal Musalam Barakat, donde
Confidencial   detallan la conexión de Chávez Abarca con una organización
           de cubanoamericanos en Estados Unid
           Arnaldo Monzón y Ramón Medina (Luis

Cassette video : Informaciones transmitidas por las cad
Nº. 5.   acciones terroristas contra Cuba.

Cassette audio : Grabación de la llamada telefónica de
Nº. 1.   Cruz León a Karla, esposa de Fran
Confidencial   8/9/97 a las 23:20 horas.

Cassette audio : Grabación de la llamada telefónica
Nº. 2.   Francisco Chávez Abarca) al detenido
Confidencial   el 8/9/97 a las 23:40 horas.

Cassette audio : Grabación de la llamada telefónic
Nº. 3.   Abarca al detenido Raúl Ernesto Cruz
Confidencial   00:40 hora.

Cassette audio : Grabación de la llamada telefónica rea
Nº. 4.   al detenido Raúl Ernesto Cruz León el
Confidencial   hora.

Cassette audio : Grabación de la llamada telefónica rea
Nº. 5.   (Francisco Chávez o Manuel Gonzál
Confidencial   Herrera desde Guatemala el 9/3/98 a l

Cassette audio : Grabación de la llamada telefónica rea
Nº. 6.   (Francisco Chávez o Manuel Gonzál
Confidencial   Herrera desde Guatemala el 10/3/98 a

Confidencial
Hoja Nº. 3

Cassette audio : Grabación de la llamada telefónica realizada por Pedro Humas
Nº. 7.   (Francisco Chávez o Manuel González) a Miguel Abraham
Confidencial   Herrera desde Guatemala el 10/3/98 a las 13:30 horas.

Cassette audio : Grabación de la llamada telefónica realizada por Jazid Iván
Nº. 8.   Fernández Mendoza o Miguel Abraham Herrera desde
Confidencial   Guatemala el 12/3/98 a las 21:05 horas.

Como constancia de lo antes expuesto, firman la presente:

Por la delegación de los E. U. A.   Por la delegación de la República de Cuba

Augustine Rodríguez   **Coronel Adalberto Rabeiro García**
Departamento de Justicia de los   Jefe del Departamento de Instrucción Judicial
Estados Unidos de América   Dirección de Contrainteligencia

CORONEL WA
DICO DEL

CERTIFICO: Q
Evidencias a l
pruebas docum
República de C
Departamento
es la que
oficiales.........

Y para que as
Junio de mil n
BATALLAS DE

Coronel Walki
Jefe Depar
Ministe

MINISTE

José D. M
Jo Cibano
des Victor
Caras Ret
cies firma
dudes de
CERTIFIC
FUNCION
LA HABAN
GUARDA E
CENTRO
USAN EN
EN FE DE
FIRMA Y
LA HABA

The political response of the U.S. government was not long in coming. Only three months after that meeting, on September 12 of the same year, during an FBI operation carried out at dawn, Gerardo Hernández Nordelo, Ramón Labañino Salazar, Antonio Guerrero Rodríguez, Fernando González Llort and René González Sehwerert were arrested in their homes."

"How many more human lives have to be lost before the FBI fulfills its duty and arrests the real criminals and terrorists from within the U.S. population itself?

"Is it perhaps that this 'struggle against terrorism' is pure rhetoric?"

Ramón Labañino Salazar

"The majority of Cuban-Americans today, 40 years on, are still active in terrorist initiatives against Cuba. They are well known by the U.S. state security authorities because they belonged to these very bodies and because it was through them that they learned about the technical resources and their working methods."

Fernando González Llort

The government took the first step against them by placing them in solitary confinement in punishment cells during the first 17 months of detention. This was to be the beginning of a long list of violations of the most basic human rights committed during this process.

RNANDEZ VALDES, JEFE DEL DEPARTAMENTO
DEL INTERIOR..

que aparece al final del Acta de Entrega de
de los Estados Unidos, donde se da a conocer
periciales, sobre acciones terroristas contra la
ponde al Coronel Adalberto Rabeiro García, Jefe del
ón Judicial de la Dirección de Contrainteligencia, y
onario acostumbra a utilizar en los asuntos
....

expide la presente a los diecisiete días del mes de
noventa y ocho. "AÑO DEL 40 ANIVERSARIO LAS
LA GUERRA DE LIBERACIÓN"..

Valdés
ídico
of

CUBA
ONES EXTERIORES
JURIDICA

lia P. Alvarez Dorts
María Silvia Fernán
a Pedraza, lo Manuel
as Ponce: Funciona
icar Autenticaciones
spedidos para aut

ER ES AUTENTICO DEL
DE ESTE DOCUMENTO
A LA SEMEJANZA QUE
REGISTRADA EN ESTE
SMO ACOSTUMBRA A
ES:
LA PRESENTE CON LA
MINISTERIO.

7 JUN 1998

CONFIDENCIAL

SECUENCIA DE ACCIONES Y PLANES TERRORISTAS CONTRA CUBA A PARTIR DE 1990

FNCA

LEYENDA

PRIMERA ETAPA
(RESURGIMIENTO DEL TERRORISMO)

SEGUNDA ETAPA
(ESCALADA TERRORISTA)

Is it possible to put on trial in the community of Miami five people who acknowledged from the first day of the trial that they are agents of the Cuban state?

In order to answer this question affirmatively you would have to say that the people of Miami have no opinion on the Cuban government and on those who defend it, and there in Miami a verdict of innocence may be pronounced by the members of the jury without fear of the community reacting.

Consider that these men, according to the accusation, infiltrated in groups of political and economic power within the community.

Let us see how some potential jury members responded:

David Cuevas:
"I would feel slightly intimidated and perhaps a little fearful for my own security if my verdict did not coincide with that demanded by the Cuban community."

Then he added:
"If you want to know the truth, I would be a bundle of nerves. . . . I believe . . . that I would be afraid, have real fear for my own security if my verdict did not coincide with that of the whole Cuban community."

Mr. Glanery:
"It would be very difficult taking into account the community in which we live."

Michele Petterson was also worried about the community's reaction in the case of a verdict of innocence:
"I think I would be worried about the reaction that it could cause . . . . I don't want riots or anything of the sort that happened during the Elián case."

Mr. Pareira, another potential member of the jury, declared:
"I would be worried about how others would see me. . . . I don't like the Mafia mentality that interferes with what I think is a system that works."

Jess Lawhorn Jr., banker:
"I believe that I am concerned about how public opinion could affect my ability to carry out my job afterwards. . . . How it could interfere with my ability to do business in the community."

A sociological study carried out in the community of Miami Dade, less than a month before the jury was selected, compared with another national poll in the United States.

People ready to support an armed action on the part of the U.S. government to overthrow the government of Cuba:

Cubans in the Miami area	49.7%
Non-Cubans in the Miami area	26.0 %
National sample in the United States	08.1%

People ready to support an armed action on the part of Cuban exiles to overthrow the government of Cuba:

Cubans in the Miami area	55.8%
Non-Cubans in the Miami area	27.6 %
National sample in the United States	05.8%

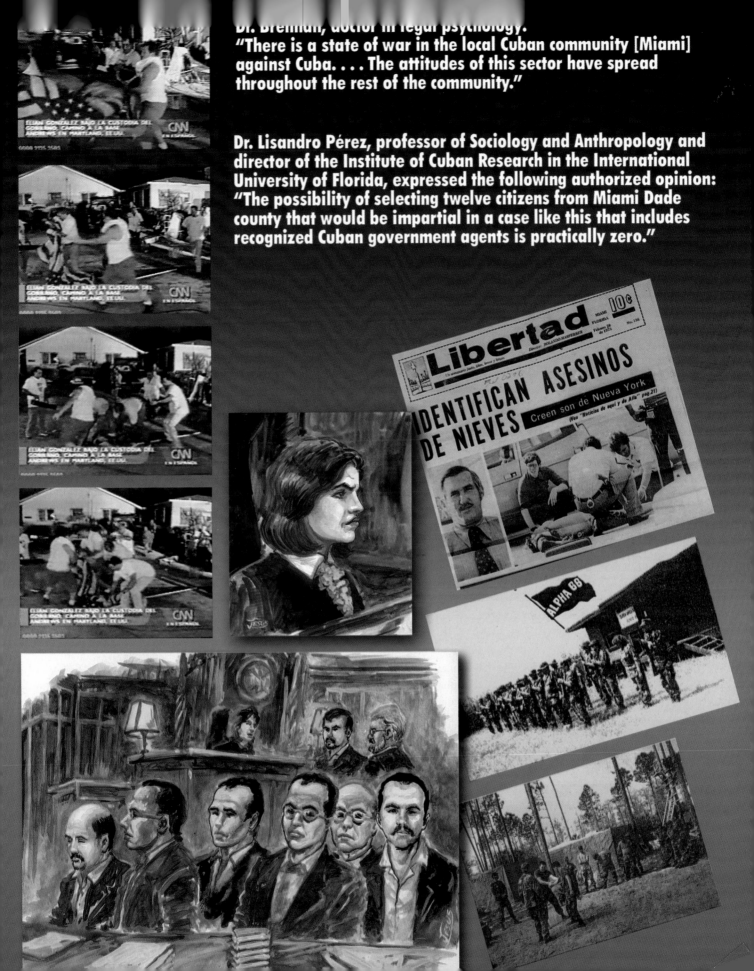

Dr. Brennan, doctor in legal psychology.
"There is a state of war in the local Cuban community [Miami] against Cuba. . . . The attitudes of this sector have spread throughout the rest of the community."

Dr. Lisandro Pérez, professor of Sociology and Anthropology and director of the Institute of Cuban Research in the International University of Florida, expressed the following authorized opinion: "The possibility of selecting twelve citizens from Miami Dade county that would be impartial in a case like this that includes recognized Cuban government agents is practically zero."

The defense presented as expert witnesses three high-ranking retired U.S. officials, who gave their authorized opinions in this regard. The U.S. Army Major General (retired) Edward Atkenson, former Director of Military Intelligence of the CIA and senior fellow at the Institute of Land Warfare, answered.

"They [the Cubans] are not a threat to us. . . . I don't think we worry about Cuba at all."

Referring to the evidence, his replies were as follows:

"In your review of all the materials, did you ever come across any instructions for people to get hold of classified material?"

"No."

"Did you ever find any specific instructions tasking to get hold of top-secret materials?"

"No."

"Did you ever come across any instructions directing agents to find materials that would be harmful to the United States?"

"No."

"There was no alternative other than to rely upon men who, being committed to a just cause, were prepared to voluntarily fulfill this honorable duty against terrorism. To give warnings of the danger of aggression."

Antonio Guerrero Rodríguez

"We have dedicated our lives to fight terrorism, to prevent actions as atrocious as these from taking place. We have endeavored to save the lives of innocent human beings, not just in Cuba, but also in the United States itself; today we are in court to be condemned precisely for preventing actions such like these. This sentence cannot be anything other than ironic and unjust!"

Ramón Labañino Salazar

Rear Admiral Eugene Carroll, with 35 years of service in the U.S. Navy, and current deputy president of the Center for Defense Information in Washington, declared:

"Cuba is not a military threat to the United States."

In a similar vein, Mr. Charles Elliot Wilhelm, General of the U.S. Marine Infantry, who toward the end of the nineties was chief of the U.S. Southern Command until the time of his retirement, said during his statement to the jury:

"My view was that Cuba's Armed Forces posed no conventional threat for the United States."

WITNESSES HOSTILE TO THE DEFENSE:

"JOSE BASULTO admitted the terrorist activities he had engaged in against CUBA during his youth, that he had not publicly renounced his violent past, and likewise acknowledged his current terrorist activities against CUBA in violation of the laws of that country, U.S. laws and international laws."

Transcript of the trial, March 12, 2001.

The witness RODOLFO FROMETA decided not to base on the Fifth Amendment and testify in relation to his activities with the terrorist groups ALPHA 66 and COMANDOS F-4. In his statement, he acknowledges, among other things, the following:

- The paramilitary training activities both groups carried out in the south of Florida.
- Armed raids in CUBA using southern Florida as a point of departure.
- The smuggled weapons and explosives held by both groups.
- That he was arrested in June 1994 when he attempted to purchase C-4 explosives, anti-tank weapons and Stinger anti-air rocket launchers for an undercover FBI agent. Following his arrest he negotiated a deal with the District Attorney in southern Florida pleading guilty in exchange for one year of domicile arrest, being freed on parole until the time of the trial.

"RICHARD NUCCIO, former presidential advisor on Cuba to BILL CLINTON, testifies in relation to the terrorist past of the president of "Brothers to the Rescue", JOSE BASULTO, and his attempts to provoke a reaction on the part of the Cuban government, the repercussions of which for both countries, CUBA and the USA, were viewed with alarm by U.S. authorities."

Transcript of the trial, March 12, 2001.

"I would like the prosecutors to know that the only blood on my hands is that of my fellow comrades, dead or cowardly murdered in countless attacks and terrorist activities carried out against my country by people who today freely walk through the streets of this city [Miami]."

Gerardo Hernández Nordelo

The witness for the defense **DEBBIE McMULLEN**, investigator in the Office of the Public Defender, presented to the court the real reason for their presence in Miami, via information confiscated from the five accused: control and follow up of the activities being planned against Cuba in this city:

- **Operation Arcoiris**: Aimed at monitoring a plan by the following terrorists: **ORLANDO BOSCH** and **DARIO LOPEZ CASTRO** for the assassination of **FIDEL CASTRO**.
- **Operation Morena**: Aimed at monitoring the terrorist activities of **ROBERTO MARTIN PEREZ, CANF** leader.
- **Operation Paraíso**: In relation to the plans of the Democratic National Unity Party (PUND) and the CANF, to bury weapons in the Bahamas that would later be used against **CUBA**.
- Boats in the Miami River being prepared to take explosives to Cuba and the proposal of the accused **GERARDO HERNANDEZ** to pass on information to the FBI via an anonymous phone call.

Transcript of the testimony by DEBBIE McMULLEN, April 12, 2001.

"The defense witness, **PERCY ALVARADO GODOY,** established a link between the Cuban American National Foundation (CANF), the lobbying organization with offices in Miami and Washington, and the terrorist activities in Cuba."

Transcript of the testimony by ALVARADO GODOY, April 10, 2001.

"I sincerely trust that one day Cuba will not need people like me, who voluntarily and out of devotion to our country and our people, will come to this country to fight terrorism."

Fernando González Llort

MIAMI: WHERE THE MOTIVATION TO CONFRONT TERRORISM IS PROHIBITED AND CONSIDERED ANTICONSTITUTIONAL.

"The fight against terrorism is the motivation of the accused and motivation should not be aired in front of the jury."

Official documents from the trial. Motion confined to the district attorney, 2000.

"The court strongly advises that witnesses exercise their right to base on the Fifth Amendment so that terrorist activities against CUBA are not made public."

Official documents from the trial. District attorney motion from the District attorney's office, March 20, 2001.

"Whether terrorism is committed against innocents in the United States or Cuba, Israel or Jordan, Northern Ireland or India, it is evil and it is wrong; but the terrorist acts by others cannot excuse the wrongful and illegal conduct of this defendant or any other."

Judge Joan Lenard. Transcript of the trial sentence of René González Sehwerert, December 14, 2001.

"As a further special condition of supervised release the defendant is prohibited from associating with or visiting specific places where individuals or groups such as terrorists, members of organizations advocating violence, and organized crime figures are known to be or frequent."

Judge Joan Lenard. Transcript of the trial sentence, December 14, 2001.

"I firmly believe that one can be a Catholic and be a good person, be a Jewish and be a good person, be a capitalist, Muslim or communist and be a good person, but there is no such thing as a good person and a terrorist. You have to be sick to be a terrorist, just as you have to be sick to believe that there is such a thing as good terrorism."

René González Sehwerert

WHAT ARE THESE PATRIOTS DEFENDING?

Any Cuban citizen has the possibility to study from primary school up to obtain a Ph. D. without having to pay a single cent. Education is free and no teacher who wishes to work is unemployed.

Cuba has the highest school attendance rate amongst the countries of the hemisphere.

Its pupils are the best in the world in terms of knowledge of language and mathematics.

The country also ranks first in terms of teacher-pupil ratio.

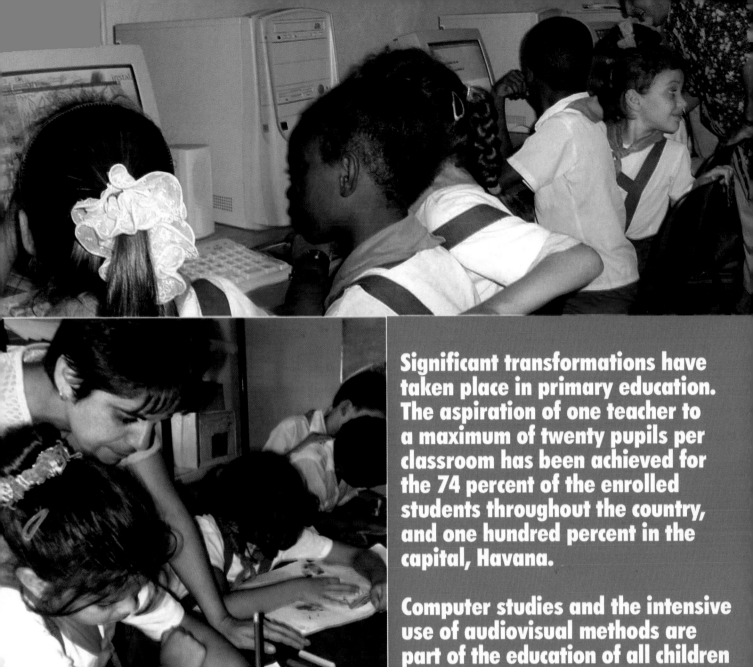

Significant transformations have taken place in primary education. The aspiration of one teacher to a maximum of twenty pupils per classroom has been achieved for the 74 percent of the enrolled students throughout the country, and one hundred percent in the capital, Havana.

Computer studies and the intensive use of audiovisual methods are part of the education of all children and young people in the countryside and in the cities.

NOT ONE OF THEM · IS CUBAN ·

Almost 120 million children of primary school age in the world do not go to school. Not one of them is Cuban.

Cuba has developed techniques to teach literacy via radio with texts elaborated in five languages—Creole, Portuguese, French, English and Spanish—, techniques that are being applied in different countries. A similar program, of exceptionally high quality, is about to be released whereby literacy is taught via television. These programs are Cuban initiatives and are genuinely Cuban. We are not interested in the exclusivity of the patent. We are willing to offer them to all countries of the Third World.

Special education takes charge of over fifty-five thousand children and young people in 428 schools, and there are also facilities provided in hospitals and at home via visiting teachers. The introduction of television and computing is revolutionizing a teaching system that is full of humanity and love.

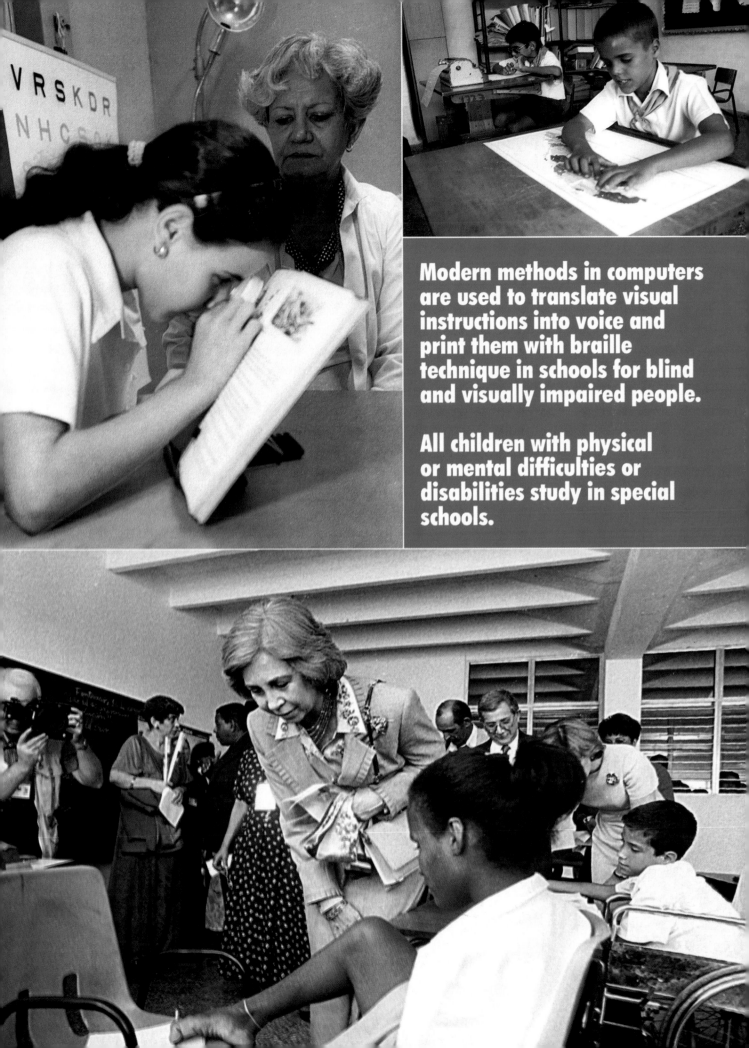

Modern methods in computers are used to translate visual instructions into voice and print them with braille technique in schools for blind and visually impaired people.

All children with physical or mental difficulties or disabilities study in special schools.

Solar panels installed in 2368 tiny rural and mountainous region schools, in very remote areas, have made it possible for schools that have very few pupils, some with only one child attending, to enjoy the benefits of television, video and computers.

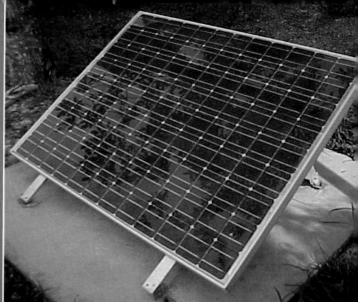

A total of 250 million children under thirteen-years old in the world are forced to work to survive. Not one of them is Cuban.

Over one million children are forced into child prostitution and tens of thousands are victims of the trafficking of body organs. Not one of them is Cuban.

Thousands of children in the world live on the streets. Not one of them is Cuban.

NOT ONE OF THEM · IS CUBAN ·

Infant mortality is 6.5 per thousand live births, meaning that Cuba has the lowest rate among countries of the Third World. Life expectancy at birth is 76 years.

We have a family physician program that guarantees free medical treatment to the entire population. These family physicians' premises are located within the neighborhood of the population they attend on.

Cuba has a unique National Health System that is universal, free and accessible to all members of the population. It is characterized by its community participation, a high degree of networking and its internationalist outlook.

All children are vaccinated without charge against thirteen illnesses, the majority of which have been eradicated.

Infectious or contagious diseases such as polio, malaria, neonatal tetanus, diphtheria, measles, rubella, post-mumps, whooping cough, dengue, have been eliminated; others, such as tetanus, meningococcical meningitis, hepatitis B, leprosy, meningitis via hemophilia and tuberculosis are completely under control.

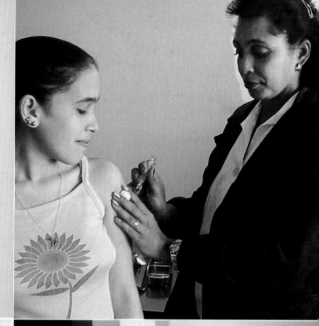

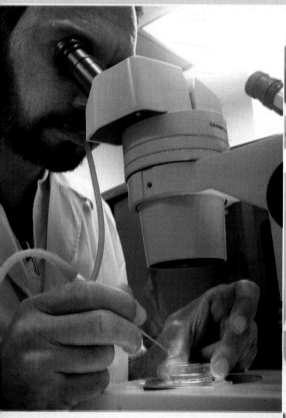

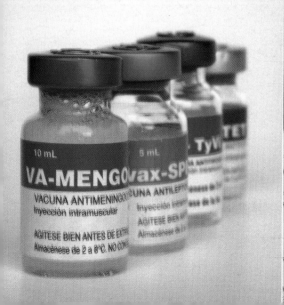

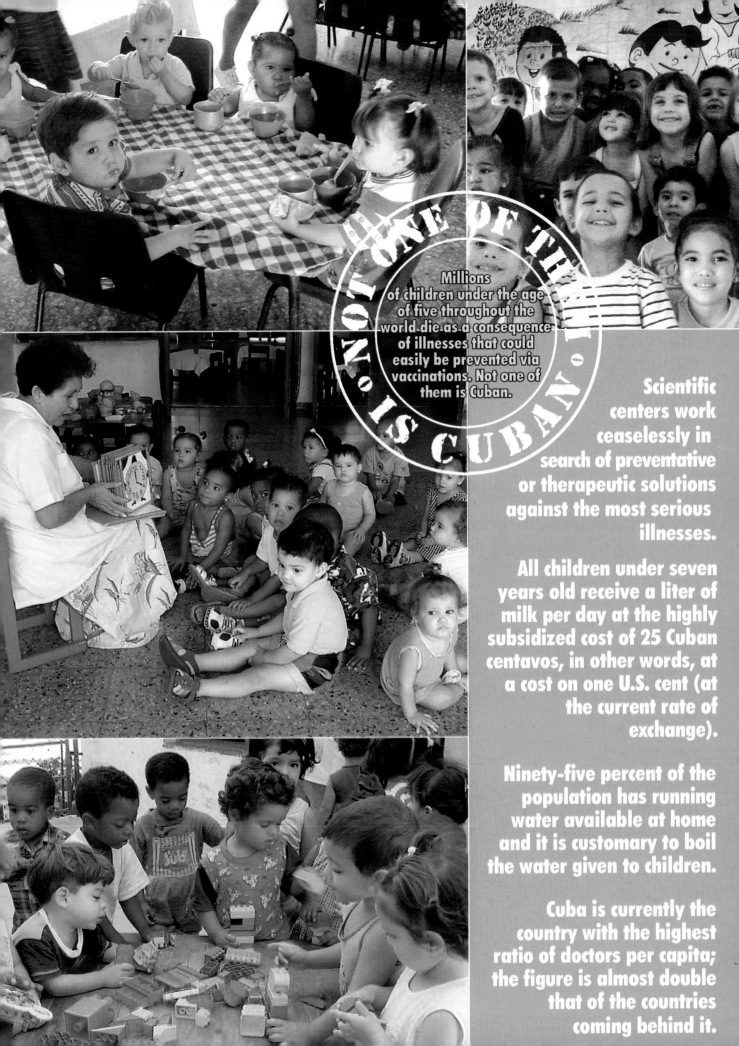

NOT ONE OF THEM IS CUBAN

Millions of children under the age of five throughout the world die as a consequence of illnesses that could easily be prevented via vaccinations. Not one of them is Cuban.

Scientific centers work ceaselessly in search of preventative or therapeutic solutions against the most serious illnesses.

All children under seven years old receive a liter of milk per day at the highly subsidized cost of 25 Cuban centavos, in other words, at a cost on one U.S. cent (at the current rate of exchange).

Ninety-five percent of the population has running water available at home and it is customary to boil the water given to children.

Cuba is currently the country with the highest ratio of doctors per capita; the figure is almost double that of the countries coming behind it.

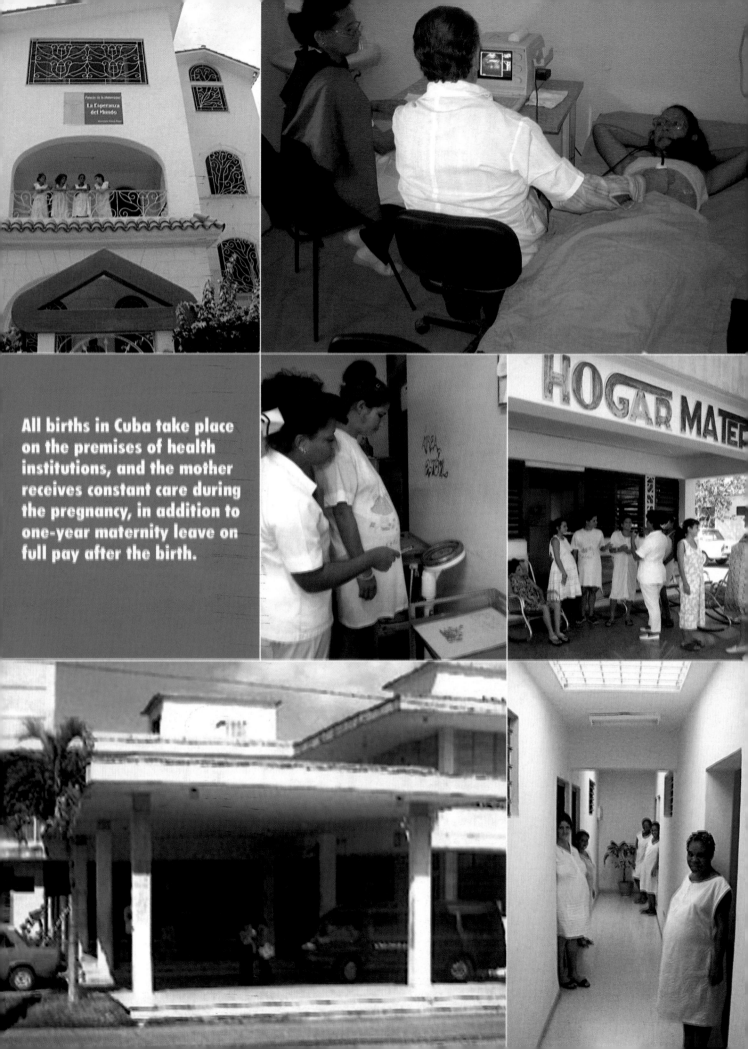

All births in Cuba take place on the premises of health institutions, and the mother receives constant care during the pregnancy, in addition to one-year maternity leave on full pay after the birth.

52,202 health workers have given their services in 92 countries around the world.

International cooperation comprises a range of activities including specialized medical care, ministerial advisory services, the development of hygiene education campaigns, epidemiological and hygiene programs, teaching staff on placement in Medical Schools and Faculties, and lecturing on masters and postgraduate courses.

Currently, 3000 specialists in General Medicine, together with other health professionals, are working in the most remote areas of 18 Third World countries. Their use of preventative and therapeutic methods save hundreds of thousands of lives every year and preserve or restore the health of millions of people without charging a single cent for their services.

Cuba also provides international aid via its professors in the Latin American Medical School (ELAM). Over 9000 students attend the school, out of whom 7557 are from 80 different countries, representing 100 different ethnic communities, 69 of which are Latin American and 31 are African.

Physical education is developed and promoted in Cuba together with a whole range of sports as part of the education program and as a contribution to the all-round education of its citizens.

The amount of technicians and teachers has risen to 30,914, ensuring that there are sufficient to cover the national needs, a ratio of one per 355 inhabitants, a figure that is considered to be among the highest in the world.

There is a University of Sports in the country with 14 faculties and an enrolment of 9664 students, with 1260 professors.

There are a total of 12,072 physical education professors, one per 183 students.

Over the years, 43,000 professionals in physical education and sports have graduated from academic and scientific Cuban sports institutions; most of the graduates have been at university level.

There are over 4000 high-performance athletes, but the source is limitless given that sports form a key part of the school curriculum, making it the base of a pyramid, at the tip of which are the elite athletes.

The most important sports competition in Cuba is carried out during the High-Performance National School Games, in which an average of around 8000 athletes take part in 29 sports every year.

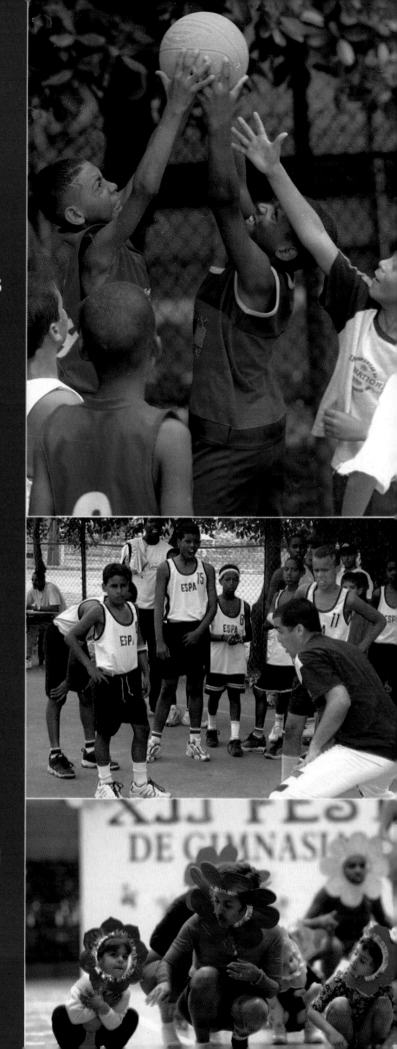

International activities are increasing, and Cuba has signed 128 sports cooperation agreements with 95 countries on 5 different continents: 71 with governmental organizations and 31 with Olympic bodies.

The International School of Physical Education and Sports has 1200 students that are from 33 African countries, 17 from Latin America, 5 from Asia, and 16 from the Caribbean; a total of 71 countries.

11,000 Cuban technicians are providing their services in 100 countries throughout the five continents of the world.

From the time of its participation in the 1970 Central American and Caribbean Games in Panama, Cuba has come at the top of the list, with 1492 gold medals, 739 silver medals and 555 bronze medals making a total of 2786 awards obtained. Out of this total, 82 percent were obtained after the triumph of the Revolution.

In the 1971 Pan-American Games in Cali, Cuba came second in the list of countries for the first time, only overcome by the United States. In 1991, an important development occurred when the United States were beaten by Cuba during the Havana games.

A total of 640 gold medals, 454 silver medals and 407 bronze medals, that sum 1510, have been won in the Pan-American games, out of which 96.7 percent have been won since 1959.

In the Olympic Games, Cuba has won a total of 56 gold medals, 47 silver medals and 41 bronze medals, making a total of 144 medals; 97 percent have been won since the triumph of the Revolution.

Cuba has won the title of World Champion in 12 different sporting areas 112 times since the Revolution; 25 of which were on more than one occasion.

A total of 90 percent of our Olympic and World Champions have emerged from the School Games.

Promoting artistic and literary creation, the production and publicizing of artists' endeavors, the protection and enrichment of our cultural heritage and the critical assimilation of the cultural expressions and messages they produce, via the participation of the population in a widespread socio-cultural movement, driven by the artistic vanguard and cultural institutions for the sake of attaining a comprehensive cultural development of our society has been and is the essential focus of Cuban cultural policy. The Cuban state has designated significant resources for this purpose.

Book-publishing programs in diverse territories have reached the figure of more than 11,169 titles and 601,690 copies.

The International Book Fair traveled to thirty cities in 2003 and was visited by 3,569,356 people who bought 2,911,966 books. The Cuban population is just over 11 million inhabitants.

Events such as the Ballet Festival, the Fine Arts Biennial, the Festival of New Latin American Cinema, the Theater Festival, the Caribbean Fiesta, the Ibero American Culture Fiesta, the May Romerías Festival, the Festival of *Trova* (Trobadours), the Cucalambeana Event, the Benny Moré Festival of Music, the Jazz Festival, the (Cubadisco) Disc Festival, the Popular Art Fair and others encourage the relationship between the public and art.

Artists' training schools have been developed throughout all provinces of the country; they offer courses and develop the talent and vocation of over 2000 young people. Tens of thousands of others do the same in vocational schools, which are the source of pupils for these professional institutions.

The mass training of art school instructors in fifteen art schools throughout the country is currently taking place with an enrolment figure of 11,700 students.

In the mountainous regions there are 43 Houses of Culture, which promote cultural activities in the most remote areas.

There are over 360 public libraries offering their services in the country today.

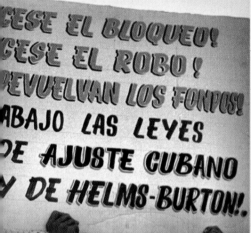

LAS IDEAS VENCERAN A LAS ARMAS

¡CESE EL BLOQUEO!
¡CESE EL ROBO!
¡DEVUELVAN LOS FONDOS!
¡ABAJO LAS LEYES
DE AJUSTE CUBANO
Y DE HELMS-BURTON!

A people has never had such sacred gains to defend, or such profound convictions to fight for, to the extent that they would prefer to disappear from the face of the Earth rather than renounce the noble and generous achievements for which many generations of Cubans have paid the high price of the lives of their best children.

FOR DEFENDING
THESE GAINS AND
FIGHTING TERRORISTS
TRYING TO
UNDERMINE THEM,
ANTONIO, FERNANDO,
RENÉ, GERARDO AND
RAMÓN WERE
CONDEMNED TO:

Antonio Guerrero Rodríguez, condemned to life imprisonment and 10 years more

". . . in the end, we shall rest free and victorious in front of that sun which we are denied today."

Antonio

Fernando Gonzalez Llort, condemned to 19 years imprisonment.

"The first duty of any self-respecting person is to his or her country. Throughout the years of my imprisonment, I will always carry with me the dignity I have learned from my people and their history."

Fernando

René Gonzalez Sehwerert, condemned to 15 years imprisonment.

"... we will continue to appeal to the American people's vocation for truth. And we will do so with all the patience, faith and courage that we draw from the crime of being honorable."

René

Gerardo Hernández Nordelo, Condemned to two life terms and 15 years imprisonment.

"My only regret is that I have but one life to give for my country."

Gerardo

Ramón Labañino Salazar, condemned to life imprisonment and 18 years more

"I will wear the prison uniform with the same honor and pride with which a soldier wear his most prized insignias!"

Ramón

Why such aberrant sentences?

To what you have read, add the following:

Miami-Dade. An impartial location?

Only in Miami is a byelaw passed demanding that the persons who wish to do business with the County, must declare under oath that they will not do business either directly or indirectly with Cuba or its citizens.

Only in Miami does the owner of a venue have to cancel a performance by Cubans after receiving death threats and having had a Molotov cocktail thrown at his property.

Alpha 66 afirma que atacó hotel

Por SANTIAGO AROCA
Redactor de El Nuevo Herald
1/6/95
Miembros de la organización

Atentado contra el Centro Vasco

Empleados miden el jueves una ventana cuyo cristal fue destruido por coctel Molotov en el Centro Vasco.

Dueños reconsideran presentación de artista cubana

Only in Miami does a dance performance almost lead to a riot due to the Cuban nationality of the dancers.

Only Miami withdraws from the prestigious Pan-American Games after spending almost quarter of a million dollars on acquiring the rights to be the setting because they discovered that Cuban athletes were to take part.

Only in Miami is the painting of a Cuban artist reduced to ashes by its purchaser who had just spent 500 USD buying it.

Only in Miami do the terrorists, prosecutors and police agree that the violent activities carried out against Cuba should be tolerated and publicized.

Only Miami has a long history of terrorist threat, bomb explosions, attacks and murders against those who express a different opinion or question the most extremist line.

FUNDACION NACIONAL ANO AMERIC

ESTAMOS EN GUERRA

The injustice of Charge 3.

An additional absurd and vile accusation was made against Gerardo Hernández: to conspire to commit premeditated murder. This is a charge without any legal pretext, endorsed by the government during the second indictment, presented eight months after detention in the search for a political charge against the accused. It was presented as if he were responsible for the death of those who lost their lives on February 24 in an incident that took place when the Cuban air forces, exercising their legitimate right to national sovereignty, brought down two planes belonging to a known terrorist group which, from Miami, had violated Cuban territory on numerous occasions to provoke a response, for subversive reasons and to carry out sabotage.

This is a unique case. It has to do with a country defending its sovereignty. The court violated the doctrine of the State Act, which has been clearly and repeatedly recognized by the U.S. Supreme Court.

As it is evident, no proof against Gerardo existed, no witness, nothing linked him with what happened then.

Acknowledging that it was impossible to prove the accusation against Gerardo, the attorney asked the Appeal Court on May 25, 2001, as an emergency motion to modify instructions to the jury arguing that **in the light of the evidence presented to the court, this represents an insurmountable obstacle for the United States in this case and will probably result in the failure of the accusation in this charge . . . since it imposes an insurmountable obstacle to this district.**

THE APPEAL COURT DID NOT ACCEPT THE ATTORNEY'S REQUEST AND AS A CONSEQUENCE THE JURY HAD TO DECIDE WHETHER GERARDO WAS GUILTY OR INNOCENT OF THE CHARGE IMPUTED TWO YEARS PREVIOUSLY. SOMETHING HAPPENED AT THAT POINT THAT COULD ONLY HAPPEN IN A MIAMI COURT: WITH UNUSUAL SWIFTNESS, THE JURY DECLARED GERARDO GUILTY OF FIRST-DEGREE MURDER, SOMETHING WHICH THE ATTORNEY HAD PREDICTED WOULD END IN FAILURE.

The government used the Classified Information Procedure Act (CIPA) to prevent the accused and their defense lawyers from accesing to documentation which formed the basis of the accusations.

The court repeatedly refused the right to Rule 16 of the U.S. Penal Procedure Law on evidence that the Prosecutor said they possessed and decided selectively which part of this would be presented in the trial. The defense lawyers did not have access to more than 80 percent of the evidence.

One of the defense lawyers, at the time the sentence was being pronounced against his client, said, "Your Honor, we began this trial over a year ago, it is going to end, and I still don't know the basis of the accusation against my client."

The Classified Information Procedure Act (CIPA) allowed the government to restrict the quantity of classified information that would be revealed during the trial, to edit it according to their desires, and compelled the defense lawyers of the five accused to reveal prior to the trial what evidence would be used in their defense, which represented major obstacles and violations of the constitutional rights of the accused.

The CIPA forced the Defense to spend a lot of time attempting to declassify tens of thousand of documents prior to the trial, documents that should not have been classified under any circumstances as they did not represent a threat to the U.S. Government, as was acknowledged during the trial by high-ranking U.S. officials who testified for the defense and for the prosecution.

The five Cuban defendants were held in preventative custody for 33 months before sentence was passed on the charges. They were isolated for almost 17 months prior to the trial and 48 days after the verdict, in special cells, known as the "hole," designed for prisoners with serious disciplinary problems, with no access to television, radio or press, conditions that, according to the rules of the Bureau of Prisons, should not exceed 60 days.

In February 2003 they were put again in solitary confinement, with all contact with the outside world cut off, including correspondence, legal and consulate visits; all of this took place during a crucial period of the legal process, when the lawyers were preparing their appeal reports and communication with their clients was vital.

Olga Salanueva, René González's wife, and Adriana Pérez, Gerardo Hernández's wife, have been denied visas to visit their husbands in prison.

The injustice committed against the Five has generated an intense solidarity campaign inside and beyond the United States. There are over 200 committees formed in 75 countries, including the United States, and in every continent, lobbying for the freedom of the Five.

Libertà per i cinque!

Gerardo Hernández Nordelo

Ramón Labañino Salazar

René González Schwerert

Fernando González Llort

Antonio Guerrero Rodríguez

¡¡LIBEREN A LOS CINCO YA !!!

Free the five

Ivette González Salanueva in John Lennon Park, Havana, Cuba.

The U.S. Government does not allow this little girl to visit her father in prison.

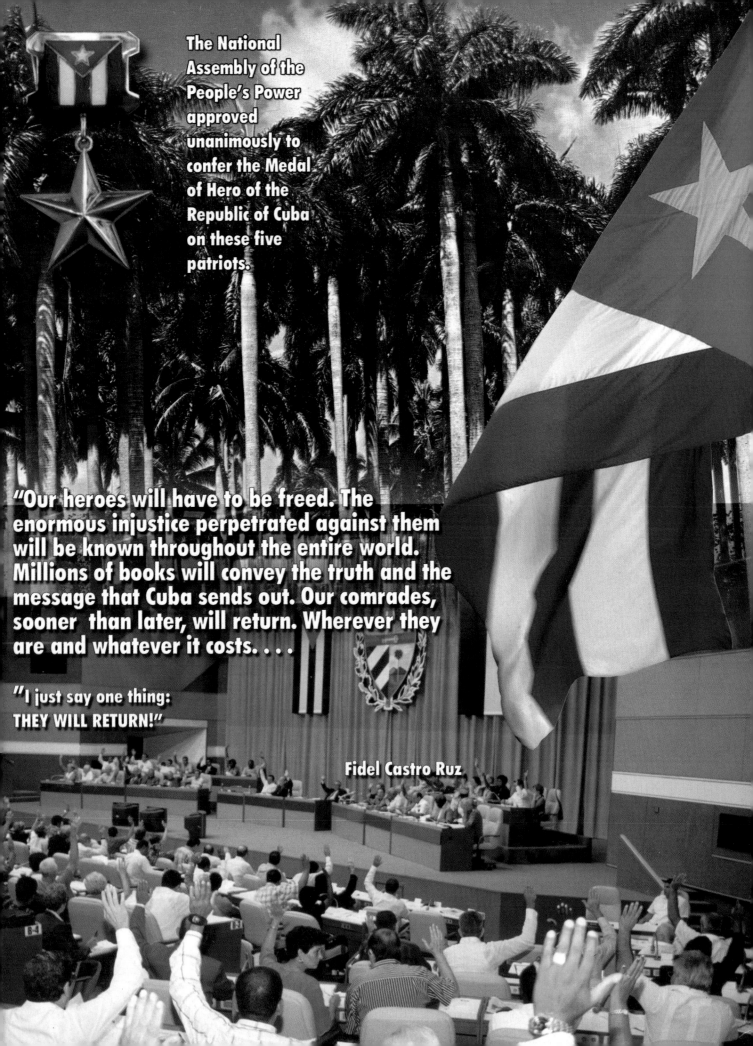

The National Assembly of the People's Power approved unanimously to confer the Medal of Hero of the Republic of Cuba on these five patriots.

"Our heroes will have to be freed. The enormous injustice perpetrated against them will be known throughout the entire world. Millions of books will convey the truth and the message that Cuba sends out. Our comrades, sooner than later, will return. Wherever they are and whatever it costs. . . .

"I just say one thing: THEY WILL RETURN!"

Fidel Castro Ruz

UNITED

Human Rights Commission

NATIONS

On May 27, 2005, the United Nations Human Rights Commission's Working Group on Arbitrary Detentions approved the following decision:

The deprivation of freedom of Antonio Guerrero Rodríguez, Fernando González Llort, Gerardo Hernández Nordelo, Ramón Labañino Salazar and René González Sehweret is ARBITRARY, and contravenes Article 14 of the International Convention of Civil and Political Rights.

After issuing the opinion, the Working Group requested from the [United States] government the adoption of the necessary measures to remedy this situation, according to the principles expressed in the International Convention of Civil and Political Rights.

The Group discussed the case at the request of the Cuban Five family members, and subsequently evaluated the arguments supplied both by them and the United States government.

To reach this conclusion, the Group took into consideration the following arguments:

"The trial did not take place in an objective and impartial climate, as it is required"

"The [United States] government has not denied that the climate of predisposition and prejudice against the defendants in Miami persisted and contributed to picture them as guilty from the very beginning."

"The [United States] government did not challenge the fact that a year later said government admitted that Miami was not the adequate place to hold a trial, where it was proven that it was virtually impossible to choose an impartial jury in a case relate to Cuba."

"The government [of the United States] has not refuted the fact that the defense lawyers had a very limited access to the evidence, since the case was classified by the government as national security", a fact that "undermined the necessary balance between the prosecution and the defense and negatively affected its capacity to present evidence against it."

The fact that they were "held in solitary confinement for 7 months", determined that "communication with their lawyers, access to evidence, and therefore, the possibility of having adequate defense was weakened."

"These three combined elements are so serious that it confers to the deprivation of freedom of these five men a character of arbitrariness against Cuba."

This declaration confirms the essential arguments of the defense, included in the appeal before the 11th Circuit Court of Appeal in Atlanta on May, 2003.

On August 9, 2005, the *Circuit Court of Appeals in Atlanta* released its decision on the case of the Cuban Five by which it reversed the convictions and ordered a new trial.

The court acknowledged the right of the Five to be tried impartially in a non-hostile climate and to have a fair trial as contemplated in the Constitution of the United States.

"In this case, the new trial was mandatory, due to the creation of a perfect storm when the wave of intense feelings of the [Miami] community and the ample publicity, both before and during the trial, was combined with the inappropriate references of the prosecution".

IN THE LIGHT OF THE STATED ARGUMENTS, THE CONVICTIONS OF THE DEFENDANTS ARE REVERSED AND WE ORDER THAT A NEW TRIAL BE HELD."

Atlanta, AUGUST 9, 2005

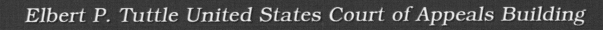
Elbert P. Tuttle United States Court of Appeals Building

56 Forsyth Street, NW, Atlanta,
GA 30303 Clerk's Office Main
Phone: (404) 335-6100

Back in Miami, eight years after having been unjustly condemned, three of the Cuban Five (Tony, Ramón and Fernando) were submitted to a new judicial event. Once more they were taken to the cells of the Federal Detention Center in Miami. Once again a courtroom of the Federal Court of Florida's Southern District, where the trial was held for months before a prejudiced jury, and where it seemed that prosecutors and judge competed head to head to be the Number 1 in a long chain of errors and violations that would lead to a verdict of guilty on June 2001, and would continue with the unjust and excessive sentences that were pronounced on December of that same year. Later on, there was a spire of distortions, bad faith, errors and apathy until they pretended to close the case of Gerardo and René, and return the case to Miami for the second time, for resentencing of Antonio, Ramón and Fernando.

Once again prosecutor Caroline Heck Miller and Judge Joan Did no clarified behavior?

First it was Tony, on October 13. One again his chivalry and the serenity of a gentleman that raises his head "with the always promised kindness." No matter that he is facing the same woman that pretended to bury him in prison for life. No matter that the prosecutor that charged him of being a spy now says that he did not handle any secrets or harmed US national security.

In the courtroom, facing the judge, is a model prisoner without a single report for indiscipline, a poet, an artist, a painter. The man that has given chess and painting lessons, the English and Math teacher. He arrives with an illegal life sentence plus ten years, and is resentenced to 21 years plus 19 months of jail.

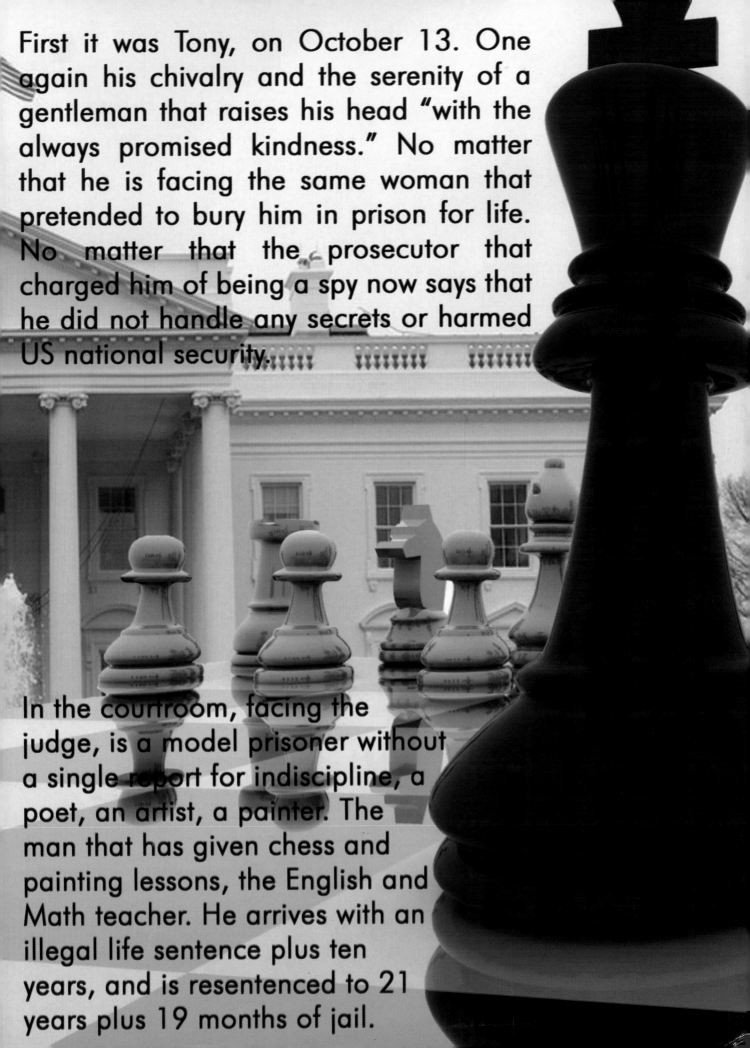

Ramón follows, unbreakable, who was asked to give up, that he betray his country and his ideals; but he leaves treason to cowards. It was December 8 (the "Blessed Virgin"). Early in the morning the faithful went to church to honor her, young boys and adults with their bouquets of carnations. But there was no miracle for this kind man, not even justice. Perhaps the Virgin never knew that Downtown, a few feet from the church, in the courtroom, the same crime was perpetrated again. Neither a terrorist nor a spy, they did not find a weapon nor a secret document. He also arrived with an illegal life sentence (plus 18 years) and was resentenced to 30 years.

Lastly, Fernando. He has served eleven years, but is accompanied by the dignity he has learned from his people and its history. His hearing is the same day of the religious commemoration, the day when acts of charity are made. It was a mockery, like giving only a crumb of bread to the hungry or a simple drop of water to someone dying of thirst. He comes with an unjust sentence of 19 years, and is resentenced to 17 years and 8 months. The judge, ever so generous, has reduced his sentence by one year and four months to a man who did no wrong.

It is not easy to take stock of the new hearings for resentencing and the results. The three heroes should have been set free, as well as Gerardo and René, for they have committed no crime. The presence of th
Five in the United States is well known and demonstrated:

the defense of their homeland and their people against criminal acts cropping up from South Florida and perpetrated by terrorists financed by the Cuban American extreme right, with the consent and blessing of the US government.

What in Criminal Law is known as "state of necessity", a circumstance for exemption of criminal accountability that justifies the alleged act and legitimizes the action.

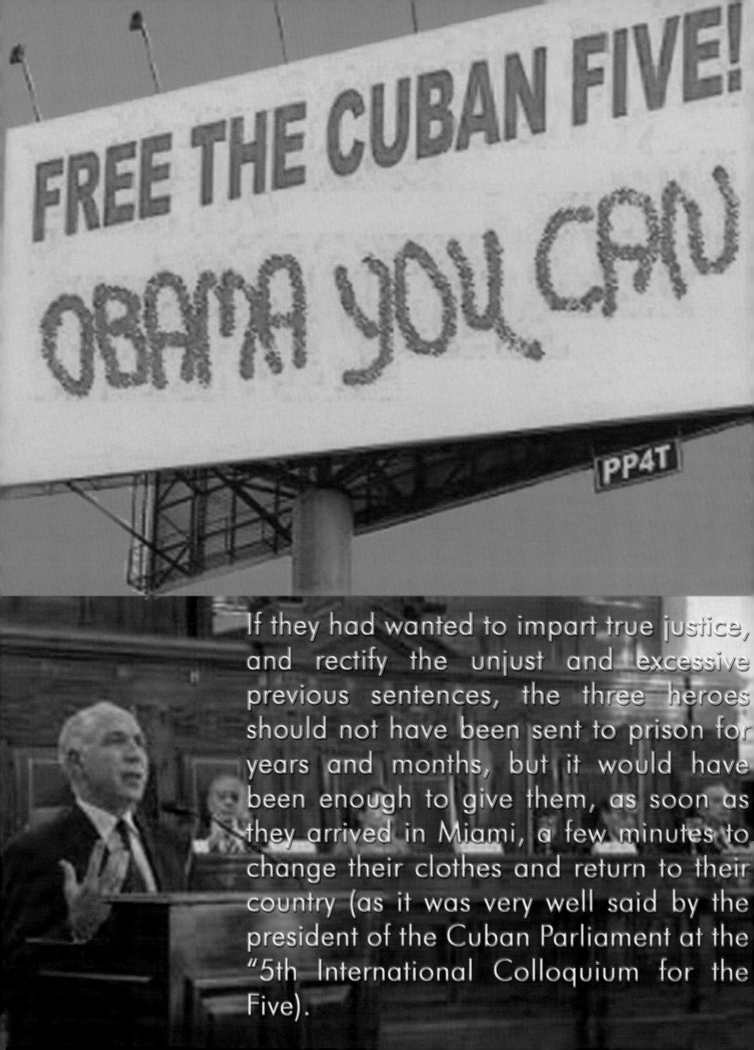

If they had wanted to impart true justice, and rectify the unjust and excessive previous sentences, the three heroes should not have been sent to prison for years and months, but it would have been enough to give them, as soon as they arrived in Miami, a few minutes to change their clothes and return to their country (as it was very well said by the president of the Cuban Parliament at the "5th International Colloquium for the Five).

Nevertheless, juridically speaking, the result of the resentencing hearings is positive, not only because there are no life sentences for Antonio and Ramón, but because of the fact that the government of the United States was forced to admit there had been no harm to national security, and that the existence of a strong international movement that demands the immediate release of the Five from prison harms the image of the US judicial system before the international community. District Attorney Miller must have swallowed hard when she said that it was necessary to "calm down the waters in dispute that swirl around this case." And those waters are a wave of solidarity that carries the truth on high until it is known throughout the world and enters the White House with an overwhelming thunder.

And why was not Gerardo there? If Tony's and Ramón's life sentences were annulled for unfair and excessive, why not Gerardo's? If there were no state secrets nor harm to national security, ¿why Gerardo's life sentence was maintained for that alleged crime?

And is René's sentence fair? René was not even charged with the most serious offenses, of which his comrades were accused, although unproved. That he did not commit any crime. That he only was and is an antiterrorist, the reason for which Judge Lenard gave him an additional and unbelievable punishment: she forbade him from coming near the terrorists once he served his sentence.

The 345 Solidarity Committees in 109 countries will be multiplied. The cry for justice will reach the White House. This is a battle that will be won by the solidarity of men with just causes.

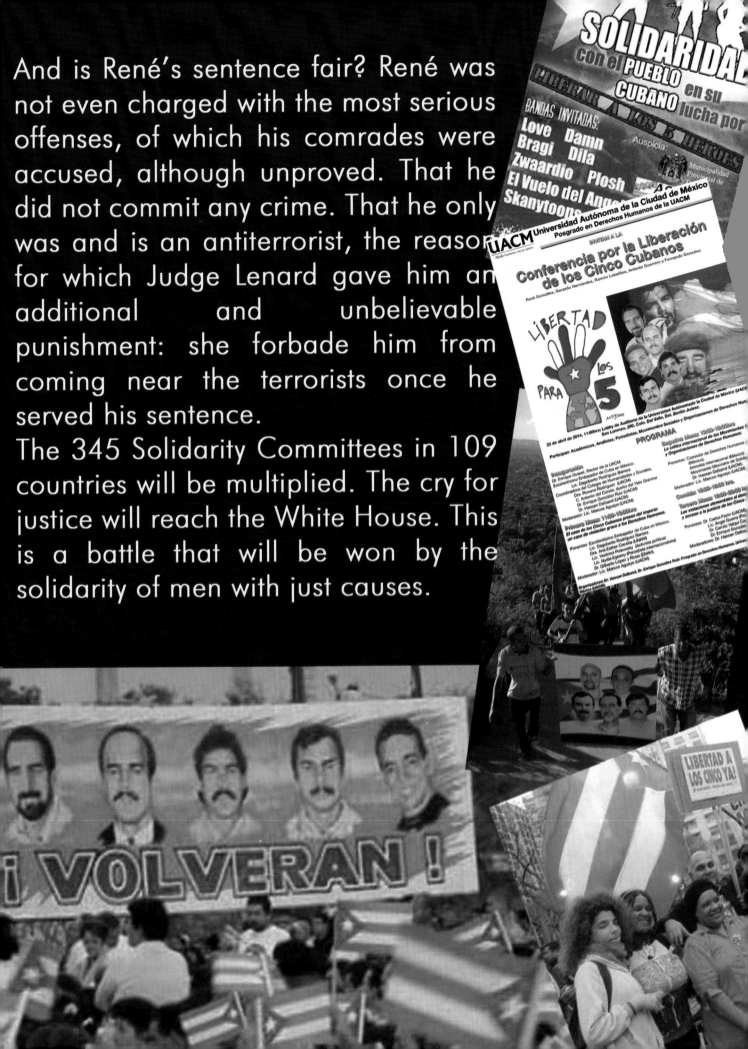

René in our Homeland

On April 3, two days after the death of his father Cándido, René filed a motion with the Southern District Court in Florida, through his lawyer, requesting authorization to travel to Cuba to be with his family in those difficult circumstances.

The decision to authorize René's travel is completely in line with the conditions established for his supervised release, which permit him to travel to Cuba with the approval of his probation officer or judge.

As the people of Cuba know, in September of 2011, after René completed an unjust sentence of more than 13 years in prison, he was arbitrarily retained in the United States, far away from his family in Cuba, to serve an additional sentence of three years of supervised release.

SATURDAY MAY 4, 2013

René will be able to stay in Cuba

Judge Joan Lenard agreed, on May 3, to the request filed by René González to modify the conditions of his supervised release and remain in Cuba, in exchange for renouncing his U.S. citizenship. Réne González, Hero of the Republic of Cuba, must appear at the United States Interests Section in Havana to begin this process, which will conclude when he is issued a certificate of loss of citizenship by the U.S. Department of State. One day earlier, the U.S. government had communicated to the court that it was not opposed to René's request.

René is no longer a U.S. citizen

On Thursday, May 9, at 2 p.m., René González Sewherert officially became just "a Cuban patriot." At that time, in the offices of the U.S. Interests Section in Havana, he received the document that certifies that he renounced his U.S. citizenship, a procedure that will allow him to remain in Cuba.

"Now I am simply a Cuban citizen, a Cuban patriot, something that I've always been anyway, without that implying any ill-will whatsoever toward the U.S. people or the country where I was born," the antiterrorist fighter announced yesterday in a press conference, after holding up the certificate that he had requested from the U.S. Interests Section on May 6, along with his attorney, Phillip Horowitz. René explained that he had to renounce his U.S. citizenship outside of U.S. territory, and that he had requested that process earlier but that the U.S. Attorney's Office refused his request, alleging his "lack of credibility." After arriving in Havana on April 22 due to the death of his father, he and his lawyer resubmitted his request.

The process of requesting and receiving the certificate was characterized by a "cooperative attitude on both sides," he said, but "that does not mean that they granted my request as a humanitarian gesture; instead, it was because they had run out of excuses to deny

However, "I am not going to feel completely free until my four brothers are back in our Homeland with their families," he said, announcing that from now on, he would be dedicated to promoting their cause. "I am in Cuba, but we are still the Five," he said.

JUVENTUD rebelde

24 DE ABRIL DEL 2014 15:16:14 CDT

DIARIO DE LA JUVENTUD CUBANA
EDICIÓN DIGITAL

Fernando returns to our country

Fernando González Llort, Hero of the Republic of Cuba, came home to his country at midday today, Friday, after serving a long and unjust prison term in the United States for fighting terrorism.

This Cuban antiterrorist fighter was released yesterday, Thursday, after fully serving the sentence handed down after the rigged trial of the Cuban Five, whose effort and sacrifice was aimed at protecting the Cuban and U.S. people from the hatred of the counterrevolutionary forces and imperialism.

Along with his four comrades—Gerardo Hernández, Ramón Labañino, Antonio Guerrero and René González, all of them Heroes of the Republic of Cuba— Fernando maintained impeccable discipline from the moment the Five were arrested in Miami, on September 12, 1998.

For preventing acts of terrorism, Fernando unjustly paid the price of 15 years, five months and 15 days of his courageous life. These long years of his absence caused suffering for his mother Magali, his sisters Marta and Lourdes, and his beloved wife, Rosa Aurora.

Today, a shared embrace, sitting all together around a table at home, in their country, will no longer be a recurring dream.

Fernando the giant

Gerardo Hernández Nordelo, the Cuban antiterrorist hero who has borne the brunt of imperialism's revenge, in the form of two life sentences for crimes that he never committed, sent a brotherly message of solidarity from the Five on the eve of Fernando González Llort's release from prison.

The note sums up the dignity, love and integrity of these good Cuban men.

"Each one of us Five is inevitably—and obviously—more or less 'something' than the others.

"In the same way that Ramón is the tallest, closely followed by René, Fernando is the least tall, and I stole second place in that category from Tony by a hair. (Although the 'hair' part is a manner of speaking). Given his 'title,' we sometimes referred to Fernando—affectionately, and also out of our deeply-entrenched professional habit of avoiding names among each other—as 'the little guy.'

"All of this might seem irrelevant or even frivolous, but at this time of joy and anxiety, when just a few hours stand between him and his freedom (and hopefully his return home, as well), as I remember so many demonstrations of greatness by our brother, I have contemplated the irony of calling this giant 'little.'

Fernando celebra su aniversario 49. Foto: Cubadebate

"When they arrested us, Fernando had extra reasons for feeling anguish, pain, and frustration.... To use baseball slang—a sport he really loves—he had pitched whole games, but his mission in Miami at that time was as a quick relief player. He was supposed to return to Cuba shortly. His wedding was coming right up. His fiancé, Rosa—a real warrior who has sacrificed everything in her life for him—practically had her wedding dress on. But with all of that, we never heard 'the giant' make a complaint.

"I was there when his lawyer at the trial, Joaquín Méndez, warned him, with all of the force of his profession to back him, that given the lesser gravity of the charges against him, any self-respecting defense lawyer would have separated his case from the rest of us, as a strategy. Fernando's response, like Rene's to a similar proposal, was resounding and unequivocal.

"Fifteen-and-a-half years later, Fernando, like René, will leave prison with his head held high. They did not give him anything for free, either. His sentence was the maximum possible, and the time discounted for good behavior was well-earned, something they had to give him by law.

"Those of us who love and admire him are celebrating today. Convinced that our struggle will be strengthened by another who holds our banner high, we send him a big hug and we say to him:

Congratulations, Giant!
Thank you for your example!
California, February 25, 2014.

Victorville Federal Prison
Gerardo Hernández Nordelo

The Editorial Capitán San Luis thanks the following for the contributions:

The archives of the newspapers and weeklies Granma *(Delfín Xigués),* Juventud Rebelde *(Violeta Martínez),* Tribuna de La Habana, Vanguardia, Surco; *the journals* Bohemia, Cuba, Prisma, Moncada, Verde Olivo; *the institutions: Agencia de Información Prensa Latina, State Security Historical Research Center (Dr. Hevia Frasquieri), Center for Studies on the United States (José Hernández, Teresa Gámez), Ministry of Public Health (Dr. Eduardo Sacca, Dr. Pablo Feal, Dr. Erick Martínez), Ministry of Education (Dr. Miguel Llivina), Ministry of Culture (Lucía Sardiñas, Ana Mayda Álvarez), Ministry of Justice (Dr. Juan José García), Ministry of Fishing, Ministry of Foreign Affairs (Fernando Remírez, Rafael Dauzá), National Assembly of People's Power (Ricardo Alarcón, Miguel Álvarez), Cuban Institute of Civil Aeronautics (León Dueñas), Pedro Kourí Institute of Tropical Medicine, National Institute of Physical Education and Recreation (Pedro Cabrera, Mario L. Garrido, José Luis Anaya), Cuban Institute of Radio and Television (Ovidio Cabrera, Ana María Hernández, Margarita Miarey), Revolución Studios, Museum of the Ministry of the Interior, Museum of Literacy (Luisa Campos), Museum of the Revolution, Museum of the Battle Against Counterrevolutionaries, Museum of the Marcha del Pueblo Combatiente, Museum of the Batalla de Ideas, Mundo Latino, Empresa Provincial de Servicios Necrológicos (Rogelio Haury, Luciano Antonio Díaz, Iraldo Ávila), Fotomecánica DA-VINCI de Cuba S.A. (Alberto Gil Rodríguez), Impresos de Seguridad (Juan Marrero), Video 8 and the photographers Alberto Díaz (Korda), Osvaldo Salas, Jorge Oller, Rigoberto Romero, Liborio Noval, Mario Díaz, Miguel Viñas, Raúl Abreu, René Rodríguez, Raúl Corral (Corrales), Francisco Altanuga, Mario García Joya and Ernesto Fernández.*

To the Nobel Prize Winner for Literature Gabriel García Márquez and to the Cuban writers Martha Rojas, Marilyn Bobes and Emilio Comas for their contributions to the texts on Elián González, Adriana Corcho and the abduction of the fishermen. To the painter and drawer Ernesto Rancaño (the cover illustration of the story of Elián González).

To the family members of Gerardo Hernández Nordelo, René González Sehwerert, Antonio Guerrero Rodríguez, Ramón Labañino Salazar, Fernando González Llort (prisoners unjustly detained in U.S. prisons for fighting terrorism).

To the mothers, fathers, widows, widowers, brothers, sisters and friends of the victims of terrorism waged against Cuba.

Publisher's Note

The terrorist activities covered in this book are only a sample of what the Cuban people have suffered for over four decades. During this period 3478 people have died as a result of these activities while a further 2099 have been injured or disabled. Damage to the Cuban economy is calculated to be 121 billion USD.